PERSPECTIVES ON LOSS AND TRAUMA

This book is dedicated to the hundreds of students who have participated in the author's class on loss and trauma at the University of Iowa over the last decade. Collectively, they have taught me more about ability of the human spirit to face, endure, and grow from daunting adversity than has any amount of academic work on this topic.

PERSPECTIVES ON LOSS AND TRAUMA
ASSAULTS ON THE SELF

JOHN H. HARVEY

Sage Publications
International Educational and Professional Publisher
Thousand Oaks ▪ London ▪ New Delhi

For information:

Sage Publications, Inc.
2455 Teller Road
Thousand Oaks, California 91320
E-mail: order@sagepub.com

Sage Publications Ltd.
6 Bonhill Street
London EC2A 4PU
United Kingdom

Sage Publications India Pvt. Ltd.
M-32 Market
Greater Kailash I
New Delhi 110 048 India

Printed in the United States of America

Library of Congress Cataloging-in-Publication Data

Harvey, John H., 1943-
  Perspective on loss and trauma: Assaults on the self/ by John H. Harvey
    p. cm.
Includes bibliographical references and index.
ISBN 0-7619-2161-3 (pbk.)
1. Loss (Psychology) 2. Psychic trauma. 3. Wounds and injuries.
4. Grief. 5. Bereavement –psychological aspects. 6. Adjustment
(Psychology) 7. Life change events. I. Title.
BF575.D35 H39 2001
155.9'3–dc21   2001001021

06   07   10   9   8   7   6   5   4   3

Acquiring Editor:	James Brace-Thompson
Editorial Assistant:	Karen Ehrmann
Production Editor:	Denise Santoyo
Editorial Assistant:	Kathryn Journey
Typesetter/Designer:	Denyse Dunn
Cover Designer:	Jane Quaney

Contents

Acknowledgments

While I take full responsibility for the contents of this book, I wish to thank the reviewers of an earlier version of this manuscript: Paul Rosenblatt, Ann Weber, Robert Weiss, Ronnie Janoff-Bulman, Robert A. Neimeyer, Alban L. Wheeler, Scotty Hargrove, and Kevin Oltjenbruns. Their input was invaluable in making the final product as strong as it is. Each provided sage advice about loss questions and work in the context of their detailed reviews.

I also wish to thank Sage Psychology Editor Jim Brace-Thompson who believed in this project and was encouraging throughout the writing process, and Sage Editorial Assistant Karen Ehrmann who helped make the final work on the manuscript bearable in the context of time constraints.

Finally, I wish to thank the thousands of research participants who have participated in my research in this field. A final acknowledgment is saved as the book's dedication to the students in my loss and trauma class at the University of Iowa.

1 Introduction to the Study of Loss and Trauma

Midway this life we're bound upon I woke to find myself in a dark wood, where the right road was wholly lost and gone.

—Dante, *The Divine Comedy*

In its most fundamental form, this book is about those events that represent our "dark wood" or that keep us up at night or that disturb our peace and make us ache and yearn for former times or altered outcomes. That dark wood of which Dante wrote awaits each of us. Sometimes, the dark wood encloses us much sooner in life than at the midpoint. Both loss and trauma spin us into dark woods. They are assaults against the self that diminish us but that also sometimes help us grow and give back to others.

Many times, the sense of loss is connected to a perceived failure. As an example, the famous baseball player Ted Williams, who was often hospitalized with heart problems in 2000, is said to have obsessed about his failures. The *New York Times* interviewed him in January 2000 and concluded, "The man who merely batted .344 in his career, the last man to bat .400 for a season, said 'I still can't sleep at night, thinking about the failures.' "[1] Such is the nature of life; we spend an inordinate amount of time and energy on problems that sometimes are insoluble.

This book considers the nature of major losses, such as the deterioration of one's own body due to aging and disease, and the loss of a loved one in a quick, violent way, such as an airline disaster. Major losses such as these often result in an experience of trauma. I view loss as the most central idea in this book. Trauma, as discussed here, refers to a special category of experience connected to loss. When a loss is experienced as traumatic, the loss usually involves some type of sudden, violent death, or the threat of such a death.

In the context of loss, people often experience a sense of missing something very important, a sense of incompletion, and a feeling of disappointment. The experience of loss can deplete our self-esteem and morale and make us struggle to find the strength to go on living. This book is about losses, losses that include the subtle processes of disease and aging, the cataclysmic events of war, and the untimely death of close others. Traumatic events, which include losses in war as well as deadly airline and automobile accidents, fundamentally are about loss. Loss is the phenomenal state we experience when these types of events occur; it is the disquiet that, over time, becomes the source not only of anxiety and depression but also of hope and generosity.

As I argue throughout this book, loss is the fundamental human experience that underlies many emotions, both negative and positive. Loss is also the key meaning that people associate with trauma. Dealing with loss can lead to growth experiences such as the development of the ability to reach out to help others and the courage to endure pain with hope.

The present volume is meant to be a general survey of work on loss and trauma. It builds on previous works in which I have argued for a unifying conception of the major losses in people's lives (Harvey, 1996, 2000). As the reader will discover in the following discussions of the general literature, I take a broad view of the nature and consequences of loss. I view loss as encompassing events such as death, divorce, traumatic injuries, war, violence, and genocide. In addition, my treatment of loss includes the loss of one's employment, home, and possessions, and experiences of loss related to one's identity, such as prejudice and stigmatization. Each of these topics is reviewed in a general way in this book. Each of these topics has its own distinct and extensive literature. Thus, in no way does this book represent the fullness of work on such phenomena.

This book's content parallels material I have addressed in teaching a large lecture course on loss and trauma (that enrolls about 175 per term) over the last several years. Students, who tend to range from juniors through graduate students, regularly comment on the value of breadth in learning about and becoming more sensitive to loss-related phenomena. They invariably tell me at the end of the term that the material contributed to their greater appreciation of the pain that many people have experienced and do experience in dealing with major losses. They invariably tell me that focusing on this topic in depth helps them deal with their own major losses. They often speak of how the stories, ideas, and voices of survivors contribute to their ability to exhibit greater compassion and empathy in interacting with people who have experienced a major loss. I hope that the present volume contributes to similar experiences for readers, both for those in formal courses and for those who just want to learn more about loss and trauma.

In the discussion that follows, I present some detailed definitions. This definitional groundwork is necessary because the dialogue about loss can quickly become ambiguous if attention is not paid to the nuances of loss. I present the idea of a "major loss" as the primary focus for the field of loss and trauma. We need to have at least a general theoretical framework for understanding what a major loss is relative to a "minor loss." The latter, such as losing a pencil that does not have much meaning, is omnipresent in our lives. The former, such as losing a spouse to death or divorce, fortunately, is less omnipresent, although when it happens it seems to have a crescendo of impacts in all areas of our lives, extending across time and space.

Knowledge of the common elements of loss can enhance communication across different disciplines involved in the care of those affected by loss. Such improved communication can lead to greater cooperation among professional and nonprofessional caregivers and hence improve integration of care.

A Social-Psychological Approach

My parent field is social psychology, and I take a social-psychological approach to loss and trauma. By that, I mean that I emphasize people's interpersonal relations and focus on thoughts, feelings, and behavior directed toward others. In addition to this emphasis on social interaction, I also believe that even in our constructions of ourselves we are intrinsically social beings (Mead, 1934). Who we are and become is a function of our social relations. When we experience our greatest losses (e.g., the loss of a parent), they are social losses—of interaction, companionship, love, compassion, and the human touch.

This social-psychological approach also emphasizes the importance of people as storytellers, meaning makers, and account makers (Harvey, Weber, & Orbuch, 1990). We are all storytellers. We all have in our memories a multitude of stories. As people share their stories with others, they name and shape the meanings of their unique life experience. They also pass on their heritage of stories to their confidants. When confidants or listeners become new tellers, they too reshape the original stories, incorporating their own particular issues and matters of moment. Thus, the same story is never retold as exactly the same story.

Harvey et al. (1990) define account making as *the act of explaining, describing, and emotionally reacting to the major events in our lives in storylike form about important events in our lives.* They suggest that this account making often begins in our private reflections and is then communicated in the form of an account to other people in whom we confide. When a major loss occurs, confiding our feelings to close others becomes an essential act of coping and adapting. As is often true, both persons in a confiding situation may be telling stories of loss and comforting each other It is the reciprocal communicative act that makes this experience a powerful social event, and as noted earlier, this act has implications both for the listener and the teller. As suggested throughout this book, constructing stories and confiding in others about our grief are among our most significant tools for confronting, understanding, and addressing our losses.

Although talking and confiding are believed to be our most effective tools for addressing our losses and grief, not everyone marches to the same drummer in their manner of adaptation. Some may adapt by adopting a stoic approach in which they confide in few, if any, close others. Still others may effectively avoid the issues or distract themselves.

Definitions

The definition of a major loss used in this book is the loss of something in a person's life in which the person was emotionally invested. The loss can involve an important person or some other entity. Emotional investment, then, becomes a key factor in defining major loss. We all experience an array of minor losses, from losing notes to losing strands of hair, on a daily basis. But major losses are events of another magnitude. By "emotional investment" I mean that we imbue these events with emotional meaning and in reaction to them we behave in ways that reflect the fact that they matter to us. They do not go away from our reflection and memory easily. In fact, we may hang on to them intentionally and memorialize their value in our lives.

This latter point about memorial work relates to the concern some analysts of loss raise about "the need for closure" after major losses. I do not agree with the popular wisdom that we should seek closure. As I argue often in this book, I do not know if closure is possible. I think that the best we can do is to learn to live *with* loss. It transforms us, and we learn new meanings through it.

For example, at remembrance events in 1997 for those who died on TWA Flight 800 in 1996, Joseph Lychner, a Houston businessman who lost his wife and two young daughters—his whole family—in the disaster, was asked whether the memorial events might help him "move on" and achieve closure regarding his losses. He said there was no moving on and closure for him and that he did not want closure. Rather, he wanted to continue remembering and honoring the family he loved so much and to dedicate a significant portion of his life to an area in which his wife was an activist (criminal justice). Is his response in some way a small clue about the psychopathology related to loss or "complicated mourning"? My answer is no. Lychner's logic is similar to that of others who, in the wake of devastating losses, have dedicated themselves to making contributions to others based on their experiences, a logic that resonates with Erikson's (1963) idea of generativity.

Traumas, by definition, involve major losses. People perceive trauma as fundamentally involving loss. All losses are not traumas, but all traumas involve loss. As discussed in detail later in this chapter as well as in Chapter 8, traumas are formally defined as unusual events involving loss to the individual—whether a death, the loss of body parts or functioning, the loss of a job, the loss of one's home, or the loss of one's trust in others or in the safety of the world (Janoff-Bulman, 1992).

Nuances of Defining Major Losses

Before going too far, it is important to consider the nuances of the definition of major loss. People perceive many types and magnitudes of loss. Losing one's umbrella at a restaurant is very different from losing an important person because of a nonresolvable interpersonal conflict. Although it may be somewhat arbitrary, it is important to try to provide commonsense, logical boundaries in defining major loss. People perceive many types and magnitudes of loss. In terms of magnitude, some losses are perceived as relatively minor (e.g., the loss of a minor, insignificant possession), and others are relatively major (e.g., the loss of one's parents). In evaluating our losses over time and in observing others' losses, we learn that losses are relative. Over time, we learn to view losses on relative continua, involving perceived impacts, complexity, and the level of difficulty of dealing with the loss.

In everyday life people make discriminations between relatively minor and major losses, and the psychology of loss will be most useful when it focuses on what people mean when they say they've suffered a major loss in their lives. This reasoning has a parallel in Wakefield's (1999) definition of a mental disorder as harmful dysfunction. Major loss, like harmful dysfunction, may be seen as an intuitive concept that has developed in human cultures and that similarly often involves reasoning by analogy in common sense discourse (Cosmides & Tooby, 1999; Kirmayer & Young, 1999).

I believe that a combination of subjective and objective markers is needed for delineating the boundaries of the definition of major loss. The following elements should be included in defining a major loss: (a) a subjective indication by the individual that she or he has experienced a major loss and (b) an objective concurrence by knowledgeable others. For most situations (e.g., death of a spouse, loss of a valued job), it is unlikely that these two indicators will be divergent. What we need to consider, however, are important cases in which they may differ.

What if an individual perceives that she or he has experienced a major loss but objective outsiders do not agree? I would ask, how "objective" are the outsiders? In the 1950s in the United States, persons of color might have concluded that they had experienced many major losses associated with prejudice and discrimination (e.g., regarding limitations in what schools children could attend or what jobs adults could find and hold). Outsiders in their environment, however, may not have agreed. But we might investigate and conclude that the individuals' subjective feelings of loss were tenable and that the outsiders did not agree because they were biased. We might determine that the outsiders were socialized *not* to see the major losses in the lives of persons of color. Hence, in such situations, the individual's own subjective view takes priority in defining major loss. People who were the target of prejudice in these situations most definitely would see their experience as involving major loss. They might also believe that they gained from the suffering. But the experience of loss very likely will be primary in their thinking and their emotional responses.

There are other situations in which the individual's subjective view does not contribute as much to our understanding of that person's significant loss as do the views of outsiders. When a person experiences a brain injury, he or she may be unaware of its severity and how the injury may change his or her life. In this case, doctors and people close to the injured person may have a better sense of what the person has lost. In such situations, the views of "outsiders" take precedence in defining the nature of the loss.

There is yet another type of situation that occurs frequently that needs discussion. Often, people who have been involved in close relationships become embroiled in disagreements regarding which member of the couple has been harmed by whom and how much harm has been done. Third parties such as therapists, mediators, or judges and juries may be called on to resolve these disputes and determine which person has suffered, or suffered the most, and possible methods of redress.

Thus, we see that there are subtleties to the definition of major loss that need to be entertained in our analysis. Perhaps the interpersonal conflict area is the one that is most replete with disagreement about how loss is defined. Even in this case, however, after a relationship has been dissolved, both parties can usually look back and conclude that each person involved has suffered a major loss.

An Extensive Literature

Behavioral scientists and social commentators have done extensive analysis and research on loss and associated grief work. The following discussion mentions a fragment of that literature that informs the later discussion of different types of loss and how people deal with them.

Judith Viorst's (1986) classic book on loss titled *Necessary Losses* deals with many of the natural losses that people incur as a part of living. Viorst points out that natural losses, such as the loss of one's sexual virginity, the loss of friends as we move from place to place, and the loss of physical health as we age, are natural and come in due course for every person. Some experience more "out-of-season" losses, such as those who die early in life or at midlife because of accidents, cancer, AIDS, or other fatal illnesses. Viorst eloquently says of loss,

> [Losses are] natural, unavoidable, inexorable. And these losses are necessary because we grow by losing and leaving and letting go. . . .
>
> For the road to human development is paved with renunciation. Throughout our life we grow by giving up. We give up some of our deepest attachments to others. We give up certain cherished parts of ourselves. We must confront, in the dreams we dream, as well as in our intimate relationships, all that we never will have and never will be. Passionate investment leaves us vulnerable to loss. And sometimes, no matter how clever we are, we must lose. (p. 3)

But does everyone who experiences these losses experience growth as a consequence? I doubt it. I argue in this book that the key to transforming losses into something positive is doing the hard work of the mind and spirit that gives our losses meaning. We can accomplish this work when we actively try to learn and gain insights from our losses and to impart to others something positive based on the experience. Not all of us will be inclined to search diligently for meaning in our losses. Not all of us will want to learn from them. Not all of us will use loss experiences to motivate us toward helping others who also are struggling with diminished hopes and resources. Some are too diminished themselves to even consider how they might try to help others. The power of Viorst's book, however, is that she highlights the fact that people experience *a plethora of types of loss in a full lifetime,* and they sometimes learn to grow and accomplish great humanitarian deeds, even in the midst of their own "dark woods."

In *Treatment of Complicated Mourning,* Therese Rando (1993) provides a comprehensive discussion of the nature of loss as it pertains to psychological intervention. She suggests that there are primary losses and secondary losses. A secondary loss, according to Rando, is a physical or psychosocial loss that coincides with or develops as a consequence of the initial loss. The primary loss is the loss of the presence of the loved one, and the secondary losses have to do with the many things that the lost loved one could have contributed to the bereaved survivor. The survivor may have financial difficulties associated with the loss and may even have to relocate as a result of the loved one's death. Each of these ripple effects is considered a secondary loss. Some people are overwhelmed by a key loss in their lives at one point, never fully deal with the loss, and then suffer even more in response to losses later in life. Psychoanalysts have long contended that nonmastered losses in the past—such as the unresolved death of a parent when a person is young—will interfere with mourning a later loss (Volkan & Zintl, 1993). Other types of losses that are particularly difficult to overcome are the loss of a child, the loss of someone through suicide, and any kind of loss that occurs unexpectedly or early in the life cycle.

George Levinger (1992) presents a useful set of distinctions about the nature of perceived loss. He notes that the extent to which a person *perceives loss* (or a deprivation in personal resources) after the death of a close other depends on several factors: How close (or involving or interdependent) was the relationship? Did the death occur unexpectedly or did it occur only after a protracted period of illness? If the individual's death involved a long terminal phase, a survivor can probably begin the process of mourning (which may involve story development and confiding) in anticipation of the death. Levinger posits that when a dying person expresses a clear desire to stop living, it helps that person's loved ones to accept the ultimate death. In fact, they have a clearer answer to the question of why he or she died—the individual wanted to, perhaps in the context of suffering from a terminal illness. Levinger also suggests that when there is a prolonged severe illness prior to death, a survivor may begin to pull away emotionally from the dying person; this is a defense mechanism that helps the survivor better accept the certainty of the impending death and begin the mourning process.

Along the lines of Viorst's position, Robert Weiss (1988) made the following valuable statement about the relative nature of healing from loss:

> Loss is inescapable. Deaths, estrangements, and separations are part of life. Recoveries tend to be either more or less adequate; only rarely can they be said to be either complete or entirely absent. Most of us have character structures influenced by partial recovery from loss. . . . Loss and pain are inescapable, but permanent damage should not be. (pp. 50-51)

Colin Parkes (1988) notes that grief following bereavement is aggravated if the person lost is the person to whom one would turn in times of trouble. Faced with the biggest trouble ever experienced, this person repeatedly turns to a confidant who is not there. Parkes suggests that such a situation, which often occurs when a spouse dies, is exceedingly difficult to resolve: "The familiar world suddenly seems to have become unfamiliar, habits of thought and behaviour let us down, and we lose confidence in our own internal world" (p. 55).

Laurie Palmer's (1987) poignant book *Shrapnel in the Heart* tells many stories of surviving relatives of individuals killed in Vietnam who have left notes and very personal memorabilia at the Vietnam Memorial Wall. These messages have been written as part of the survivors' attempts to release their feelings and to make sense out of something that was essentially senseless—the loss of life of tens of thousands of soldiers and innocent Vietnamese citizens. In large measure, the fact that the Wall exists as a memorial site made it appropriate for the relatives of Vietnam soldiers to be expressive. As Palmer said after she had tracked down a sample of persons who had left memorabilia, "People, I found, not only want to talk about the person they lost in Vietnam, they need to talk. It is a deep yearning in many, suppressed because of the wildly erroneous notion that by now they should be 'over it' " (1987, p. xiii). The Wall made it appropriate to be expressive because it represents a nation's official homage to its fallen sons and daughters. The Wall stimulated expression because it represents a material expression of grief! It expresses grief in the enormous number of names of those who died. It expresses grief in its blackness. It expresses grief in that it features a chasm into the earth—like a grave. But it also expresses hope as it rises out of the earth at its ends. The Wall provides a symbolic place for those who grieve Vietnam losses to come and share with others who grieve, and for all to come and stare in sadness and awe.

Emphasizing People's Construction of Meaning

This book emphasizes the ways in which people construct meaning and the use of accounts or stories to communicate meaning. This perspective focuses on how, when, and why people search for and construct meaning in connection with their dilemmas of living.

Several influential theories in psychology emphasize people's search for meaning. Such an emphasis can be found in Heider's (1958) seminal ideas that led to attribution theory in social psychology. Kelly's (1955) personal construct theory also embraced this perspective. Some of the most systematic recent work on people's search for meaning in situations involving severe stressors has been done by Thompson and colleagues (e.g., Thompson & Janigian, 1988).

Why is meaning so important to our lives? As suggested by theorists such as Heider (1958), when people feel that they have an understanding of events, they feel a greater sense of control in dealing with those events. As has been pointed out by Thompson (1998), some stressors may be so daunting that they defy direct actions designed to establish control. Still, a person may feel a sense of secondary control through accepting the situation and making the best of it, whether cognitively, behaviorally, or emotionally. Finding meaning is usually instrumental to finding hope and feeling a sense of agency in coping with loss (Snyder, 1994).

A focus on the meanings individuals perceive in events is essential in understanding the psychology of loss and trauma. Frankl's (1959) classic book, *Man's Search for Meaning,* tells how he survived Nazi death camps and developed an optimistic view of human potential. Frankl provides penetrating insights into the power of people's ascription of meaning in allaying pain and suffering, even in situations involving horror, degradation, and deprivation. Frankl emphasized acts of meaning such as reaching out and connecting with someone else, making a creative work, and adopting an attitude of hope as steps that may facilitate the construction of meaning in a larger sense. People often have difficulty finding hope in their lives because of the meanings they give to personally challenging or devastating loss events.

U.S. naval officer Admiral Mike Boorda's suicide in 1996 is illustrative of this point. Boorda had the honor of being the only enlisted man to rise to the highest officer position in the Navy. When he committed suicide, he apparently felt that his accomplished career was about to be defamed and that he and the Navy were about to be humiliated by news stories suggesting that combat medals he had worn were not deserved. Thus, he apparently decided that he had only one way out of this dilemma. He killed himself just prior to an interview with *Newsweek Magazine.*

What prevented Boorda from reconstructing the meaning of his situation in a way that made the ultimate act of self-destruction unnecessary? We do not know, but I do suggest that his own unique experience of loss and the imputation of meaning to that loss played a critical role in his decision. It is probable that Boorda could not assimilate a great humiliation with his self-image. He must have felt that he would be faced with a situation that would produce massive shame, humiliation, and loss of self-esteem. In his mind, it may have been a hopeless situation. We all rely on images of ourselves to make meaning out of our life experiences. When those images cannot be maintained, we may give up on life.

We are constantly constructing and reconstructing meanings, and we continually construct and reconstruct ourselves in the process (Mead, 1934). In life crises, this constructive enterprise can be one of our most effective antidotes to depression and the loss of hope. Echoes of Frankl's (1959) conception of the necessity of finding meaning can be found throughout the scholarly and popular literatures on how people adapt to severe stressors (e.g., Lazarus & Folkman, 1984; Radner, 1989; Rosenblatt, 1983).

Contextualization of Loss Experiences

Throughout this book, I propose that people often conceive their losses in terms of accounts or stories that contextualize the major events of their lives (Bruner, 1990; Coles, 1989; Harvey et al., 1990). Associated with these stories are perceived chains of events, not unlike the idea of perceived causal chains advanced by Brickman, Ryan, and Wortman (1975). Perceived causal chains are involved in attributions of responsibility for accidents. These investigators provided some often neglected evidence and ideas regarding how people make judgments about chains of causes in making causal and responsibility judgments. I posit that people are especially prone to perceive relatedness among their personal losses and possibly in their causes. In people's stories involving major losses, they may assimilate different loss events occurring at quite different points in time as related and meaningful to who they have become.

Behavioral scientists also engage in such reasoning about chains of causal loss events. For example, in follow-up research to their long-term program of work on the effects of divorce, Wallerstein and Lewis (1998) followed 130 children of 60 middle-class families in which the parents had divorced. The children, now in their late 20s and early 30s, were between 2 and 6 years old at the time of the divorce. They found that these adult children displayed the following characteristics: (a) lower-paying jobs and less college education than their parents, (b) unstable father-child relationships with their own children, (c) a fear of commitment and of the prospect of divorce in their own early adult relationships, and (d) a vulnerability in adolescence to drugs and alcohol. Whether or not one accepts Wallerstein and Lewis's particular findings, their reasoning about such causal chains of loss events associated with divorce is not unusual.

The Experience of a "Pileup" of Losses

Series of losses may appear to us as a "pileup" of losses (Viorst, 1986). "When it rains, it pours" is the expression we learn to use for times when losses such as deaths or accidents or illness in our personal lives come in multiples. Life stress and distress may be at their highest during these periods. As noted by Stroebe, Stroebe, and Hansson (1993), multiple losses occurring for an individual in a brief period of time are often associated with multiple bereavements that are unremitting over time. But there is more to the "psychologic" of multiple losses in contributing to distress. Questions of whether we deserve our fate (Lerner, 1980) or whether our experience is typical may be critical in our response.

People in their "golden years" frequently point to the number of funerals and memorial services they regularly attend. A mediating variable in the influence of perceived chains of loss events may be the sense of whether or not the losses seem warranted in terms of justice or timing (Janoff-Bulman, 1992). As we move toward our senior years, we expect to lose family and friends. Such loss is a natural concomitant of time. However, to have these experiences in our youth or even at midlife is more statistically unusual. Hence, it may seem more unjust. This is a topic that deserves empirical attention, both in terms of what our norms of justice are and what each of us feels is just or appropriate in our own lives in terms of loss.

Ellis (1995) tells the story of her 9-year relationship with Gene Weinstein, a prominent sociologist who died of emphysema after years of battling the disease. This is an incredible story of multiple losses converging in the lives of two people over a relatively short period of time. Ellis was 24 when she met Weinstein who was 44. She was a young doctoral student at the school where he taught.

Although Ellis describes their relationship as a strong love affair, she also wrote of many loss issues that they experienced. These issues included the following experiences: Ellis spent almost 9 years in her 20s and 30s caring for a man whose health was deteriorating as each year went by, such that he was unable to take care of most of his bodily needs and functions by the time he died. She had to alter her own early academic career in terms of how it would affect Weinstein's health. They had to deal with their relationship dynamics, which included many difficulties and conflicts that interacted with his condition. They had to deal with the stigma of being unmarried lovers and encounter academics who were uncomfortable with them and hospital and insurance personnel who would not treat her as his legal significant other. Ellis writes of numerous instances of anger, frustration, passed-up dreams, and despair that besieged them during parts of their relationship. In addition to all of these losses, 3 years before Weinstein's death, Ellis's younger brother was killed in the crash of the Air Florida jet in the Potomac River in 1982.

In the end, though, Ellis's story is one of courage and hope. In her provocative narrative, she shows how she and Weinstein constantly negotiated between denial and acceptance. She reveals their psychic defenses and emotional complexities in situations of overwhelming loss that could have been construed as bordering on hopeless. Ellis (1995) concludes with the idea that the negotiation of her relationship with Weinstein, as well as their story, cannot end yet and will likely be a lifelong enterprise.

The idea of contextualized loss experiences goes well beyond the notion that we tend to cognitively work on (negotiate) losses and assimilate them over time and circumstances. Dealing with loss events may lead to secondary losses (e.g., of energy, resources, morale) and stigmatization (Rando, 1993). Loss events of grand proportions may have cascading effects for decades, if not centuries into the future. Holocaust researchers such as Peskin, Auerhahn, and Laub (1997) and Bar-On

(1995) have provided evidence suggesting that the effects of the Holocaust continue for second and even third generations of families whose loved ones were murdered. Beyond that, emerging media stories, such as the admitted role of certain Swiss banks who have held money and possessions stolen by Nazis from Jews for more than 50 years, reveal further aspects of the web of complicity that attended the Holocaust and that reverberates in its implications among nations and individuals alike.

Psychologists and other behavioral scientists have inadequately theorized about and investigated the meanings of loss associated with the Holocaust and other acts of genocide. Psychologists' general study of genocide (e.g., Staub, 1989) is a topic that should be a part of the domain of a psychology of loss and trauma.

A Set of Basic Ideas

From the literatures on diverse types of major loss, do we have a set of basic ideas about loss phenomena? By "basic ideas," I mean principles of loss and adaptation to loss that are generalizable across different phenomena. I think we do, and I offer my view later to present part of the set of basic ideas. About 15 to 20 such ideas are presented here (italics are added to indicate what I call a basic idea). The reader will see overlap among the ideas and may view some of the ideas as more basic than others. But the main reason for this exercise is to further our understanding of ideas and principles of loss and trauma.

Bereavement, mourning, and grief are commonly used terms in the loss and trauma field. These terms have been used interchangeably in the literature. I do not offer strong distinctions, although some writers (e.g., Rando, 1993) have suggested that grief is the more private and mourning the more public, socially approved response. In this latter vein, bereavement may be seen as the composite of private grief and public mourning. My own preference is to try to understand the processes associated with bereavement, mourning, and grief. Are they different processes? I am not convinced they are; hence, the reader will see that I tend to use these terms interchangeably.

The basic idea of *perceived control and predictability* is probably the most general and prevalent idea in the field of loss and trauma. Because of its centrality, I deal with it at some length here. As will be evident throughout this book, the sense of having control and being able to predict events is critical to feelings of well-being and hope and to the ability to cope and function (Seligman, 1975). The value of control and predictability is also often revealed in the news. Mary Schmich, columnist the *Chicago Tribune,* told of how in February of 1994, 48-year-old Wisconsin businessman Donald Booth took his daughter Amanda, aged 16, to Chicago so that she could take a series of tests to determine her interests and aptitude. Booth then decided to stroll along Michigan Avenue. As Schmich says, that decision was a fateful one for Booth and his family:

> And in that fleeting moment of a freakishly mild day, a chunk of ice the size of a microwave oven slipped from a high ledge. It hurtled toward the ground and hit Booth in the head. He died immediately.
>
> Every spring and winter since then, "falling ice" signs have popped up like dandelions in Chicago's high-rise business districts. And each year when the signs appear, weak protection from the winter thaw, I wonder what happened to Booth's widow, Dawn, and to the three children who lost a father so unpredictably.[2]

As I review in the chapters on war and genocide, Frankl's (1959) seminal work on the importance of people's *search for meaning* derived from his own survival of Nazi concentration camps. It has helped generations of people better appreciate the importance of the meanings we attribute to the events in our lives. Frankl argued that meaning or purpose in living was as important or more important than food for the survival of the prisoners. He believed, and his life showed, that if we can attribute meaning in constructive ways, we can endure many circumstances that otherwise we might be too daunting for survival. Frankl believed that we could find meaning in our lives by creating work, making something with our hands and minds, extending ourselves to others by doing positive acts, and adopting a positive attitude toward the suffering that we must endure.

In the preceding example of the Booth family, this family no doubt has searched for and found meaning in their tragic loss. Ms. Dawn

Booth has searched for and found a ray of meaning in the horribly unlucky loss of her husband. As she said to Mary Schmich, "Whenever I see an icicle, I think about it. I look at it as the enemy." In describing Dawn Booth's life in the wake of her loss, Schmich writes, "Not a day goes by that Dawn doesn't think about Don, and some days she's convinced he's thinking about her." According to Schmich, Dawn Booth admits that this is a kind of strange thing. In this same column, Schmich also recounts a story Ms. Booth about a friend whose son died as a high school senior. The friend, looking for proof that her son was still around in spirit, asked for a sign. She and her husband started seeing dimes in peculiar places. The symbolism of this affected the Booth family too. They now see dimes in strange places. Schmich quotes Ms. Booth as saying, "I was walking along a lake one time, it was very bare, and I was talking to my son. . . . All of a sudden we looked down and there was a dime. We both started crying."

Schmich concludes that the dead may live on in unexpected ways for those they leave behind. I believe that is true. Those with whom we were very close leave with us parts of their personalities, ideas, and ways of going about life—they may also leave genetic traces with us! In effect, they do not die until we die and take with us the images, influences, and expectations that they implanted in our minds in our time together.

The idea of *shattered assumptions* derives from Janoff-Bulman's (1992) important work on people's assumptions and illusions about the world and how they may be dashed when tragedy occurs. Janoff-Bulman contends that we are socialized to believe that the world is a benign place, that it is a meaningful place, and that we are worthy people. Each of these assumptions is susceptible to being shattered when events such as acts of senseless violence occur in our lives. The Booth's tragedy shattered the assumptions and life courses of the surviving family members. Janoff-Bulman writes extensively about the growth that people may experience after coming to grips with tragedies and the shattered assumptions that result from them. From these losses, we may develop new and more realistic assumptions. Essentially, we may learn to be tougher about the nature of life and how it regularly involves losses for ourselves and others. That is just the way it is. To successfully adapt, we have to learn to make the best of it.

An idea related to shattered assumptions is that of *justice.* Lerner (1980) posits a just world theory to refer to people's belief that we get what we deserve and deserve what we get in life. As suggested in the discussion of shattered assumptions, sometimes our intuitive psychology of justice does not conform to the facts. We have to adjust to the reality that the world is not such a just place and that good people may experience terrible and unjust events in their lives. Adjustment to this fact of life is one of the most challenging and yet maturing steps most of us will take as humans.

An important derivative of Lerner's theory is that we often derogate victims. We think that something they did must have contributed to their loss. We must be on guard for this knee-jerk reaction to victims. I think that the study of loss and trauma is a wonderful antidote to the just-world tendency to derogate the victim. We learn quickly that we can just as readily *be the victim.*

The idea of *grief work* builds on Lindemann's (1944) conception that people need to engage in a process of working through grief and that adaptation does not readily occur unless such work is done. As I argue in this book, it is what we do through time, and not time, per se, that helps us cope with major losses. Grief work is similar to another set of concepts used in this book. The concepts related to grief work include the following ideas: working through loss events, account making for loss events, and searching for meaning (and meaning making). Each is work, not unlike demanding physical work. Each is not completed in any "quick and dirty" way. I think that is one of the reasons people do not like to hear about the critical nature of grief work in adaptation. We all find it difficult to think that we may have to spend a lifetime working on an important death or dissolution in our lives. Yet all evidence leads me to think that it is true—another one of those "that's just the way it is" realities that the sooner we recognize, the better.

The major outcome variable in the loss and trauma field is that of *adaptation.* Rando (1993) emphasizes adaptation as a state of coping that we may achieve with work after a major loss. I prefer this term to the terms *recovery* and *healing,* because adaptation is more descriptively accurate in conveying the state people can most readily achieve in their adjustment process. Through the adaptation process, I believe that we make the loss a part of who we are. Adapting after a loss includes the following critical ingredients and processes: cognitive and emotional work, reflection, confiding in close others, and the psychological experience of peace, (Harvey, 1996). Theoretically, the alternatives to adaptation are physical and psychological disorders (e.g., Pennebaker, 1990).

According to the general view of adaptation presented in Chapter 11, to find peace, we do not avoid working on our thoughts and feelings about the loss. At the same time, we go on with what have to do in life. Eventually, though this work, we are more at peace. But the loss stays with us.

One of the most important consequences of major loss is *identity change* (Harvey et al., 1990). All through life, each of us takes on new identities. Yet no stimulant of identity change is more potent than that of major loss. As discussed in Chapters 2 and 3, when people lose close others through death or divorce, a major chunk of who they are is lost as well. They then must become "new people," no longer Ms. Jones's husband, but now a widower after Ms. Jones's death or Ms. Jones's ex-husband. Such a reality can be a shattered assumption of the first rank. As Janoff-Bulman (1992) argues, it also can be the stimulus for great and valuable growth and change.

The term *generativity* refers to Erikson's (1963) idea that people may use their experiences, including their losses and stresses, to give something to future generations, such as understanding, perspective, corrective actions, and resources. As documented in this book, such has been the response of many persons surviving great losses. I believe that generativity is one of the most important ideas a person can learn or better appreciate through a broad and in-depth study of loss and trauma. Fiske (2000) discusses how generativity may have an evolutionary-adaptive basis in human life. This aspect of generativity is evident across countless examples of giving by persons suffering great loss and pain.

After a major loss and in the midst of continuing pain, so many have shown generativity by dedicating their lives to "giving back" to others based on their experience and what they learned through their loss. Frankl's (1959) example again stands out and helps us better understand the towering importance of generative acts. Unlike other survivors of and writers on the Holocaust (e.g., Weisel, 1960), Frankl developed a very positive view of what humans could do based on his experiences—which included losing his wife and his mother and having his father die in his arms. He used this positive view in the development of a therapy for loss, depression, and other states of mind involving despair. This therapy is called logotherapy.

As discussed in various chapters, *disenfranchised grief* is a central idea in the field and helps us understand people's sense that they are not supported by others in their loss and mourning. Disenfranchisement pertains to the idea that some people's mourning response is not seen as acceptable because their loss experience is stigmatized by the public. For example, in the mid-1980s AIDS patients often encountered various types of reactions from others that reflected the stigma associated with being homosexual. Any person or group who experiences loss in the form of discrimination and prejudice and who cannot find ready support for their loss experience may be said to be experiencing disenfranchised (vs. franchised) grief. Doka's (1989) compilation of writings on this topic is important in helping us understand how widespread disenfranchised grief may be in our world. One group who probably experiences considerable disenfranchised grief is children who cannot articulate their pain or ask for help and who do not have strong support from adult caretakers.

Another concept discussed often in this book is that of *survivor's guilt*. Survivor's guilt refers to regrets that people have about their own survival when their loved ones or friends or colleagues do not survive. This idea is also related to *ambivalence*. In discourse about loss and trauma, ambivalence refers to the feeling a person may feel toward a deceased loved one at the time of their death (Raphael, 1980). Ambivalence is common when there was hostility in the relationship before the death occurred. There are a number of illustrative situations involving survivor's guilt. The survivor may have been in an airplane crash and survived whereas others died. He or she may feel guilty about being so lucky—maybe the survivor occupied a seat near the impact point that killed fellow passengers. Or this type of guilt may refer to feelings of regret that others who are similar in age or other characteristics died a young, "out-of-season" death, while the survivor goes on with life (Rando, 1993).

Survivor's guilt may also refer to the guilt one feels about not visiting a loved one before that person's death. On a related dimension, survivor's guilt may refer to the belief that significant unfinished business existed between the survivor and the deceased person when the person died (e.g., that there were major imperfections in the relationship that never were satisfactorily addressed). Many students have told me that they regret not having had the opportunity to be with a grandparent or other loved one, or to tell the grandparent how they felt about them before the grandparent's death. Rando (1993) also discusses guilt deriving from the survivor's feeling that he or she contributed in some way to the loved one's death.

A final idea that I believe is central to loss and trauma is that of the psychological experience of *intrusive imagery* (Horowitz, 1976). Intrusive imagery is a part of the *schemata* that develop after major losses. The schema idea refers to our mental landscapes or maps of what has happened to us. I believe in this phenomena and have provided some evidence to support the view that major losses stick with us in our minds and have an effect on our moods and general psychological condition (Harvey, Flanary, & Morgan, 1986). Part of what contributes to these mental landscapes is the fact that we fairly regularly encounter environmental stimuli that remind us of our losses. Inevitable reminders of our loss stimulate images of the lost other or the loss event. It is impossible not to encounter these stimuli. They are the lyrics of music. They are in common sightings, such as of the first snow of the year, or the sight of two lovers enraptured with each other or a funeral procession. They are endemic to our physical worlds, and they have the power to evoke thoughts, feelings, and images.

Horowitz (1976) discusses how people come to grips with major loss by developing new schemata of who they are (see earlier discussion of identity change). I believe that these schemata, however, are open to repeated inputs from the environment and reflect self-generated (as in dreams) concepts of who we were and what happened in times past and particularly what happened in moments of great despair and pain. Students in my loss and trauma courses have often told me about their dreams of interactions with deceased loved ones or with former lovers with whom they no longer interact. Such dreams may be quite functional in assisting with grief work and may be generated by events that happen in the daytime or by stimuli so complex we cannot begin to understand them.

Trauma: Conceptual Background

Trauma is a specific term referring to extreme psychological and physiological reactions to major losses, such as the death of close others. Traumatic reactions may be so severe as to constitute posttraumatic stress disorder (PTSD), which is a particular diagnostic category in psychology and psychiatry. As discussed further in the chapters on war and genocide, traumatic reactions may involve loss of concentration, sleeping and eating problems, flashbacks, and nightmares. Although people sometimes exhibit such extreme reactions to loss that we refer to their reactions as reflecting PTSD, more generally, we all exhibit posttraumatic stress responses in our lives. Such responses do not meet the criteria of PTSD, and the individual experiencing such stress is more able to function in a normal way than if he or she is experiencing full-blown PTSD. Nonetheless, posttraumatic stress may lead to quite significant psychological and physiological reactions, such as some loss of concentration and difficulty sleeping.

Figley (1993) provides a useful short history of the field of traumatic stress. He notes that what is now called traumatology began with an ancient Egyptian physician's reports of hysterical reactions, which were published in 1900 B.C. in *Kunyus Papyrus* and became one of the first medical texts (Veith, 1965). Figley (1993) defines traumatology as the investigation and application of knowledge about the immediate and long-term psychosocial consequences of highly stressful events and the factors that affect those consequences. This field evolved mainly within the last two decades, encompassing research as well as therapy and application. The onslaught of studies of PTSD after the Vietnam War was a major factor in contributing to the development and refinement of this field. The Society for Traumatic Stress Studies was born in 1985 and now publishes a leading journal, the *Journal of Traumatic Stress.*

Figley (1993) suggests that PTSD-like reactions have been reported in some form in every century. The symptoms of flashbacks, dissociation ("out-of-body" type experiences), and startle responses were viewed as works of God, the gods, the devil, or other types of spirits (Ellenberger, 1970). Figley (1993) attributes the use of trauma as a scientific term to replace religious terms depicting these reactions to Franz Mesmer, an 18th century physician. Other important early figures were Martin Charcot, who was the first to demonstrate that hysteria had psychological origins (Charcot, 1889), and Pierre Janet, who was the first psychologist to study and treat traumatic stress (Figley, 1993). Figley (1993) also notes that Janet first recognized that the inability to integrate traumatic memories was the core issue in posttraumatic stress syndrome. Janet was also the first to describe the symptoms now considered to represent the diagnostic criteria for posttraumatic stress syndrome.

Figley (1993) traces more recent developments in traumatology to concern about "concussion of the spine," a phenomenon associated with train wrecks. Erichsen (1882) wrote a book that described how such concussions could occur as a result of the violent shock of a railway collision, and he indicated how such experiences could account for what later would be described as PTSD symptoms. Page (1885), a surgeon working for a railway in England, then suggested that survivors of railway accidents who complained of symptoms such as sleep disturbances and startle responses were suffering from "nervous shock." Figley (1993) points out that Page was one of the first physicians to suggest a psychosocial origin for what had been a mysterious disease.

After this late 19th-century literature on trauma, war-related stress became the context for continuing work on trauma in the 20th century. Ideas about melancholia in the U.S. Civil War and "shell shock" in World War I became assimilated into the later concept of PTSD. As Figley (1978) indicates, it was initially believed that a predisposing character or personality defect accounted for why some individuals developed combat-related PTSD. This position changed during the

Vietnam War, with personality-predisposing characteristics no longer viewed as necessary factors in PTSD.

Figley (1993) describes how the highly related topics of stress and coping evolved separately from that of traumatic stress. Hans Selye is viewed as the pioneer developer of the study of stress. Selye (1956) defined stress as, "the state manifested by a specific syndrome which consists of all the non-specifically-induced changes within a biologic system" (p. 64). He discovered the biological stress syndrome, referred to as the general adaptation syndrome. Selye suggested that some degree of stress is inherent in our biological systems, with the complete freedom from stress being death.

Figure 1.1 presents a model of the effects of a traumatic event, including the coping steps involved in the search for meaning and attribution aimed at explaining the event. Note the early occurrence of "shattered assumptions" and the later "existential confrontation" (see further discussion in Chapter 11 on adaptation), and the final step of transcendence or generativity.

"Missing" Something: A Central Experience in Loss and Trauma

People show grief differently. Some show profound grief over their losses in visceral reactions that leave no doubt about their meaning. Others also show unmistakable signs of grief over losses but in less demonstrable ways. In a recent study in Romania (Harvey, 2000), I observed a man (probably) in his 20s over a period of time who looked for donations on Bucharest's subways. I called him "The Slider" because he slid around the floors of subway cars on his one partial leg; his other leg was missing. I saw what I perceived to be grief in this man's eyes. He showed no tears or overt signs of pain about his obvious struggle to survive. He seemed hardened to his losses—not just the loss of his legs but of his youth, dignity, and ability to make a regular income. However, what was so poignant about this young man was the sense of loss in his life. Life seemed so grim and such a grind. I hope that I was pro-

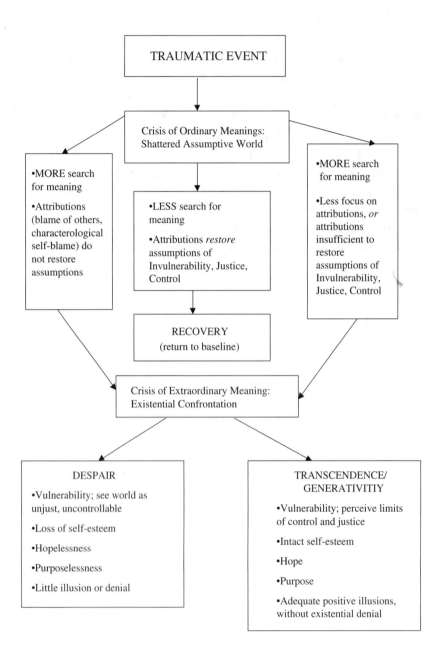

Figure 1.1. Trauma Scenarios

jecting these feelings onto this man and that in reality he did not regularly entertain them. But I fear that indeed there was a sense of something "missing" in his life. He missed his legs. He missed interaction with friends and close others as he traveled the subway cars. He missed even a modicum of a normal life: If only he could have had an easier time making a living or dealing with merchants. He was so short he could not begin to reach many merchants' counters.

It is probably true that one of the most central meanings of major loss can be described best not with words but with *images of missing other or something* that occur at the immediate point of learning of the loss, especially an unexpected loss. In word form, these images and feelings approximate these expressions, reported by people reflecting on their first reactions to sudden, debilitating loss:

Oh, my God! Oh no, please no! It can't be true.

She wasn't there anymore. I felt so empty.

This can't be real. We were happy and laughing only hours before. I couldn't believe the lifeless body I discovered.

I can't feel anything. It doesn't feel real.

I cried hysterically, and then I went numb; kind of like I was watching myself from the outside.

After someone's death, the images and feelings often pertain to the physical entity being gone, perhaps swiftly and unexpectedly. The first experience of missing a key body part after amputation may produce images and feelings not unlike those experienced after the loss by death of a loved one. After a death, or a dissolution or a divorce, the images and feelings often relate to a sense of a void left by the person who becomes "missing," and even "missed." Psychologically, in the long run, a loss is best represented by the sense of missing, being bewildered, being without, and even being hopeless in some cases. After learning about a great personal loss, people often report that they felt numbed and overwhelmed.

Images that convey the sense of missing a deceased loved one were described by C. S. Lewis in *A Grief Observed* (1961), a book of notes following the death of his wife Joy Davidman. Lewis, who was a writer, teacher, and theologian in England, had been a confirmed bachelor well into his midlife when he met Davidman, an American poet. They fell deeply in love and married. Within a few years, however, her advanced stage of cancer was discovered. Perhaps her death was even more devastating to Lewis because of the whole set of unexpected events—being single so long, then falling in love overnight and quickly getting married, and then just as quickly losing that which had brought Lewis his greatest happiness. Lewis was inconsolable in his grief. He soon began the notes about his grief that not only helped his healing but that also served as a beautiful memorial to his love for his wife. These notes also stand as a magnificent contribution to anyone who has lost a loved one. Consider Lewis's expression of what it felt like to miss Joy:

> Her absence is like the sky, spread over everything. . . .
> I have no photograph of her that's any good. I cannot even see her face distinctly in my imagination. Yet the odd face of some stranger seen in a crowd this morning may come before me in vivid perfection the moment I close my eyes tonight. No doubt, the explanation is simple enough. We have seen the faces of those we know best so variously, from so many angles, in so many lights, with so many expressions—waking, sleeping, laughing, crying, eating, talking, thinking—that all the impressions crowd into our memory together and cancel out into a mere blur. But her voice is still vivid. The remembered voice—that can turn me at any moment to a whimpering child. (pp. 11, 16-17)

Conclusions: Emphasis on Basic Principles

At the core of this book are the assaults on the self that form the terrain of most human lives. They include death, dissolution of close relationships, disease processes and losses that come as a result of aging, accidents, the loss of one's job, and more global losses, such as in war and genocide. The latter are often assaults against our selves in a collective sense.

Loss is a fundamental aspect of the lives of all people from earliest childhood. Although each loss event has unique characteristics, there are common features of different types of loss. Although people cope with and react to loss in unique ways, there also are common responses to loss as we will see across the different topics explored in this book. In subsequent chapters, the reader will see a presentation of fundamental types of major loss events, from death and dissolution/divorce to violence and war and the Holocaust. Also included are special topics such as stigmatization, life span losses and aging, and international perspectives on loss and coping. I believe that this spectrum samples well both the central loss experiences and the diversity of loss experiences and coping reactions.

As can be seen in the many ideas and references in this chapter, the field of loss and trauma is a broad, interdisciplinary one. The idea of loss as a broad unifying experience is a new and emerging concept. I have argued for an encompassing view of major loss that takes the traumatic aspect of many losses into account. I believe that this view is conducive to the generation of theory and research and to the development of ideas that can assist people at all levels of education and work as they deal with loss and trauma in their own lives and assist others facing loss and trauma. The final chapter of this book focuses explicitly on personal adjustment strategies for dealing with the inevitable losses we all will experience. I believe that this field can be both a stimulating arena for intellectual discourse and research and a valuable repository of stories and ideas about loss and adaptation.

This book emphasizes a distinct set of principles in the study of loss and trauma. The following principles are reexamined for each of the phenomena presented:

1. *Our major losses are relative.* They are relative to other losses we have experienced and to those experienced by others. By seeing them on relative continua, we are better able to make sense of them and see them as part of the whole of the human experience.

2. *Our major losses have cumulative effects.* When a new major loss occurs, we are not affected by it alone but also by other major losses that interact with it in our minds and that are recalled in our experience, some of which have been only partially addressed and resolved.

3. *When major losses occur, they contribute to new aspects of our identity.* We are different based on the consequences of those losses. As the *Wall Street Journal* reported in a series on grief in the workplace, losses can lead people to reshape their identities and careers.[3] This article described a man who had headed a large communications firm who changed his career after his 24-year-old daughter died of a brain aneurysm. He went from being a corporate executive to a consultant and a poet as a result of his loss. The grief over the loss of his daughter inspired him to write poetry for grieving children.

4. *Major losses involve adaptations related to our sense of control.* We may adapt to a degree through the use of coping strategies. In an article on grief, a reporter for the *Kansas City Star* told the story of how one man reacted when his 69-year-old father died of lung cancer: "I used to be a happy person. I want this depression to go away. I don't want to be like this. . . . I need myself back."[4]

5. *Valuable coping strategies for dealing with major losses include working on the meanings of the losses and learning how to give back to others based on our lessons of loss.* This principle is repeated in many versions throughout the chapters of this book.

For many of the phenomena discussed in the following chapters, we will see how these five principles operate. I argue the relevance of these principles in situations involving many types of loss: the death of close others, prejudice and stigmatization, war and violence, genocide, accidents and disease, unemployment and hopelessness, and suicide and aging.

Notes

1. From *New York Times*, January 12, 2000, p. C27.
2. "Tragic Death," by Mary Schmich, *Chicago Tribune*, January 24, 1999, sec. 4, p. 1.
3. Column on Work & Family, Sue Shellenbarger, *Wall Street Journal*, January 20, 1998, p. 1A.
4. Article by Eric Adler, *Kansas City Star*, November 10, 1997, p. 2A.

2 Losing Loved Ones to Death

They say when you bury your parents, you bury your past. And when you bury your spouse, you bury your present. But when you bury your child, you bury your future.

—Anonymous

Life is short but love is long.

—Epitaph for 11-year-old boy, Mells Churchyard, Somerset, England (1960)

At the same time that I was writing a draft of this chapter I was also preparing to give a talk at Indiana University regarding the abduction and possible murder of a female student at that university in the summer of 2000. This talk was difficult because of the open-ended nature of the loss of this person and the fact that her parents would be present at my talk. In such situations, what can you say to the loved ones of a person who may or may not still be alive, when every passing day represents another point in the seemingly unending anguish of the parent awaiting news or developments? The family of the lost student was exceedingly brave, but this type of loss initiates a long-term experience of devastation for the people closest to the missing loved one.

In some cases, the death of a loved one is not as painful as other types of loss situations, including those involving missing (and presumed dead) relatives. As described in Chapter 1, Carolyn Ellis's (1995) grief and anguish in watching her lover die a slow, agonizing death during the last years of their 9-year relationship speaks to the great breadth and depth of losses that survivors may experience in observing their loved ones die a slow and painful death. Thus, the death of a loved one may or may not be greatly devastating depending on the circumstances of that death that determine the extent and nature of the loss.

The importance of the "circumstances" surrounding a loss was revealed powerfully in Sittser's (1996) memoir *A Grace Disguised,* in which he tells the story of coming back from an outing in 1991 with his wife, mother, and four children. He was driving the family van when another person's negligence intervened. While he was rounding a curve at night, Sittser's van was hit by a drunk driver going 85 miles per hour.

In the blink of an eye, three generations of Sittser's family were dead: one child, his wife, and his mother. How could he ever cope with such a great loss? Would he feel guilty for being on the road at night with his family? How could he and his remaining children go on? In light of such a tragedy, could there be a God? Where was the justice in this situation? These are among the questions Sittser addresses, and he concludes by saying that his faith has been the only force helping him get to the point of writing about his experience, doing his job as a single parent, and even trying to forgive the drunk driver.

As R. Weiss (personal communication, September 5, 2000) has suggested, the experience of the death of a person we love has many meanings to us. It may involve a sense of being abandoned. It may involve a sense of helplessness in the face of death. It may involve a dashing of hopes and expectations about the future with the loved one. It involves the eventual recognition of life going on without the physical presence of the loved one.

The Death of Loved Ones

A number of prominent psychological analyses of what makes people happy have pointed to the importance of having close, loved ones. These studies indicate that close relationships are critical to the feeling of happiness and the sense that life is personally meaningful (Baumeister, 1991; Myers, 1992). Thus, when a close loved one is taken from us, our grief, mourning, and sense of despair may be profound and long-term. For those closest to us, there simply is no substitute person. The deceased person related to us in a unique way and greatly contributed to our satisfaction with life, giving us a feeling of being blessed. What we lose in these situations is more than the presence of the loved one and interaction with that person. It is often the assumption that the person will be present for many years (Janoff-Bulman, 1992). There will be many stories about the loss of loved ones reported in this chapter. There is no strong evidence available in the literature specifying clearly the types of death of loved ones that cause the most devastation in the lives of survivors. A key principle in evaluating the scope of a loss for survivors was articulated by Harvey (2000): *The survivor is the person whose perception and imputed meaning counts the most in our understanding of the nature and extent of loss. The survivor defines the power of a loss in his or her feelings of devastation and the extent and depth of mourning.*

What is clear for all who must endure such pain and mourning is that love was an original condition for its ultimate occurrence. As Robert Weiss (1988, 1998) has argued, only the loss of relationships characterized by deep, close attachment triggers powerful grief. So there is an irony in the grief to be reported here. It is that such grief could occur only when people loved the lost person and had an extraordinary bond of closeness with him or her. What, then, is wiped away in death is the continuity of that bond, which in large measure is composed of people's memories of being together, of the beloved one's smile, voice, and particular mannerisms and expressions. These countless memorial traces continue to exist and sometimes bubble up into the consciousness of the survivor. A "survivor," then in some sense, is really the "victim" of a loss, in that he or she will continue to experience these wonderful memories of a past love with the knowledge that no further memories can be created.

In the following discussions, I first consider loss of a loved one through death and then loss that occurs through the breakup of a relationship. In the latter discussion, I compare these two types of loss.

A Survey of the
Bereavement Literature

Grief is defined as a person's emotional reaction to the loss event (DeSpelder & Strickland, 1992) and as a "process of realization, of making real inside the self an event that has already occurred in reality outside" (Parkes, 1972, p. 53). The *Diagnostic and Statistical Manual of Mental Disorders* (American Psychiatric Association, 1994) defines bereavement as a psychiatric disorder if it includes symptoms characteristic of "a Major Depressive Episode . . . such as insomnia, poor appetite, and weight loss" (p. 684) that last at least 2 months after the loss. The *DSM-IV* goes on to note that "normal grief" could include (a) guilt about actions taken or not taken, (b) thoughts in the survivor that he or she would be better off dead, and (c) hallucinatory experiences of hearing or seeing images of the lost person. The *DSM-IV* suggests that prolonged impairment of daily functioning, marked slowness of movement, and preoccupation with worthlessness would begin to move the grief experience toward disorder status, or what also is called "complicated mourning" (Rando, 1993).

As C. S. Lewis (1961) implies about grief, it is a type of experience that most people anticipate with dread. Lewis himself died within 2 years of the death of his wife Joy, and it is believed that Lewis's profound grief hastened his death (Bregman & Thiermann, 1995). In principle, however, grief is an adaptive reaction and essential to recovery. Lewis (1961) suggested the power of recurrent thoughts and images of the loved one when he said,

> There are moments . . . when something inside me tries to assure me that I don't really mind so much, not so very much, after all. Love is not the whole of a man's life. I was happy before I ever met Joy. I've plenty of what are called "resources." People get over these things. Come, I shan't do so badly. One is ashamed to listen to this voice but it seems for a little to be making out a good case. Then comes a sudden jab of red-hot memory and all this "commonsense" vanishes like an ant in the mouth of a furnace. (p. 7)

Working from a combined biological and psychoanalytic perspective, John Bowlby (1960, 1979), the late English psychiatrist, made important contributions to our understanding of grief. Bowlby argued that grief instinctively occurs and is focused on resolution and adaptation. Bowlby conceived a developmental theory of attachment based on his research with children and their mothers. He framed his analysis of grief within the context of the mother-child relationship.

In this scheme, the child has great fear of being abandoned by the mother. When the mother leaves, the child uses both crying and expressions of anger to get the mother to return. Anger is an attempt to ensure that absences are not prolonged. But when the loss is permanent, crying and anger responses are no longer adaptive. Depression soon occurs, as does an inability to initiate and maintain action. This early stage of shock and numbness is eventually replaced by detachment from the loss. Bowlby views this detachment as an essential step for the reorganization of one's life in the absence of the deceased close other. Reorganization then leads to new attachments. Grieving is the process that permits detachment, reorganization, and new attachments to occur.

Bowlby (1980) concluded that there are two forms of pathological mourning. Both can reach various degrees of severity; however, a less severe instance is difficult to distinguish from "normal" grieving. The first category of pathological mourning is chronic, and it is characterized by intense and prolonged emotional reactions to loss—it is as if the mourner is stuck in an adrenaline-fueled fit of emotional expressiveness. According to Bowlby, the second form involves the prolonged absence of conscious mourning. This delayed form of mourning has been described extensively by counselors who work with the bereaved. The person who is not able to mourn consciously typically suffers vague physical and psychological symptoms (e.g., headaches, tension, insomnia) but does not readily relate them to the loss. It is as if this mourner is stuck in being "numb" or in the early phase of grief. Such a mourning pattern also frequently involves cheerfulness on the part of the mourner, sometimes with such zest that it may appear to be exaggerated to the outsider.

Wortman and Silver (1989) have contended that this latter type of behavior may not signify mourning at all. Rather, these people may show an absence of grief because they feel no distress. Kleber and Brom (1992) suggest that both schools of thought may be correct. Some

indeed may have no distress and show no symptoms of mourning—
however devastating the loss. Others, though, and possibly the majority of those who show delays, may be kidding themselves and trying to
kid their friends and associates. They often do not even accept sympathy and compulsively try to take care of others encountering various
types of difficulty.

In the grief area, Bowlby's theory of attachment has proven to be one
of the most useful stimulants for contemporary theory and research
(Cochran & Claspell, 1987). His ideas, for example, have been influential in the investigation of adult attachment in close relationships
(Hazan & Shaver, 1987) and attachment and bereavement in general
(Shaver & Tancredy, 2000). Presumably, people who have more secure
attachments in their close adult relationships experienced a sense of
security in their early relationships with their mothers. Those who are
more insecure or avoidant, however, are posited to have encountered
ambivalence or abandonment in their relationships with their mothers.

Harvey (1996) argues that we all likely will experience unresolved
degrees of grief throughout our adult lives. We incur too many losses
not to have these lingering feelings and issues. Researchers of the grief
experience have tried to determine what is an "abnormally long" period of grief. But it seems that this question cannot be easily answered.
It is clear that the first year after a death, especially an unexpected
death, brings with it many anniversary-like reminders of the loss to
survivors.

Holidays, birthdays, and other special days are often times of acute
anguish for survivors. Probably the most critical question about extended, deep grief concerns the societal stereotype that it is time to
"move on" with life after some period of grieving. But grieving is one of
the most individual of all human responses. There are no set truths
about how to lose someone dear to us and then "put it behind us." In
fact, many losses are never "behind us." They are often at the forefront
of our thoughts on a daily basis. We may go on with our work, find new
intimates, and otherwise seem to be achieving normality. Yet these
losses are there and are seen as fundamental reductions of who we are
and what we are about as human beings. They are harsh facts that define

us and cannot be sugarcoated or filed away and brought back when we wish to consider them.

Hopefully, the survivor can move to a point at which it is possible to remember regularly and positively the lost other, while at same time take constructive steps toward establishing a life without the other and the personal identity that attaches to the other. Often, the survivor needs to recognize that the deceased person likely would want her or him to achieve this new identity.

As many scholars have noted, different types of loss and resulting grief directly affect the length and depth of the grieving experience. Fulton (1979) conceived a distinction between "high-grief" deaths versus "low-grief" deaths that has merit. A high-grief death is characterized by intense emotional and physical reactions to loss. A low-grief death is less affecting emotionally, and the bereaved is able to cope more readily. The death of a child would be the classic high-grief death. The death of a person who had reached a quite advanced age and who had lived a long and fulfilling life would be a low-grief death.

Another type of grief has been posited. It is "disenfranchised grief." Orbuch (1988), in discussing nonmarital relationships that end, and Savage (1989), in discussing the death of an unborn or stillborn child, both point to the devastation of these experiences for the people involved. As a society, we do not typically provide the same types of social support for people who experience these losses that we do for people who experience marital dissolution or the loss of a child who was born and lived for some period of time. In a certain sense, "loss is loss," and each loss deserves due consideration of its meaning in the life of the survivor and requires a time for healing.

Many people must experience disenfranchised grief, because for various reasons they lack a community of close, caring others. Early in the AIDS epidemic, persons dying of AIDS and their loved ones often encountered this type of grief. In recent years, increasingly, various homosexual communities have been diligent and effective in addressing the mourning needs of persons dying with AIDS and those close to them. Still, for many, an AIDS death is a stigmatizing type of death. Others, too, including the homeless, still must silently experience their own instances of disenfranchised grief. Because some people have in one way or another become alienated or isolated from close others, there are millions of people who likely experience much unrecognized grief and anguish. And that is *in addition to* the normal grieving experience that we all regularly experience!

Another type of grief has been conceived as "anticipatory grief." According to Schoenberg, Carr, Peretz, and Kutscher (1970), anticipatory grief refers to the feelings inspired by prior knowledge of an impending death. With such knowledge, the survivor is better able to prepare psychologically for the death. Whether or not anticipation is helpful to a person's ability to deal with the extent and depth of a loss, it likely does reduce the initial shock. However, that may be the extent of its ameliorative power. The survivor still may have to deal with substantial issues pertinent to the relationship that has ended and to the new life that must be developed.

One of the most sophisticated longitudinal studies of grief was carried out by Parkes and Weiss (1983). They studied 70 widowers and widows, conducting interviews at 2 weeks, 8 weeks, 13 months, and 2 to 4 years after the spouse's death. Parkes and Weiss identified the following types of grief: (a) unanticipated—in which the survivor has great difficulty in moving on and often shows avoidance, self-reproach, and despair; (b) conflicted—in which the survivor goes up and down, showing ambivalence toward the lost loved one; and (c) chronic—in which there is a long-term intense yearning for the deceased loved one. This last type of grief occurs especially among those who had been quite dependent on the loved one. Because the survivor's sense of security and safety had been reduced considerably in one fell swoop, the survivor has little direction in reestablishing his or her life.

In the 21st century, do we grieve in the same ways that we grieved in the 19th century? A valuable book titled *Bitter, Bitter Tears* by Paul Rosenblatt (1983) provides some insight about this question. He examined hundreds of tattered, dusty diaries written by persons who had remained behind in the Eastern United States while their loved ones went West looking for fortune. Many of these adventurers were men who died or disappeared, often leaving behind young widows. Rosenblatt found an outpouring of emotion and yearning for the lost other. He noted that the grieving processes of these survivors were similar to the grieving processes of people in the 21st century. Their depression, despair, and sense of hopelessness were frequently displayed in the diaries, which were used for venting feelings and trying to reflect on the different meanings of their loss.

One view of grief is that it can be the prelude to positive developments in a survivor's life. C. S. Lewis (1961) said, "Still, there are enormous gains" (p. 49). Cochran and Claspell (1987) eloquently argue that a key activity involved in grieving is a search for meaning that leads to insights, glimmers of understanding, and the learning of principles that help us clarify our philosophy of living and a more mature view of oneself and other people. Survivors who begin to search diligently for meaning often develop a story of resolve and hope and grow emotionally as a consequence.

Finally, some people choose to develop a mental reality that involves some type of regular activity oriented toward a lost loved one. An important book edited by Klass, Silverman, and Nickman (1996), titled *Continuing Bonds*, explores the idea that grieving individuals often choose to construct continuing mental relationships with their deceased loved ones. One may see a sign of this bond in cherished pictures of the lost other that a grieving person places strategically around his or her life space.

Diverse Grief Responses

When is a grieving reaction, whether in the form of crying out, depression and despair, or running fast to avoid thinking and feeling, so prolonged or intense that it is considered to be abnormal? That is a question that is exceedingly difficult to answer in the abstract. As I discuss here, people grieve in different ways. Commonsense logic suggests that when a person feels that he or she is not able to function because of grief, then the person needs to seek professional help.

The usual early reactions to the death of a loved one are shock, a feeling of numbness, and denial. In addition, the person usually experiences a lengthy period of highs and lows—with the lows involving various degrees of depression and inertia. After the loss of her husband at age 34 one woman reported, "When he died, I just felt empty, numb. I was in a fog."

In a moving and inspirational firsthand account of the sudden heart attack and death of her husband, who was in his 40s, Elizabeth Neeld (1990) describes vividly her own early reactions at a memorial service for her husband:

> The congregation is now beginning the final hymn: "Amazing Grace." I listen, but I am not present at a memorial service on July 4 . . . I am far away.
>
> In a big white room in a house in Texas. . . . It's Sunday, and the *New York Times* covers the floor . . . [my husband] Greg says, "Hey, I haven't heard our concert this morning. Isn't it about time?" And I go over to the piano I've had since I was a little girl and begin to play, "Amazing Grace, how sweet the sound." (p. 18)

She suggested that this scene was typical of the many scenes of intense closeness with her husband that raced through her mind in the early days after his death. She was experiencing the "missing" state that was described in Chapter 1 as being at the core of major loss. She continued with the following description of her experience:

> In the days and weeks following, I must have told the story [of my husband's unexpected death] a thousand times. . . . I took little notice of the strange things that were happening to my body—or to my mind. My appetite disappeared. For days I felt no hunger. It was more than two weeks before I remembered that there were good things in the world to eat. . . . I lay awake for hours when I went to bed. (p. 19)

Neeld's report is similar to that offered by many individuals in describing their early reactions to the sudden loss of a loved one. Neeld became seriously depressed the summer after her husband's death. An encompassing sense of hopelessness and depression are common in these situations in which a devastating loss comes without notice. As Meg Woodson (1994) said in *The Toughest Days of Grief,* "The smell of hopelessness and helplessness pervades the bog of our grief. Difficulties loom in the darkness as impossibilities. Taking initiative comes hard; being sucked into thick, clinging depression doesn't take initiative" (p. 30). In her classic book, *On Death and Dying,* Elizabeth

Kubler-Ross (1969) describes the stages of denial and isolation, anger, bargaining, depression, and acceptance that she believes characterize the experience of people who know that their death is imminent. Certainly denial and isolation, anger, depression, and acceptance occur as part of many people's set of grief responses. Grief theories have suggested a number of other phases of grief, including disorganization, undoing, guilt, and integration. Stage or phase theories of grief have been criticized for indicating or implying the presence of lockstep sequences of experiences and suggesting that deviations are abnormal (DeSpelder & Strickland, 1992). In fact, however, people's grief reactions are variable. Some grief experiences involve only a small subset of the aforementioned stages, and some of these reactions may occur at any point during the grieving process. Commenting on the experience of stages of grief in her memoir of her husband's death, former New York Congresswoman Bella Abzug wrote, "I still have tremendous pain. . . . I haven't found any five stages, just tremendous sadness."[1] In the following sections, reactions to different types of loss are considered. For example, a common reaction on the part of parents who have lost a child is a feeling of guilt and responsibility—even if there was no way they could have prevented the death. A principle that seeps through this entire chapter on the loss of a close relationship through death is that there are universals associated with every grieving reaction. The idea of "missing" that I have frequently mentioned is one such universal, as is the idea that powerful grieving of a major loss irrevocably changes who people are in some significant ways. Paradoxically, at the same time, each loss is special and different. Each grief reaction bears the individual's own idiosyncratic stamp of meaning and identity.

In considering the following types of losses, it should be emphasized that contemporary research on bereavement is challenging the idea that everyone who loses a loved one will experience severe or chronic grief (Bonanno, 2000). Increasingly, also, there is pause about the link between pathology and grief or the view that everyone must resolve grief.

The Death of a Child

> I still feel my son's absence every day of my life. But it's overcoming the challenges that are placed in our way, that make life worth living. (Mary Tyler Moore, describing the effects of the suicide death of her son Richie in 1980)[2]

> "Hi, I'm Meg Woodson, and my son Joey just died," I said to strangers on elevators when I went alone to a conference. (Meg Woodson, *The Toughest Days of Grief*, 1994, p. 30)

A parent's grief is arguably the most inconsolable, incurable kind of grief. Parents usually expect to outlive their offspring. They usually imbue their children with many plans and hopes—some of which did not materialize in their own lives. Thus, the loss of a child can dash all of these expectations that the child will live a long, "normal" life and accomplish much—including continuing the bloodline of the family. A frequent reaction of parents to the loss of a child is that of survival guilt: "It is not fair that she died before me." As discussed by Corr, Nabe, and Corr (1994), other types of guilt include the following: death causation guilt (that one had a role in the death), illness-related guilt (that the parents' neglect led to the child's fatal disease), and moral guilt (that the loss of the child is punishment for the parents' moral transgressions).

Weiss (1993, 2000) has argued that parental grief often includes intense wishes to protect and soothe the lost child, to hold and comfort the child. According to Weiss, parental grief may also include survivor's guilt and guilt about being unable to protect the child from death. A parent may feel this protective need even though the child's death was in no way the fault of the parent.

As part of people's attempts to cope with major loss, they may be creative and contribute to the welfare of others (similar to the idea of "generativity," or giving to future generations). Parents who grieve the losses of their children have expressed their grief through many positive artistic and scholarly works. I note some such helpful works in this discussion. However, I first describe a particularly engaging project as an example of contributory grief work.

In 1988, Pan Am 103 exploded over Scotland on a flight from Germany to the United States. A bomb caused the explosion of the plane, most likely planted by two Libyan terrorists. Many of the individuals killed on this flight were Syracuse University students returning to the United States from Europe where they had been pursuing studies in art and other fields. These students' parents have formed one of the most powerful special cause lobbying groups ever established because of a tragedy. Not only have the parents been effective in urging the U.S. government to find and indict the persons who were the likely perpetrators of the bombing, they have also contributed many beneficial works to the memory of their young, talented daughters and sons who perished. They also created a scholarship program in honor of the Pan Am 103 students that funded its first group of scholars in 1994.

The most gripping work by the Pan Am Flight 103 parents has been a sculpting project started by one of the mothers. Susan Lowenstein is a gifted sculptor who has created a number of female figures in bronze cast form and placed them on the Syracuse campus as a memorial to the students who died. The women who served as models for the figures are mothers of children who died. The expressions they show illustrate their inconsolable grief at the very moment they heard about their children's deaths. In this sculpture piece, called "Dark Elegy," these female figures kneel, lie, and stand while they weep, shout, and try to shrink away from the darkest moment of their lives. As I viewed these figures, I thought that no greater testament to the loss of these young persons could have been created. It is a monument to the love their mothers felt for them. It is a place where generations of students, parents, and others can go and look and shed their own tears.

A sense of being haunted is a theme expressed by many parents who have lost children. The Pan Am parents reflect this theme. As I note in a later chapter on haunting, writers such as David Morrell, who created the Rambo series of novels and movies, have devoted books and parts of their lives and careers to expressing their feelings about their deceased child and what the child meant to them. Morrell's 1988 book, *Fireflies,* describes the loss of his son Matthew, who died of cancer at age 14. Matthew was very special to his father. He had great sensitivity, was a budding musician, and brought many friends to his family's home. For Morrell, Matthew's death was staggering. Ironically, it occurred at a time when the Rambo books were bringing Morrell much fame and wealth. But without Matthew, it did not matter.

Fireflies refers to a hallucinatory experience Morrell reports that he had a few months after Matthew's death. In the experience, Matthew appeared to Morrell as one of hundreds of fireflies and transmitted message to him. Through this message, Matthew told Morrell to re-establish his hope and begin to contribute to others who had lost children, thereby giving Matthew's life and death greater meaning. Writing this story of Matthew and speaking to organizations for grieving parents were Morrell's ways of working on his grief, moving on with his work and relationships and honoring Matthew.

A particular kind of loss occurs when an only child dies and leaves behind a single parent. Evelyn Gillis (1986) was a single mother of a 22-year-old daughter who was killed in an automobile accident. She notes some of the special deprivations experienced by a single parent upon the death of his or her only child:

> We face the absence of support from another adult who would share the same feelings of loss and grief. . . . We alone carry the responsibility of the funeral arrangements. After the funeral, when other people return to their own homes and families, we are left to face the reality of the child's death, alone in a house that offers nothing but silence. . . . We cry out to have another person alongside who knows, really knows, what the death of the child means, someone who shares those special memories of how our family once was. (p. 315)

Gillis indicates that it took years for her to reestablish her life without her daughter. She would often go to the cemetery and grieve for hours at the grave of her daughter because she lacked the energy to drive away. At some point she knew that to come out of her absorption in mourning she would have to give of herself to others. But she also felt it was better not to love or give, lest she again lose someone she loved deeply. She finally began to recover with the aid of a chapter of the Compassionate Friends organization (whose focus is on helping bereaved parents) where she worked as a sibling leader in her group.

Many who lose a child go into a shell, seldom showing the depth of grief that resides within them. Journalist Bill Moyers described the tor-turous grief that his father kept inside and what he believed were the physical effects of that grief on his father:

> When my brother died of cancer in 1966 at age 39, my father began a grieving pro-cess that lasted almost 25 years. During that time he suffered from chronic, debilitat-ing headaches that could not be cured. At one point, a doctor tried to tell him that his headaches were related to his grief, but he persisted in treating the pain as a medical problem, and the torment continued. After my father's death at 86, I thought about he could have been helped. (quoted in Powell, 1994, p. 42)

The Death of a Spouse
or Significant Other

Reactions to the loss of a spouse or romantic partner can vary, but there is a set of factors that make the devastation more severe. As de-scribed earlier, Elizabeth Neeld experienced a wrenching sense of grief when she suddenly lost her husband. She had an intimate, long-term relationship that unexpectedly came to a sudden end. The unexpected-ness and suddenness, the relative youth of the victim, and the closeness of the bond all appear to contribute to the extent and depth of the grieving experience.

Joie White is another widow who felt a powerful sense of grief when her husband died suddenly. White's husband, Jason, was killed while on duty as a police officer in Washington, D.C., in 1993. Ms. White, who was 30 at the time, was described in a *Washington Post* article as em-bracing the memory of her husband by totally immersing herself in the trappings of his life. In effect, as described in a later chapter, she is still haunted by this loss. She said that for a long period after her husband's death, she waited by the front door for him to return at his normal 11 p.m. arrival time. She was in total denial and continued to tell people that her husband didn't die. It finally hit her when she was filling out an application to return to school soon after the funeral. She said, "I thought I was going to have a nervous breakdown, because that was the first time I actually had to state that I was a widow."[3] Instead of admitting she was a widow she wrote that she was married. Soon, however, her denial gave way to anger. About 6 months after the loss of her husband, she went to see a therapist in an effort to begin to be able to have a new life and a new identity. Her road back may be long.

The effects of losing a close relationship in early life or midlife can be staggering for the survivor, who may grieve in a profound way for years. Raphael (1983) reviewed evidence suggesting that continued intense bereavement may contribute to early death. One such indicator is an increase of almost 40% in the death rate of widowers over the age of 54 during the first 6 months of bereavement. Suicide is also a danger during this very early stage. Raphael reports evidence indicating that the suicide rate among a large sample of widows and widowers was 2.5 times higher in the first 6 months after the loss than in the fourth and subsequent years. Short of death, a survivor's mental and physical health is often impaired during the intense bereavement period that usually last for months but can last for a much longer time span.

The death of a spouse or romantic partner is one of the most researched topics in the grief literature. Widows and widowers have been frequently studied. Particularly valuable discussions may be found in Glick, Weiss, and Parkes's (1974) analysis of the first year of bereavement and Shuchter's (1986) analysis of the dimensions of grief. Glick et al. (1974) followed a group of 49 widows (originally) over a period of years and developed this informative conclusion about recovery after the first years of bereavement:

> Most components of the grief syndrome—feelings of shock, of abandonment, and of loss of part of the self, for example—seemed to be a response to the loss of the husband, and so to have faded as the loss receded into the past. Loneliness, however, seemed to be a reaction to the husband's absence. . . . It did not fade with time.
>
> By the end of the first year . . . some widows were dating, generally without the emotional reliance on the man or men they were seeing. (p. 84)

The follow-up interview, held 2, 3, or 4 years after death of their husbands, revealed however that a good many were engaged to remarry or had already remarried. None of these described themselves as still lonely, although most continued to sorrow for their loss of their husband.

Sometimes when widows looked back on the first year of their bereavement they could single out events they felt had special significance for their recovery. Some spoke of incidents in which they asserted for the first time that their lives must continue and that they must look forward and not back. (pp. 212-213)

NBC *Today Show* host Katie Couric lost her husband in 1998 to colon cancer when he was 42. She is now raising their two small children by herself. In an interview in *Good Housekeeping*, Couric noted the value to her of having others acknowledge the horrible loss she had experienced. A few months after her husband's death, she expressed the profound nature of her feelings of loss:

Nothing really comforts me . . . I still can't believe it. When I think about it, it just permeates every cell in my body. You can forget about it temporarily. But then the grief comes like a huge wave and like a horrible invasion of your heart and soul.[4]

In his analysis, Shuchter (1986) interviewed widows and widowers as well as others who had lost close relationships to death. He provides a useful comment on the renewal of romantic relations after losing a spouse or lover:

The widowed person who has begun to expose his or her vulnerability and opens up to someone else carries a whole set of emotional responses that have been associated with being in love, making falling in love easy once the barriers are down. (p. 245)

He goes on to describe a woman who fell in love a few months after her husband's death. She said that the chemistry was there when they just said hello and that she decided she would marry him early on— recognizing that later she would learn a lot more about him. Shuchter notes that this couple may be in for difficult times because the woman most likely has not begun to complete her grieving. It is probable that she will often have experiences with her new husband that initiate strong feelings of loss—possibly without recognizing it, she may associate events and cues in her new family with her dead husband and be thrown into feelings of missing him. Furthermore, the woman very likely will make some invidious comparisons between her new husband and her dead husband. In many ways, these difficulties are the same that people who divorce after long marriages and then remarry quickly experience. The situation is not hopeless but must be approached by both partners with patience and respect for the continued grieving process. To the extent that the woman in this example does not recognize and affirm her grief, it is likely that she will be troubled and the new relationship ultimately will be troubled as well.

An interesting finding emerging in the past two decades is that the immune systems of widows and widowers apparently are affected by loss and grief. In a study reported by Schleifer, Keller, and Stein (1979), it was found that bereaved husbands' lymphocyte responses became less effective 2 months after their wives died from breast cancer. Why would a person's immune system be less able to cope with potential threats after the death of a spouse? There probably are many reasons, but depression, loneliness, and social support may be involved. Depression and loneliness are common experiences for a survivor after a loved one has died. Social support may buffer the survivor somewhat against the effect of physical disease potential. A confidant—someone with whom one is quite close and to whom one can express pain—often is a critical resource that we all need much of the time, but particularly in times of stress or great anguish.

I conclude this section with an excerpt from Herbert and Kay Kramer's (1993) *Conversations at Midnight* (which is discussed again in the chapter on experiencing dying). This husband and wife team wrote this book about death as Herbert was in the process of dying of cancer. It is a valuable book on dying for anyone who is close to death and for that person's loved ones. So much of our lives with our closest loved ones who survive us live on in their minds after our deaths in the form of images and memories. The following excerpt reveals the poignancy and vividness of some of these images. It is a narration by Kay of her experience in the moments that she watched the undertaker take Herb's body from their home soon after his death:

> Leaning against the porch pillar, I wept as I remembered the sight of him the first time he appeared at this door, the romantic arrivals during our brief courtship, the evening he arrived for our marriage ceremony, and all the times he left, usually racing at breakneck speed for Mr. Duncan's cab—coat, hat, and bag already airborne for his trip to the airport—and on to Washington in the early morning hours before the rest of the street was awake. I could see him running out the door to ride the new

bike I got him on his sixtieth birthday, and the surprise on his face the time the white limousine came to pick him up for a Father's Day picnic at Gillette Castle.

It felt as if my heart were breaking as I watched him leave this street for the last time, this street he loved, that looked so good to him each time he returned to it after every journey, this street that was home to him since 1953. (pp. 226-227)

Although Kay Kramer's memories here reveal great pain, the book as a whole and the act of writing it in the last year of Herb's life were healing and uplifting experiences for both of them.

The Death of a Parent

It's very important for us—all of us baby boomers who grew up in the biggest group in American history—to give our parents the dignity of living lives as whole as possible as long as they can.... Honor your parents and live without regret when they're gone. (President Bill Clinton in a Mother's Day interview in *Parade Magazine*)

This quotation relates President Clinton's feelings about his mother, Virginia Kelley, who died at age 70 early in 1994. Clinton was very close to his mother. She raised him by herself after her husband died very early in Clinton's life. She had an enormous influence on all that Clinton has accomplished, including his political career. Clinton reflected on how, in the middle of a hectic life, he had tried to take some time to grieve soon after his mother's death:

I have literally signed thousands of letters to friends of hers and friends of mine who wrote me to say they were sorry she had died and with some reminiscence of her.... Signing the letters, and being able to read them, was just a way of reconnecting with my mother.

It was a way of grieving that even a workaholic could understand. I've got all these things around here I've got to do. I said, "I'm going to sign these letters." So sometimes I'd sit in here [in the Oval Office] by myself for an hour and read letters, or do it at night. I'd cry and laugh and do all the things you want to do. It was a way of being alone, doing something I ought to be doing anyway, and then just kind of having images of my mother flash before my mind. It helped me to deal with it.

Yes, I think I have a pretty tough time on Mother's Day.... I recall the first time I realized she was gone. I used to call her every Sunday night.... So I come in on Sunday night from my trip to Europe [that occurred soon after Ms. Kelley's funeral] and I was in the kitchen and all but had the phone picked up before I realized: "My God, I can't do it."[5]

Going into the 21st century, more than one quarter of the population are baby boomers in their 40s and early 50s. Many are beginning to lose parents and to experience the deep void of that experience. Near his own midlife, *Chicago Tribune* writer Bob Greene lost his father in 1998. In a piece in the *Tribune,* Greene mentions the experience of being invited to give a commencement address at Ohio State University in the Ohio Stadium, the gigantic football stadium to which he often had been taken by his father. In introducing his speech, Greene mentioned the recent death of his father, who had gone to games at the stadium for more than 50 years. The crowd of 50,000 rose in unison to honor Greene's father, a lovely tribute that reassured Greene and the thousands of readers of his column.[6]

A theme that occurs throughout people's accounts of their parents' deaths is the regret of not having shared more with them emotionally and cognitively while they still were alive.

I certainly feel that way about my mother who died in 1996 and to a lesser degree about my father who died during the writing of this book in 2000. I regret that we did not spend more time getting to know each other as adults. That is a special blessing for parents and children who become good friends and confidants as adults. When we lose our parents, we usually feel a great void. Willy Loman says in the play *Death of a Salesman,* "I never had a chance to talk to him, and I still feel—kind of temporary about myself."

Anne Loew (1993) has written about the ongoing process of grief associated with the loss of a parent at age 17, a point much too early in the "normal course of life events":

> I remember telling myself, "I can't deal with these feelings now. I'll figure it out when I'm older." I wish I had let myself feel those healing feelings.
>   His death left an empty place in my life, which I now try to fill with memories and personal reminders of him—he was from Texas, so I buy a yellow rose of Texas each year on his birthday. Many entries in my diary start, "Dear Dad." It's a way of sharing my life with him.[7]

It might seem that an adult's loss of a parent has less effect than the other types of loss described in these pages. And it may be that way when the parent has lived a full and generally satisfying life and when the adult child has had much opportunity to be close to the parent. In general, however, we all have loose ends, or unfinished business, with our parents when they die. It has been reported that in the months following the loss of a parent, surviving adult offspring show a greater incidence of spousal abuse, drunkenness, and extramarital affairs, as well as conflicts among siblings (Ackner, 1993). The conflicts among relatives are quite common—even at the time of the funeral and especially at the reading of the will. Death forces survivors to be more honest in how they perceive and really feel about one another. More generally, why might such patterns be associated with a parent's death? Probably the best answer is that the death may shake up the person's life in such a way that the person feels that he or she no longer has an anchor. This type of feeling may be particularly strong when parents are close to their children (e.g., the relationship of James and Michael Jordan). The following obituary poignantly demonstrates the bond between a mother and her son:

> Theresia [who died at age 32] was a loving, caring and sensitive person. Her whole life was devoted to her young son and her dreams for his success in school and baseball. She will be missed beyond words by her son Chad.[8]

Chad's grief may always defy words. As a college teacher, I can attest to the frequent grief shown by students who lost parents when the students were still young children. It is often a bitter, angry feeling that they were dealt a terrible injustice by life. They may not have known their dead parent, but that fact too causes great consternation. You can go to the Vietnam Wall in Washington, D.C., and find grieving children of soldiers who died when the children were very young. There definitely is a sense of incompleteness that follows the child throughout life. The same is true for young children who knew their parents, but then lost their parents when they still were young children. Their agony is often intensified by knowing a loving parent only for what seems to have been a short, inadequate period of time.

Another important instance of losing one's parent occurs when the survivor is at some age below the generally conceived boundary line for adulthood. Quite young children, for example, may show feelings of unreality for a long time after a parent's death (Sanders, 1980, 1982). It

seems impossible to them that their parent could die, or leave them—
in their experience of unreality they may think the parent chose to die.
It has been argued that this is one of the main reasons young children
need to be involved in funeral or memorial services for their deceased
parent (Leash, 1994). Such involvement may help them accept reality.
Years after their parent's death, children sometimes indicate that they
felt cheated when their parent died because the adults attending the
parent were not truthful with them and did not involve them in the formal plans for grieving. Young and teenage children will grieve the loss
over a long period after a parent's death, both explicitly and implicitly.
The implicit type of grief may come through in their dreams, relationships with others, and actual physical and psychological health.

Joyce Carol Oates discusses a frequently overlooked form of loss connected to the potent experience of losing a parent. Oates knew about
this type of loss through her own mother's experience as a child.
Oates's mother was given to another member of the family to raise
when her mother lost her husband and was in desperate financial
straits. Oates's mother expressed a profound grief to Oates 80 years after this occurred, telling her, "My mother didn't want me."[9] Oates concluded that despite our ages, identities, achievements, and the like, we
are all a single age (in effect we are always children). Our parents are
still children requiring the love of parents long deceased, just as we in
adulthood are still the children of our parents, vulnerable and exposed
to their emotions.

A Child's Grief

Without intervention, research shows children aged 4 to 16 who have lost a sibling
have the highest incidence of behavioral problems.

The preceding quote is by Sara Atkins, grief counselor and leader of
Journey of Hope, a homeowners' community support group in Plano,
Texas. In this quote she describes the importance of providing support
to children who have lost siblings or parents. Worden (1996) wrote a
valuable book about children and grief. He based his arguments on his

own and others' research on children who have lost parents and siblings to death. He suggests that children must believe that the deceased is indeed dead before they can begin to deal with the emotional effect of the loss. Depending on the development of the child, he or she likely will experience most of the same cognitive, emotional, and behavioral effects of bereavement that are displayed by adults. Adolescents also show similar patterns, although they often exhibit more difficulties if, in addition to the death, they have had to cope with the divorce of their parents (Balk, 1996).

Worden (1996) suggests that children should be referred for professional help if they exhibit the following patterns: persistent difficulty talking about the dead parent; aggressive behavior; high degrees of anxiety and somatic complaints such as headaches, sleeping, and eating difficulties; academic difficulties; and withdrawal and persistent self-blame or guilt. All of these patterns are common after the death of a parent. What is essential is to evaluate how prolonged they are and whether the child is able to begin to address them with the help of close others. If necessary, it is important to provide the child with professional help.

Worden (1996) notes that his research indicates that children suffer similarly when a parent or a sibling has died. He also contends that within the first year of either type of loss, about 25% of children experiencing the loss will be "at risk," and possibly in need of professional assistance.

What I have discovered as a college teacher is that college-age young people who have lost parents or siblings often have not had much *opportunity to talk about and be expressive about these losses.* These young people often pinpoint this lack of opportunities to communicate about their loss as a factor that causes them long-term grief and the feeling that few if any other people care about their continuing experience of loss. Such reports suggest to me the importance of lifelong personal work (such as journal writing) and confiding in close others to attaining the highest level of peace and adaptation to these types of staggering loss, that always are "out of season," and sometimes perceived as unjust as well (e.g., when a parent or sibling has been killed by a drunk driver).

Relevance of Basic Ideas

As noted in Chapter 1, certain basic principles of loss phenomena are highlighted throughout the discussion of different topics related to loss. For death of close others, these principles are as follows:

1. *Our major losses are relative.* They are relative to other losses we have experienced and to those experienced by others. By seeing them on relative continua, we are better able to make sense of them and see them as part of the whole of the human experience. We saw this principle at work in people's reasoning about the loss of parents, spouses, and children, with the latter being typically the greatest manifestation of "high grief."

2. *Our major losses have cumulative effects.* When a new major loss occurs, we are not affected by it alone but also by other major losses that interact with it in our minds and that are recalled in our experience, some of which have been only partially addressed and resolved. Again, losses such as the death of children often have staggering, reverberating effects on us throughout our lives.

3. *When major losses occur, they contribute to new aspects of our identity.* We are different based on the consequences of losses in our lives. We have seen, for example, that persons who lose spouses after long, satisfying marriages must learn to think of themselves as alone, without a partner who contributes to their emotional, social, and physical welfare. Their whole identity must change.

4. *Major losses involve adaptations related to our sense of control.* We may restore a sense of control to a degree through the use of coping strategies. The death of a loved one is one of the most potent strikes against our sense of control. We can try to make reparations or regain the lost person in cases of dissolution or divorce. But we do not have that option with death. Acceptance of the death of someone we love affords us some peace and a restoration of a partial sense of control.

5. *Valuable coping strategies for dealing with major losses include working on the meanings of the losses and learning how to give back to others based on our lessons of loss.* These strategies are key factors in our effective adaptation to the death of someone close to us. The following discussion offers a further illustration of this principle.

The various chapters in this book bear differing threads of connection among underlying ideas for diverse loss phenomena. An interesting thread linking the present chapter to Chapter 8, which discusses losses connected to violence and war, is suggested by CNN's Christiane Amanpour. Amanpour has been a frequent reporter in war zones during the past two decades. She has reported from the streets of Sarajevo, the Bosnian War, the Gulf War, African border wars, and the Kosovo conflict. In late 2000, she was asked to interview persons involved in the latest Palestinian-Israeli conflict. Amanpour said she was quite reluctant to go there (and to new wars in general) because she had a 6-month-old son and worried about being killed and leaving him without a mother.

After beginning her reporting in the streets near Jerusalem, however, Amanpour began to feel that her work was all the more important due to the large number of children being killed—55 of the first 240 Palestinians killed were children. One of these children was less than 2 years of age, and another, aged 7, was captured on video by a camera crew trying to hide behind his father when he was killed by cross fire from those battling in the streets. Many of these children were killed because they refused to obey their parents by staying home and instead spent time throwing rocks and objects at Israeli forces in the streets of death.

Amanpour said, "When my son is old enough to look me in the eye and ask me, 'Mummy, why do you go to those dangerous places? What will happen to me if you get killed?' I hope I will be able to say, 'Because I have to. Because if the storytellers quit, the bad people will win.' "[10]

Patricia Weenolsen (1988) offered these words of wisdom, which summarize in a nutshell the importance of survivors' embracing their memories of their lost close relationships:

> We can never completely "get over" a major loss in the sense that all its effects are negated, that it is "forgotten." Our losses become part of who we are, as precious to us as other aspects of our selves, and so does the transcendence of those losses. (p. 15)

C. S. Lewis writes about the "double edge" of grief after losing his wife, Joy: "I not only live each endless day in grief, but live each day thinking about living each day in grief" (Lewis, 1961, p. 12).

Notes

1. From "Martin, What Should I Do Now? by Bella Abzug, *Ms.*, July/August, 1990), pp. 95-96.
2. From *Star,* July 11, 2000.
3. From *Washington Post,* March 20, 1994, p. 1A.
4. From *Good Housekeeping,* October 1998, p. 127.
5. From *Parade Magazine,* May 8, 1994, pp. 3-4.
6. From *Chicago Tribune,* December 20, 1998, sec. 1, p. 2.
7. From an article in *Parade Magazine,* May 2, 1993, p. 18.
8. Obituary in *Cedar Rapids Gazette,* June 20, 1993, p. 14A.
9. From *O Magazine,* January 2001, pp. 46-49.
10. "Internal Strife," by Christiane Amanpour, *USA WEEKEND,* December 17, 2000, para. 31. Retrieved May 18, 2001, on the World Wide Web: www.usaweekend.com/00_issues/001217/001217amanpour.html

3 Dissolution and Divorce

The sorrow of the lover is continual, in the presence and absence of the beloved: in the presence for fear of the absence, and in absence in longing for the presence. The pain in love becomes in time the life of the lover.

—Sufi master Hazrat Inayat Khan
(quoted in Welwood, 1990, p. 66)

Mother drives into river, killing herself, children.

The preceding is a headline from the *Des Moines Register,* July 12, 2000. The accompanying story indicated that this 35-year-old woman drove into the Missouri River at full speed, killing herself and her 8-year-old and twin 4-year-old sons. As she said in a suicide note, she was distraught over the ongoing conflict with her husband.

The topic of this chapter is the loss of close relationships or marriages via the decision to separate, terminate, and/or legally divorce. The preceding quotations regarding the pervasive sorrow connected to the loss of a loved one speak to the depth of loss that is inherent in situations in which lovers part. Sometimes violence accompanies a couple's decision to terminate their relationship. This is another indication of the intensity of this type of loss experience. People's emotions at the time of dissolution can range across the spectrum, from utter despair to rapt ecstasy to intense hatred and anger.

As discussed in the first chapter, Viorst (1986) describes a number of "necessary losses" we all will experience in life. We will lose our youth. We likely will lose our sexual virginity. We will part company with many friends and acquaintances over time. We likely will lose prized possessions and material property. We may lose our financial assets. We all eventually will lose our health. We all probably will lose a close, romantic relationship at some point due to death, divorce, or a mutual parting of ways. We may even lose many close, romantic relationships. Not all of us will experience divorce personally, but in light of the frequency of divorce, most of us will either experience it personally or indirectly through the effects it has on others close to us. Sometimes, it is almost as difficult to watch your son's or daughter's divorce unfolding as it is to experience the divorce process yourself.

It is hardly uncommon for most people marrying in their 20s during the last two decades to have had a relatively large number of lovers and intimate, sexual relationships prior to marriage. At the turn of the century, however, marriage and family researchers have estimated that the average woman had less than one sexual experience prior to marriage. Certainly, sexual experience with many others does not equal having close relationships with them. But these types of observations reflect the fact that people who get married today typically have had more experience with relationships than in the past. Such experience with close relationships before marriage probably will be invaluable in helping the individual evaluate potential partners and issues in relating to others. Why, then, is divorce becoming no less prominent in the early 2000s than it was in the last three decades of the 20th century? That is an enigma that cannot be addressed in a satisfying way by the literature or what will be said in this chapter. The enormity of relationship turmoil potential is a part of the culture. Many cultures share this unfortunate potential.

This experience of dating a lot, separating, and dissolving also means that the individuals involved may be somewhat cynical about the durability of close relationships. If they marry and then divorce and begin another dating period, they will probably experience still more losses of this nature. Such recurrent losses are so common that they are taken for granted. Not only that, but the effect of broken relationships may not be recognized by society (and this type of phenomena may even be seen as a disenfranchised form of grief).

People may not immediately process a succession of lovers as losses. They may feel as if they are having the time of their lives and gaining valuable experience about others. As time goes on, however, the people who were meaningful to them but who are no longer physically present will be salient in their memories. And in fact, these memories of past loves may influence the everyday existence of many people (Harvey, Flanary, & Morgan, 1986). Relationship loss is a natural part of living, a never-ending part of the cycle of searching for meaning through intimate relations. It is increasingly viewed, for better or worse, as normal (Ahrons, 1994).

The dissolution process often exacts a heavy toll of psychological pain, and possibly physical and practical devastation, on the couple as well as any children or close relatives, such as parents. Thus, this chapter is fundamentally about loss and grieving. The words of Khan are applicable for most types of major relationship loss, from death to separation and divorce.

This chapter considers a general sampling of research evidence, theory, and speculation about the following: the causes of separation (as in the case of nonmarried couples) and divorce (as in the case of married couples); the consequences of dissolution and divorce; and the recovery process. Furthermore, a discussion of affairs, adultery, and betrayal is included because these phenomena are often at the center of why we decide to divorce or why we feel pain in relationships.

A Culture of Divorce

We in the United States are a marrying and divorcing society. As we approach the 21st century, the divorce rate has risen to 1 in 2 *recent* marriages (i.e., marriages begun in the last 10 to 20 years). Also, our attitudes about divorce have been tilted toward believing that divorce is the answer to relationship problems. Thornton (1989) has provided powerful attitudinal survey data to illustrate this point. When a sample of young mothers was asked in 1962 whether couples with children ought to remain together if they could not get along, one half said they should. But when these same women were asked the identical question in 1985, fewer than 1 in 5 said they should. Why did this change occur? Had the world of marriage, sacred vows, and human commitment "gone to the dogs" in that time interval? Maybe. But perhaps in the intervening 23 years, these women had learned a lot about the difficulties, and even the hopelessness, that accompanies some close relationships. Many of these women were in relationships that dissolved. Some of the relationships involved physical abuse. There are worse states than dissolution and divorce. The suffering experienced in a truly abusive relationship is one of them.

Now in the early 21st century, the stigma of divorce is mostly gone. After a dazzling wedding in 1981, the "perfect couple," Prince Charles and Princess Diana of England, separated in 1992. Because the divorce of Charles and Diana may have raised questions related to the succession of the British throne, the dissolution of the "perfect couple" showed how common separation and divorce had become. "Perfect couples," of course, are very much the exception rather than the rule. The English royal couple endured excessive media attention as their marriage crumbled over the course of a decade. As English tabloids recounted many details of their conflicts and likely extramarital ventures, it became clear to all that this marriage was no fairy tale and would not have a fairy tale ending. Their marriage was between two people who were probably ill suited for each other, and it fell victim to difficulties that are part of the everyday world of most humans in our time.

In fact, by the late 1990s divorce had become a common phenomenon throughout the world. What is happening now in the former Soviet Union is indicative of the widespread acceptance of divorce today. In Moscow, people are responding to the extraordinarily difficult economic situation confronting them by divorcing at a record rate. According to an article by Jack Kelley in USA TODAY, 75% of all recent marriages in Moscow ended in divorce in 1992, and 62% of recent marriages throughout Russia ended in divorce. Social commentators have blamed not only the economy for the disintegration of these marriages, but they have also suggested that this trend is related to the fact that

Russians are embracing capitalism and career making. Increasingly, they are foregoing traditional relationships in which the wife stayed at home and raised children. As one 19-year-old woman, married only 6 months and in the process of divorcing her 21-year-old husband, told Kelley: "Being a housewife is not for me anymore. . . . I want to make something of myself. I want a BMW."[1]

Changing Mores: A Fading Stigma

Divorce has not only had little social stigma associated with it during the past two decades, it is even fashionable in many circles to have been divorced. As one illustration, people in their late 30s who are single are sometimes viewed as having less questionable relationship histories if they were married and divorced earlier. The line of inquiry among observers of a person who is nearing 40 and has never been married often goes something like this: "Why isn't he married? Is there something wrong with him?" It has only taken a quarter of a century for the stigma of divorce in its harshest form to fade. But the hurt, the long-term pain for the participants, and the brutality of the legal aspects of divorce have not abated with the lessening stigma of divorce.

The time during which a divorce is happening is, as Robert Weiss (1975) suggests, a time of craziness. The antics of people involved in the breakdown of a long-term relationship are sometimes beyond belief. One of the most common and strange mutual enactments is the tendency for these tormented individuals to have sex regularly during their separation. Weiss found this activity to be common among his separated sample, regardless of level of hostility in the separation. Why would sexuality, presumably an act of kindness and care for other, occur at such a time? Mainly because these two people have been sex partners previously, and in fact may have liked the sex part—they just couldn't stand the partner on other grounds. At this time, weaning oneself from sexual activity is difficult, but it is also very problematic to try to find a new sex partner (although that is commonly done). Thus, the otherwise hostile and rejecting partners may find that they still have this need in common.

It is common for people to have highly conflicted emotions at the time of separation. R. Weiss (personal communication, November 2000) suggests that the psychological effect of the separation event can be astonishing. For example, the wife may simultaneously feel free, relieved, disoriented, and abandoned.

Defining an Emotional Divorce

A major loss, such as a marital separation and divorce, initially diminishes the self (Harvey, Weber, & Orbuch, 1990). Such an event may reduce one's dignity, will, or resources. By definition, the breakup of a close relationship, takes a psychological and physical toll on the principal parties concerned, including any children involved. Probably more potent than the loss of physical resources is the loss of emotional resources during a breakup. As has been argued by Vaughan (1986) and Spanier and Thompson (1987), the most meaningful step in the dissolving sequence is that of the *emotional divorce. This is the time at which one, or (rarely) both, partners define the relationship as dead in their minds.* Once that decision has been made in the marriage, the legal relationship may go along for a short period or many years. Psychologically, however, it has ended. Whether or not they are physically separate, a dissolution has occurred when one partner's understanding that a close bond exists no longer coincides with the other partner's understanding. Next comes exiting behavior, which can be quick and explicit or slow and implicit.

Levinger (1992) wrote a valuable commentary on the loss of a close relationship. He noted that the extent to which one feels that a close relationship's ending is a loss (or a deprivation in personal resources) depends on several factors. These include the following questions: How close (involving, interdependent) was the relationship? Did the relationship end suddenly, or was the ending more protracted (as when an individual is dying slowly from a terminal disease)? Did the loss involve a lengthy period in which partners could withdraw and possibly explore new options? Levinger posited that when a dying person expresses a clear desire to stop living, it helps his or her loved ones accept the person's demise. As will be discussed in the grief chapter, Levinger also suggested that loss by death is different than loss by separation or divorce. The key differences are that death is irreversible and may have occurred due to physiological reasons; such reasons are quite different from those that involve a person's intentional decision to end a relationship.

Nonmarital Dissolution Versus Divorce

It might be thought that divorces, by definition, are more difficult for people to deal with than are nonmarital breakups. We have little evidence comparing the emotional and practical effects of the endings of different types of relationships. We do know, though, that many nonmarital divorces can be excruciatingly painful. In fact, as Orbuch (1988) suggests, nonmarital dissolution may be as painful, or even more so, than divorce because in society it usually is not officially recognized as an experience that involves great pain—which can be the case when lovers who terminate their relationship have been a couple for an extensive period of time. This pain can be found even among college students who lose a close relationship after only 6 months or so (Sorenson, Russell, Harkness, & Harvey, 1993). College-age couples may not have invested many years together and have major assets to divide and custody decisions to make. Nevertheless, they likely go through many of the steps of grieving that are encountered by persons who have been married many years.

In fact, people of all ages feel pain, confusion, and sometimes despair at the loss of closeness with others. In a "Fresh Voices" column in *Parade Magazine*, the topic posed for high school students was "Rejection in Dating—Is It Better to Hear From Somebody Else?" One male, aged 16, said, "When a girl says you could be friends, that's like the kiss of death." Victor noted still another way one knows a relationship has ended when he said, "All of a sudden, the phone calls stop—you know she's sick of you."[2] As will be discussed in a later section, one assumption regarding relationship dissolution is that the initiator fares better after the relationship has ended than does the one who receives the message. The old line "I just want to be friends" is usually received as if it means rejection. Rejection is hard for all concerned. That is why people frequently use euphemisms about continued friendship to try to moderate the effects of the bad news.

Recovery after marital or nonmarital dissolution frequently involves similar steps. The total experience often includes these steps: shock or surprise at the decision of the other to end the relationship; denial that it really is happening; an outcry that may involve quickly trying to find a new mate, or indiscriminate, frenzied dating and sexual activity for a period; and then gradually recovery. Recovery is effected in all types of loss circumstances only after the mind and body have had time to regroup and is facilitated greatly by the person's diligent work to combine staying active and hopeful with going over the details of the relationship, what went wrong, and what to do and expect the next time. At some early point in the healing, confiding in good friends is essential to recovery (Harvey et al., 1990; Pennebaker, 1990).

If such confiding cannot occur and if the individual cannot readily move beyond grieving about the lost relationship, professional counseling should be considered. I do not believe that suppression of the loss (i.e., just filing it away and not thinking or talking about it or distracting oneself to a high degree—thus eliminating the opportunity to grieve) is effective. As Pennebaker's (1990) important research on the value of confiding has shown, suppression can be quite detrimental to a person's psychological and physical health over the long term. At the same time, there may be a limit to how much one can confide to *certain friends or associates.* People with whom one is friendly but who are not perceived as "soulmate" confidants, may desert a grieving person when they believe the person either has told them too little or too much about the details of the loss (Hunt, 1966).

Many distinctions could be drawn about the nature of the separation experience for different couples. Some, including those divorcing, may experience little apparent stress and may in fact move on to another apparently happy relationship soon after the ending of the previous relationship (or even before if they have been having an affair). The word *apparent* is used here on purpose. As implied earlier, it is unlikely that people can easily escape doing a degree of emotional work in getting beyond a major loss (see discussion surrounding Wortman & Silver's, 1989, thesis on this matter in Chapter 1). Those who move too quickly will have to come back and deal with it later—or "it" will likely deal with them in the form of psychosomatic difficulties at other points in life.

When Deteriorated Relationships Do Not End

Before discussing how relationships progress toward dissolution, it is important to note briefly that not all conflict-ridden, or highly deteriorated, relationships terminate. In decades past, it was not common to end a marriage even if there was significant physical abuse occurring (Coontz, 2000). In the 21st century, however, that state of affairs more often eventuates in dissolution than it did in previous times. The main reason why people sometimes elect to stay despite the gravity of relationship problems (or the moribund nature of the relationship) is that of investment.

One wife told Ann Landers in a 1989 column that she had invested 21 years in her marriage. Her husband was a prominent, well-respected professional man, admired by everyone. Her children were in college. They had a beautiful home and were considered a loving couple. The woman her husband had been seeing for 9 years had worked for him. The wife said that this woman had had two failed marriages and her whole life was her job. She said that she did not hate the woman and that the woman was not taking anything away from her. The other woman and the husband were never seen together in public. But Tuesday night was theirs (the husband and the other woman's in the other woman's apartment), so the wife played cards with the girls. The wife said that she had the husband's name, his children, the respect of the community and more than enough sex. She ended by saying that one of these years her husband would decide that he had had enough outside activity and that would be the end of it. All she (the wife) had to do was wait. As surprising as it may seem, Ann Landers reported that she had received many such letters from women who had decided to stick by their men, even if the men were involved in seemingly interminable affairs (one or more over time). Another wife, for instance, said she was tired of sex anyway, and her husband was merely "servicing" the lonely widow next door.[3] The concept of investment and its power to keep people in troubled marriages has been carefully studied by scholars such as Heaton and Albrecht (1991) and Rusbult (1980).

Moving Toward Dissolution

As Ellen Berscheid (1999) commented in a review of a recent book on relationship issues, we have far too little insight about the different dynamics involved in the downward spiral and ultimate demise of close relationships and marriages. Berscheid (1994) comments that theory and research on the dissolution process and related variables have produced no certain package of factors always involved in dissolution. Rather, a "kitchen sink" of factors has emerged, as well as scores of theoretical conceptions of how they are related to dissolution. Longitudinal research that tracks couples over time and pinpoints elements of the dissolution process as it is unfolding is quite difficult to do. There is a paucity of such work in the relationship and loss literatures.

There likely are at least as many perceived scenarios that eventuate in the dissolution of a close relationship as there are people who have encountered dissolution in their lives. Also, there are countless factors that have been identified as being associated with dissolution. In some instances, the process of deterioration is slow and halting. In others, the progression is up and down, including periods of separation and the resumption of living together or "being a couple." In still others, the progression is as swift as a bullet. This latter type of progression is most interesting because it is most puzzling, at least to the person being left. It is as if, "out of the blue," one partner in an seemingly functioning, satisfactory relationship decides that she or he wants out and will take the steps to get out. Of course, this particular type of progression may seem as if it is "out of the blue" to the person being left. But to the other partner or a knowledgeable outsider, the progression may be more gradual and systematic in how it plays itself out.

This discussion of a couple's subjective sense of the transition trajectory of their dissolving relationship leads to the question of how similar their subjective sense is to the "objective" reality of the situation. What do the people involved think the causes were? What were the actual causes? Is there a difference between the two? What accounts for the difference if there is one? We do not have enough knowledge of the process of deterioration to know the answer to these questions. More research is needed that looks at a prospective sampling of young married couples and follows them over an extended period—presumably tracking the instances of separation and divorce on the part of some of the sample. We have some fledgling but promising work along this line (e.g., Fincham & Bradbury, 1987), but mostly we have retrospective report data on what happened. Gottman (1994, 1995) has produced some of the most coherent theory and research on relationship dissolution. However, even his work generally is lacking in the prospective research component mentioned earlier (that would involve following couples closely over time to know more precisely what is happening along the way to their demise).

Even biological factors have been associated with dissolution processes. It has been argued that an array of innate, biological factors *sometimes* may predispose people to relationship difficulty, including dissolution and divorce (McGue & Lykken, 1992). The specific predisposition might be a personality type that is diffident, retiring, and uncomfortable around people. It is suggested that these predisposing factors, including certain patterns of socialization such as the way parents and significant others model relating to others, mainly come into play under certain conditions. There is much value in studying people's perceptions, or retrospective reports. They matter greatly to the couple and should matter to the investigator as well. At the same time, we must be cautious in trying to validate their reports compared with reports of knowledgeable others and any other sort of evidence that exists about what happened in the course of the relationship. Following is just a sampling of factors that often have been identified as being centrally involved in dissolution, some of which are taken from Sprecher's (1994) analysis (see later for more detail):

- Growing apart in attitudes and interests (or never being sufficiently similar to begin with)
- Inability to give emotionally and be expressive of personal feelings
- Involvement with third parties, as in affairs
- Paying too much attention to one's career and too little to one's close relationship
- Economic difficulties that diminish people's physical and psychological resources, making them less able to deal with relationship issues (e.g., after Hurricane Andrew devastated Dade County, Florida in 1992, the divorce rate jumped nearly 30%)
- Feeling a marriage constrains one's ability to pursue one's career or life dreams
- Feeling overly controlled by the other, such that one cannot be "oneself" and pursue what makes one happy
- Physical or psychological abuse
- No longer being physically or sexually attracted to one's significant other
- The difficulties of caring for children and how that responsibility interferes with attention given to relationship needs
- Failure to understand the other's perspective and taking other for granted
- The weakening effect of religion on maintenance of marriage
- "No-fault" divorce laws

No-fault divorce laws first began in California in 1969. These laws have played a role in the breakup of relationships by making it easier to get a divorce and lessening the stigma associated with divorce. As summarized by Sprecher's (1994) research, the reasons cited by both ex-partners' for the ending of their relationship are listed in Table 3.1. This research is invaluable because it involved more than 100 couples who reported their divergent and convergent perceptions of why their relationship ended.

Entertaining Uncertainty About Causality

In trying to pinpoint some of the causes of dissolution, it is most helpful to study the perceptions of both members of a (former) couple. My colleagues and I did that in the mid-1970s (Harvey, Wells, & Alvarez, 1978), and we were struck by both the divergence of percep-

TABLE 3.1 Reasons Cited by Ex-Partners in Dating Relationships, With All Listed
Producing Intercouple Positive Correlations

Reasons referring to the couple or interaction

- We had different interests.
- We had communication problems.
- We had conflicting sexual attitudes and/or problems.
- We had conflicting marriage ideas.
- We had different backgrounds.
- We had financial problems or conflicts.
- There was emotional abuse.
- There was physical abuse.

Reasons referring to external factors

- We were living too far apart.

Reasons referring to self

- I was more involved than my partner.

Reasons referring to partner

- My partner desired to be independent.
- My partner became bored with the relationship.

SOURCE: Adapted from Sprecher (1994).

tions that often occurs at times of major conflict and by the people's inability to correctly perceive their partner's understanding of what was happening. Indeed, more recent work (e.g., Holtzworth-Munroe & Jacobson, 1985) has painted a clearer picture of the importance of mutual understanding, divergences in understanding, and recognition of such divergences as powerful elements in conflict and eventual separation. Often, there is a complex web of understandings surrounding a close relationship and major events in its history. Within these understandings reside much of what determines how successful the relationship becomes. Furthermore, and just as important, if couples are flexible regarding their understandings, they can better revise misperceptions and converge more in understandings of important issues that are key to whether the relationship survives (see Harvey, 1987, for a review of work in this area).

Gottman's Analysis of Dissolution

In Gottman's (1994, 1995) study of maintenance and dissolution, he invited couples to live in his "love lab," an apartment geared for studying the verbal, nonverbal, and psychophysiological responses of couples in various situations. By videotaping parts of the couples' interaction and obtaining psychophysiological and verbal report information, Gottman claims that he can correctly predict whether or not a couple will divorce for 90% of the couples who participate in this research. In fact, some early participants who did indeed divorce challenged him to develop intervention approaches to complement his success in predicting divorce—a challenge that Gottman and his therapist wife now have tackled with a similarly ambitious program at their Seattle Institute.

In Gottman's conception of relationship conflict, he argues that the "Four Horsemen of the Apocalypse"—factors so labeled because of the damage they can do to a close relationship—are the factors that often contribute to dissolution. These "Four Horsemen" are criticism, defensiveness (that includes even rehearsing defensive thoughts such as "I'm not going to take this any longer" in one's mind), stonewalling (clamming up about hurt feelings or motivations for acts), and contempt (which can be obvious or subtle, such as a rolling of the eyes that one's partner would not mistake for a more benign sign).

Overall, Gottman emphasizes the countless small acts that matter most in establishing the climate of a relationship—not just the specific acts during times of conflict. These small and sometimes barely discernible acts (e.g., acknowledging what a partner has said, making eye contact that reflects attention and care in conversation) go a long way toward creating a savings account of goodwill that will serve the couple well in difficult times.

The Process of Disaffection

In a valuable analysis of evidence about the divorcing process, Kayser (1994) points to three major phases of close relationship disaffection.

As shown in Table 3.2, Kayser suggests that Phase 1, "disappointment," involves anger and hurt, as well as thoughts about responsibility for the problems and behaviors aimed at repairing the relationship. This phase is followed by Phase 2, which Kayser calls, "disappointment and disaffection." This phase involves an intensification of the thoughts, feelings, and behavior of the beginning phase. Finally, the couple or one of its members reaches disaffection, which includes hopelessness, plans to end the relationship, and actual acts that end it.

Kayser's (1994) research on disaffection with a sample of 49 formerly married persons also showed that the participants believed that the partner's control, lack of intimate behaviors, and other negative traits (e.g., disloyalty, overdependence, inability to give) were at the top of the list of issues that had been faced in their relationships.

Although Kayser's analysis is valuable, people's patterns of relationship dissolution vary. For example, Table 3.2 only refers to the "blaming" pattern often shown by partners who become disaffected. However, sometimes partners become convinced that their own qualities are to blame for the problems and ultimate demise of the relationship.

Vaughan's Analysis of the Progression Toward Termination

Diane Vaughan (1986), a sociologist, wrote a book titled *Uncoupling* that presents an interesting analysis of the dissolution process. The research Vaughan reports involved the collection of retrospective reports from 103 women and men who were separated or divorced; no former partners of the respondents were included. Across her sample, Vaughan found evidence of various stages in the dissolution of a relationship. She proposed that "uncoupling" involves the following:

1. "Secrets," or the breakdown of frank communication in one or more areas of the relationship
2. "The display of discontent," whereby the initiator, in particular, begins to define negatively one or more aspects of the previously positive relationship

TABLE 3.2 Phases of Close Relationship Disaffection

Phase 1: Disappointment

    Feelings: anger, hurt, shattered assumptions

    Thoughts: heightened awareness of partner's faults; who is responsible for problems?

    Behaviors: attempts to resolve the problems unilaterally, may involve trying to please partner; avoidant and passive coping (e.g., silence) may be used.

Phase 2: Disappointment and Disaffection

    Feelings: intense anger and pain

    Thoughts: partner's negative traits seen as pattern; dilemma of staying or leaving is faced.

    Behaviors: continued attempt to problem-solve; confrontation of partner; physical and emotional withdrawal

Phase 3: Reaching Disaffection

    Feelings: anger, apathy, hopelessness

    Thoughts: making plans to end the relationship; focus on partner's negative qualities

    Behaviors: actions to dissolve the relationship; possibly counseling to help disengage

---

SOURCE: Adapted from Kayser (1994).

3. A transition from one's role as a "partner" to a more ambiguous role of "independent person," while trying to cover up one's leave taking

Because of the value of Vaughan's work as an analysis of the sequence of dissolution, let us consider the progression of "uncoupling" in more detail.

In the "secrets" stage, one of the partners, the initiator, develops a deep unhappiness with the relationship. This phase is rather quiet and unilateral. The initiator broods a lot, goes through life's paces mulling alternatives, and eventually begins to let out her or his discontent. The initiator may not be able to fully articulate the major complaints about the relationship but begins to show anger, perhaps blowing up over small matters. The initiator may also show various forms of passive-aggressive pulling away behavior such as engaging in perfunctory sexual behavior or "forgetting" to wear her or his wedding ring.

At some point, for some people, potential outside romantic relationships began to develop. Indeed, the appearance of new potential romantic partners on the scene may have been the major secret that then led to other secrets, such as the initiator's making an invidious comparison between the outsider and the present partner (e.g., regarding how much easier it is to talk with the other person than with one's partner). The outsider is a "transitional other" with whom one may discuss the problems in one's relationship and perhaps form some type of fledgling relationship. That is, the outside activity may involve movement toward romantic or sexual relations or flirtation with a directionality toward sexual relations. In Vaughan's sample, respondents who reported such outside activities also sometimes reported guilt, which then often led to further passive-aggressive behavior toward the spouse or partner. Why? Because if one can make one's partner take actions that clearly violate the relationship, then one's own guilt about personal violations can be lessened. Vaughan told of a 26-year-old man who had been living with a woman for 4 years whose account fit this pattern:

> I could never have left Julie. She was so vulnerable, I just could not do it even though I didn't love her anymore. But I started disappointing her in lots of ways. I realized I was becoming someone that I knew she couldn't like. (p. 101)

Eventually, the partner who is being left clearly gets the message, and the conflict escalates from that point. The couple may go back and forth regarding staying (or getting back) together. But the "dye is cast" at that point in terms of the secrets and their related behavioral patterns. With some initiators, the "secrets" are not affairs or possible affairs, but, rather, other forms of discontent. They too are secrets that may continue to further secrets in the form of outside relationships.

Who Is Most or Least Distressed?

As is clear from this discussion, Vaughan (1986) analyzes her evidence in a way that emphasizes the role of the partner who appeared to initiate the breakup. The initiator clearly was the person in charge beginning the unfolding events. This person was also the person feeling the best about what was happening—maybe not super happy but glad that soon she or he would be free. This person was already beginning to undergo the necessary identity transformation from that of being in a couple to being single or perhaps a member of a different coupling. The initiator also tended to make these further moves toward what Goffman (1959) once called "cooling the mark." This pattern of behavior is defined as getting the person who has been exploited in some way to calm down and not take unkindly to what has happened and involves the following:

1. Focusing on the negative qualities of the partner
2. Indicating a belief that the relationship was nonsalvagable from some earlier point to the present
3. Trying to convince the partner that the relationship was/is not savable
4. Telling other people the story of the demise of the relationship—making it public, thus strengthen one's commitment to the ending
5. Possibly seeking transitional other(s)
6. Beginning the process of grieving or mourning

Each of us who has been in a long-term relationship likely will mourn its loss. Initiators just start sooner, according to Vaughan.

On the other hand, Vaughan found that the person being left often was "out in the cold without a clue" from the start. This person's life was caving in, and she or he really did not understand why. Many of us have been in this position. It is one of life's worst conditions because we feel that we have no control over something that meant a great deal to us—another person's feelings toward and decisions about us. What we often do in such situations is make it worse. We get angry and tell the person to be gone right away; then we apologize and plead for the person to come back; then we waiver in our statements between bravado and pitifulness. The truth is we often are out of control. The control is sitting there in the other's hands and being enhanced as we flail about trying to resist acknowledging that the relationship was over sometime back when our partner developed the secret that he or she wanted out. We may start to analyze and recognize aspects of the relationship as reflecting that development. Yet that does not make us any happier. We still are losing, pardon the metaphor, our right arm, and there is no way to sew it back on. We feel abandoned by the person to whom we were strongly attached.

In his classic study of separating and recently divorced people, Weiss (1975) defined separation distress as, "a response to intolerable inaccessibility of the attachment figure" (p. 42). If the behavior of the person who initiates the breakup is clearly apparent to friends and family, that person may catch more heat about why the relationship has to end. But compared with the one being left, the initiator has a great head start toward restoring his or her self, establishing a new identity, gaining control over his or her life, and developing a new close relationship.

Does it follow, then, that we who worry about whether our relationships will end should be "quick draws" in deciding whether we get out first? No. A more rational style of relating is mutual retreat, if that must happen. A couple who discusses their relationship issues generously and regularly is more likely to achieve mutual initiation than is a couple who cannot freely and regularly discuss these issues. There is a lot of defensiveness on display in Vaughn's account of how the initiator treats the person being left at the end of the relationship. The initiator is not necessarily being morally wrong in this approach. But the behavior of the initiator will hurt the other partner to a degree that is unnecessary if a more open style of relating is adopted early on.

Vaughan's strong emphasis on the initiator versus the person being left probably does not do justice to the complexity of many endings. As Weiss (1975) has eloquently argued, based on his interviews with individuals in the organization Parents Without Partners, the matter of who actually got the dissolution ball rolling usually is a complicated matter:

> There do seem to be differences in the impact of separation on those who define themselves as leavers and those who define as left, but the differences seem to be more nearly in the character of the resultant distress than in its intensity [meaning that each will suffer more or less to the same degree]. In most separations . . . [the] marriage became intolerable for both partners; somehow one partner rather than

the other decided finally to call it quits. Sometimes husband and wife alternated in the initiation of preliminary separations. . . . Sometimes a spouse who had been un- willing to accept responsibility for ending the marriage behaved so outrageously that the other spouse could not go on with it. And sometimes a husband or wife who had insisted on separation later had a change of heart and wanted to become recon- ciled, but the other spouse now refused. In all these circumstances the identification of the one spouse as leaver and the other as left oversimplifies a complex interactive process. (p. 63)

Weiss goes on to note that when there is a more clear cut leaver in the breakdown sequence, the leaver may have some advantages but also in- curs some major costs. Chief among those costs in Weiss's sample was that of guilt. He found that such individuals may experience harsh re- actions from outsiders, such as friends of the couple. Furthermore, the leaver sometimes starts to question his or her own ability to stick to a commitment and to meet another person's emotional needs. It should be remembered that Weiss's evidence came from the early 1970s, a time when the stigma of leaving another person, in a marriage at least, likely was more substantial than it has become over the past two decades as separations have become more commonplace.

Chip Brown, writing in *Glamour* magazine,[4] provided another inter- esting perspective on who experiences the most distress when a close relationship ends. He said that as there are two roles in any breakup— the passive part of the one who is left and the active part of the one who leaves—so there are two sorts of accompanying pain: the agony of loss and the distress of guilt and doubt. Brown argued that in the long run, the first may be easier to bear. His reasoning was that the pain of loss heals more quickly and completely than the pain of guilt and doubt does. Loss is loss, Brown asserted. When someone leaves you, however much it hurts, there is nothing to be done but endure it; once you ac- cept that you have no control and can only embrace what's inevitable, you can go on. Brown suggested that guilt and doubt, on the other hand, have a tendency to fester. You look at yourself in the mirror and see the agent of someone's unhappiness. You may ask questions such as, Was it worth it? Did you make the right choice? Were you being self- ish? Will you regret your decision one day in the future and have no one to blame but yourself?

Brown went on to note that he had learned to be less consumed by the need for control in his close relationships and to disagree with W. H.

Auden's (1994) line, "If equal affection cannot be, let the more loved one be me." Brown noted that there is much irony in loving and losing: The person who takes the bigger chance by loving too much or too quickly and who then experiences great heartache if the relationship ends, may learn much from this experience and may later attain considerable tranquility about the ending, whereas the person who is more reserved about giving love and who moves first to end the relationship may learn little and be beset with the "drip, drip, drip of regret and doubt."

Infidelity

A full chapter could be committed to this important topic. We have already seen in the previous chapter that much of the violence perpetrated by one human being toward another is often directly related to the conflict and bitterness that sometimes arises in intimate relationships. People have a tendency to get caught up in complicated love dramas that often have tragic, long-lasting results, especially when there are victims (as there usually are) who feel cheated and betrayed. Of course, sometimes an affair represents a refreshing change in an otherwise stale and stagnating long-term relationship. Affairs or adultery (as in having intimate, sexual relations outside of one's marriage or primary bond) that are found out can lead to better primary relationships if the partners can learn to believe in and trust each other again. This is a big "if" though. The headlines frequently tell of an outpouring of enduring anger and deadly hostility in the context of affairs and adultery. Consider these headlines:

Wife's Night of Passion Sparks Slaughter
   A West Side hotel porter went on a murderous rampage yesterday and killed four people after finding his wife in bed with another man, police said.[5]

Love Triangle Ends in Death
   Wittenberg, Wisconsin—Pretty and smart, Lori Esker was class president when she was in high school. But friends say she was devastated when her romance with a handsome young farmer broke up. Now she's in jail, accused of strangling the woman he planned to marry.[6]

All available evidence suggests that affairs and adultery are very common in our world. They have been well studied in the literature of marriage and divorce (e.g., Hunt, 1967). For centuries, men have been the primary instigators of affairs. They still may have a lead over women in this area, but the difference between the sexes apparently is becoming smaller. The data on the extent to which affairs occur during marriage vary and are subject to respondents' efforts to give researchers what they think they want to hear—or simply the tendency to exaggerate or de-emphasize behavior that may or may not be construed as involving an affair. For example, does an affair always involve sexual intercourse? Probably not. Emotional involvement, lustful feelings, and passionate embraces with a partner outside the primary relationship over a period of time likely would be seen as constituting an affair. Or a couple might have a stumbling, halting experience of sexual intercourse on one brief occasion but never again engage in sexual or emotional sharing. Is it possible that such a brief encounter could be seen as an affair to some? As with other forms of sexual and related behavior, we at least need to be careful regarding what it is we are talking about when we say a couple is having an affair.

In general, though, the best statistics we have show a rather high absolute number of men and women participating in affairs. For example, in a 10-year study of 600 adults married or living together, Lawson (1988) found that men still cheat more than women. She found that whereas 25% of the women had as many as four affairs, 40% of the men had as many as four. But the women are coming up in the percentages. Sixty-six percent of the women and 68% of the men in first marriages had at least one affair. Lawson's figures are high in light of typical estimates—with the percentage of women having affairs generally estimated to be between 25% and 50% and between 50% and 65% for men. Also, given that Lawson's data were collected before the AIDS epidemic became such a salient factor in sexual liaisons, her data may also be somewhat inflated beyond what one would find in the 1990s. Nonetheless, whatever percentages one uses, affairs are common whether in marriage or in close relationships that do not involve marriage.

When do affairs occur? Although affairs may occur at any point during an ongoing close relationship, they are more likely to happen at watershed points both in the history of the couple and in the individual's own history. Such points would include the so-called 7-year itch time. This maxim suggests that after a significant period of time one or both partners may begin to consider the "green grass" just outside the fence and may begin to stray. Usually, relatively young married persons in their late 20s or early 30s must endure this "itch" period. Another major watershed is the time when an individual in a couple reaches what he or she perceives to be midlife. This period can occur anywhere from age 30 to age 60. If one has been married for a long time and is unhappy at that point, affairs become more likely to move from the imagery of the mind to actual behavior. Even people in relatively happy relationships may be more prone to consider an affair at midlife than at some other personal historical moment.

Finally, this is only speculation, but I think that affairs are less likely to happen when people are having a difficult time battling outside forces such as economic stress or health problems. Ironically, it is often after a couple has won a major battle with such an outside force that an affair begins.

Why do people have affairs? A typical laundry list includes the following reasons: revenge toward one's partner for some alleged wrongdoing, including his or her affair; boredom with the primary sexual relationship; frustration or deprivation with the primary sexual relationship; curiosity; a need to enhance one's sense of one's self-esteem, attractiveness or masculinity, and so on (Lawson, 1988). These are just some of the reasons that get mixed in with the many complex details of a particular love or lust story. As has been emphasized before, these "reasons" may be more excuses than true causes. But they are there in the causal repertory nonetheless and must be considered when we try to understand how people think and feel in these situations.

Sociologists, historians, and demographers (e.g., Bailey, 1988; Blumstein & Schwartz, 1983) often have emphasized the role of women's greater involvement in the workplace, especially during World War II, as a key historical event in the growth in the incidence of affairs in the United States. The idea was that women, like men before them, would sometimes conclude that they desired more freedom of sexual behavior, as well as the other freedoms they had struggled to attain (Ehrenreich, Hess, & Jacobs, 1986).

Jones and Burdette (1994) have argued that there are numerous types of betrayals in close relationships, with affairs and adultery representing one major class of such betrayals. In general, perceived violations of relationship understandings are seen as betrayals and may involve a continuum of types of behavior, from making fun of one's partner in front of others at a party to plotting to put a murder contract out on one's partner.

From a clinical perspective, Rothman (1991) raises a number of questions about the logic of affairs. A person contemplating an affair should keep in mind that his or her new affair may one day be his or her primary relationship. "One day, your new lover will also be boringly familiar—that is, if you stay together long enough" (Rothman, 1991, p. 109). Rothman also raises an important question: If you end up marrying your new lover, why should he or she believe that you will be trustworthy—or vice versa? The new relationship (that started as an affair) may be subject to the same rules of decay that dimmed the flame of the earlier relationship. We should not be too moralistic, however, because the pressures people experience in relationships are intrinsic to the human condition. The prospects of "green grass" on the other side are likely to be a part of our mental makeup throughout our lives.

This excerpt from Cheryl Lavin's "Tales From the Front"[7] addresses a scenario (and the "lines") encountered by some single persons getting involved with married people (Lavin titled the story "Smart Woman; Foolish Choices"). She tells the story of a woman named Lana.

Lana had written to Lavin about the affair that had consumed her for 7 years. Lana had met Michael when he was 41. He was married and lived halfway across the country. He was unhappily married, or so he said. According to Michael, he and his wife were not having sex. He asserted that he was going to leave his wife. Michael stated that he had never had an affair before. He said he had waited all his life for someone like Lana.

The last thing Lana wanted was an affair. Her own marriage had broken up because her husband had cheated, so she knew how much damage it did. But the affair happened anyway. The affair lasted 7 years. After several years, Lana moved across the country to be with him. The good times were unbelievably good. They traveled together all over the world. The end came in two stages. First, Michael began pulling away. He had never been very involved with his children, but he became very involved with his grandchildren. Then his parents died and his wife was diagnosed with cancer. The final end came quickly. Lana and Michael were on a business trip together. He looked at her and said that she had been so happy on the trip that he thought she should find someone so she could be with that person all the time. They were in a restaurant when he said it. Lana took her wineglass, threw it on the floor, and walked out. Lana is now full of regrets. But she is by no means over it. She says that she still loves Michael and sometimes feels obsessed with him. Lana says Michael has repaired his life and his marriage and has gone on to achieve a kind of success that he never could have achieved had he still been involved with her. Lana concluded that she was 51 and still attractive. She is, and always has been, approached continually by men. But she is not interested. She said that when you have had the fairy tale, you don't want to settle for less.

The Aftermath of Divorce: Staying Single

One of the most salient aspects of the increase in the divorce rate in the United States is that divorced people are staying single in larger numbers and for longer periods than ever before. Statistics from the U.S. Bureau of the Census[8] indicate that for people in the middle-age years between 40 and 54, about 1.5 million were divorced and still unmarried in 1970. By 1998, that figure had risen to 7.1 million (4.1 million women and 3 million men). The number of divorced people remaining single is rising because of a number of factors. For women, one well-publicized demographic factor is that there are fewer eligible men from the age of 40 up than there are women who are eligible. On the average, women outlive men by a little less than a decade. And more men than women are incarcerated.

Other reasons for women staying single through middle age are more social psychological in nature. Women frequently have well-established and nurturing social support networks of confidants and friends. These networks buffer them from some of the adverse effects of single life, such as the brooding loneliness that sometimes affects men who become single during this stage of life. Women are more independent financially now than they were two to three decades ago. They can often support themselves in this passage without assistance from a man and his resources. Women also do not define themselves in terms of their husband's career and values in the same way that they did in the past. Psychologically, one of the most important reasons for women staying single is their desire for freedom.

As one 50-year-old woman recently said after her divorce, "I could do anything I wanted for the first time in my life. . . . It was so good feeling free."[9] The abiding complaint among women divorcing after many years of marriage is that the husband was overly controlling. Close relationships with men who do not believe in equality and freedom of expression for women has become a challenge that many women are not willing to accept in the 21st century.

When we turn to the question of why men are staying single in large numbers after divorce, a different profile of reasoning emerges. Most important, men may be less willing converts to single life. Still, once they are in this state, they may not readily find women whom they want to marry. One of the reasons often cited by men for delaying remarriage is the major cost in assets and emotional resources involved in getting divorced. Some men feel that they lost a considerable amount in the divorce decisions regarding property and/or custody of children. They feel "burned." Gately and Schwebel (1992) report on work showing that younger men in their 20s may be especially crestfallen and humbled by divorce. These young men may see divorce as a major blow to their normal progression toward becoming fathers and having families. But such reasoning also suggests that these young men will quickly try to remarry and will not remain single very long.

Deciding to Remarry

What about those who decide to remarry? Millions do. In 1995, of 45 million married households in the United States 20 million were of remarried partners. At the same time, the percentage of second and beyond marriages ending in divorce has been on the order of 3 out of every 5 in the past decade. Thus, the possible wisdom of Samuel Johnson's famous line, "Remarriage is the triumph of hope over experience."

Very few people intend to stay single when they divorce or after the dissolution of a long-term nonmarital relationship. What they want is a new partner who has all the good qualities the last one did not have. Or they may want most someone who does not have the negative qualities they perceived in their last partner. Thus, people remarrying usually are saying "I want a better marriage than the one I had before." They also may be more realistic regarding what is possible and what issues may transpire in a marriage given different circumstances.

But Johnson's cynicism is well taken. There usually are many issues left hanging from the first marriage. The sooner the second relationship happens, the more salient the baggage from the first. Children and custody of them often is at the top of the list. New partners each may bring children from other marriages to the new home, necessitating a blending of people, personalities, habits, rules, and expectations for how this new amalgam of people will behave with one another. Still another potential problem includes the ex-husband's having to pay large child support payments. If this is the case, money may be tight for the new family, and this fact may be exacerbated by a decision to increase the new family by having more children.

Emotional baggage carried over from an earlier marriage is common and also may impede the new relationship. Some therapists and commentators in this area suggest at least a 2-year gap between marriages in order to mute some of the emotional and practical difficulties deriving from the ending of the earlier marriage. A period of counseling may be helpful in addressing emotional residue. One of the problems that may carry over is continued emotional attachment, usually experienced by just one of the ex-partners. Such attachment may continue for years beyond separation or legal divorce. Problems in joint-custody arrangements regarding how children are treated are also common. Children are often caught between warring "exes" who want revenge and who try to use the children to spy on their ex-partner and his or her new lovers.

An axiom of analysts of remarriage is that people remarrying have to be very careful lest they repeat similar patterns in the new marriage that were problematic in the first marriage. An excessive drinking habit, staying away from home after work, excessive criticism of one's partner, nagging, excessive rigidity and control, an inability to express feelings, and flirting with or actually having affairs with others represent such patterns. It takes a lot of caring about and desire to change them in order to actually change them.

Many people would do almost anything to make a second, or later, marriage work. At the same time, many people know that they would be quick to end a second marriage if they see signs that clearly indicate the emergence of problems similar to those they experienced in the first marriage. Furstenberg and Spanier (1987) suggest that the psychology of the remarried person who spots trouble is, in effect, "I've survived divorce before and I will again. I do not intend to put up with this very long."

One of the respondents in Furstenberg and Spanier's study echoed and elaborated on the attitude of preparation to terminate a second marriage:

> I think we also went into our second marriage with the attitude that if he woke up one morning and said "I'm not in love with you anymore (or) it's not the same for me anymore—I've met someone else," I'd say, "God bless" without any animosity. I would try my damnedest [to make the marriage work] and hope that he would try the same way, but if we couldn't work it out, then we wouldn't stay together ... it's a little different from what I thought the first time. I think the way you look on ... the next relationship—you know, that these things can be terminated—that's a matter of historical record, so there's a illusion that's gone. (p. 192)

Health

The effects on the psychological and physical health of the partners and their children are often powerful and long-lasting (sometimes positive—relief from an abusive relationship, but more often negative). One of the most debilitating aspects of divorce is the legal activity of officially splitting up assets and resources and determining custody when children are involved. These proceedings, by definition, usually are highly adversarial and may be protracted for years. For example, in 1992, in one New Jersey suburb of New York City, contested divorce trials were backed up to the point of many 3-year delays from the point of filing to the point of the trial. One outraged woman who had been married for 23 years and separated 6 years ago and who had been waiting 3 years for a divorce trial said, "This is my life we're talking about.... It interferes with my social life. If I tell a gentleman I've been trying to get divorced for so long . . . he'll figure I'm some sort of lunatic."[10]

The effects of divorce on an individual's health read like a grocery list. Divorced people have excessive rates for suicide, depression, mental illness, physical ailments and illnesses, and mortality (Stroebe & Stroebe, 1986). It is critical to remember, though, that most of these relationships are correlational in nature. That is, we do not know for certain that being divorced *caused* the problems noted. Conceivably, other problems, such as financial difficulties and other stresses could also cause these mental and physical health problems. Nonetheless, the correlation between divorce and psychological and physical problems is so strong that it cannot be readily dismissed.

The effect of divorce or dissolution is enhanced by certain situational factors. Parkes (1972) argues that a sudden or unexpected termination of the relationship is especially hurtful. Also, Parkes notes that people who share domestic and other major practical tasks in a relationship are better able to cope, and less devastated, when divorce or dissolution occurs because they have become less dependent on each other. The same likely holds for emotional independence. If an individual is highly dependent on his or her partner to meet his or her emotional needs or for friends and a social network, that individual is likely to be affected much more by the termination of the relationship than is the person who is less dependent on the other person.

Why is divorce so devastating? First, it robs us of our innocence. Each of us has the aspiration for our marriage or significant relationship to continue "until death do us part." Thus, that expectation is dashed. The result often is a hard knock to one's self-esteem, sense of control over major events, and feeling of competence in close relationships. We also tend to compare ourselves with others whom we perceive to be engaged in solid relationships. Such social comparison (see Schachter, 1959) makes more salient our loss and the possibility that we may never again experience such stability and hope. Beyond these blows, the person who loses a partner also loses the emotional support and companionship that usually go along with such relationships. Even in sadly deteriorated relationships, partners may not recognize the extent to which they were attached and, thus, may be bewildered by the bereavement at the loss of this attachment. After all, many partners have been together since they were quite young. They have often gone through many adversities together. These experiences create an attachment, even if the quality of the marital interaction is poor and becoming poorer.

Finally, there is a great loss of social identity attendant to divorce and dissolution (Harvey, 1995). We no longer are "Joan's significant other," "John's wife," or "Mary's live-in partner." We have become known in these relationship identities by our friends and family, and somehow the outside world has to learn that the identities no longer hold. The ending of the relationship necessitates an identity change in our minds as well as the minds of those with whom we regularly relate. Depending on how much we wanted this role and wanted to continue in it, the necessity to change can be daunting. But it has to be done. The sooner the newly single person can recognize the need to change his or her life, by becoming involved in support groups and working on self-improvement, the sooner the recovery will be complete. Our society, fortunately, is now more primed for the occurrence of divorce and so may better assist the person experiencing it firsthand. The high frequency of divorce has led to outsiders exhibiting more sensitivity, or caution, in how they view someone's intimate relationship. Too often, we may have been floored to discover that some long-term, seemingly well-functioning relationship no longer exists.

Vivid Memories of Loves Gone By

Related to the grieving involved in divorce and dissolution is the idea that people will continue to have many poignant and sometimes haunting memories of their past loves. These memories may intrude unexpectedly when we encounter stimuli that remind us of the lost one. They also may occur in dreams about the lost partner or in conscious attempts to dredge up images and feelings about the past relationships. For some, these vivid memories appear to be a part of the continual grieving process, in that they still have not totally come to grips with the physical absence of the other in their lives. I personally believe that just about anyone who has loved deeply and lost that love will experience such grief at recurring points throughout his or her life. I believe it is normal. Some continue to obsess about the loss, however, and do not engage in the grieving and resolution processes that are necessary to effectively live one's life and fully participate in future close relationships. Let's look briefly at some research on this topic.

In one study, Rodney Flanary and Melinda Morgan and I (Harvey et al., 1986) found that women (who were mostly in their late 20s through early 40s) reported more vivid memories of their past loves than did men. The method involved asking respondents to recall their most vivid memories of events occurring in their most significant past close relationship. A "vivid memory" was defined as a picturelike image or thought that is lifelike, striking, and evocative of strong emotion. The respondents in this study had been involved both in nonmarital and marital relationships lasting at least 2 years, and the length of time since the relationships ended averaged almost 3 years. The content of some of these memories are shown in Table 3.3.

As can be seen in Table 3.3, highly vivid memories tended to be of first meetings, first sexual experiences, critical conflict episodes near the end, and ending events. Although both pleasant and painful memories surfaced in respondents' reports, unpleasant memories were more commonly reported. Harvey et al. (1986) also found that women tended to exhibit more depression regarding the loss of these past loves than did men. It was as if many of these women continued to pine for their past loves and experienced related depressive episodes—even though at least 2 years had passed since the relationships had ended.

In a related study, Ross and Holmberg (1992) hypothesized that women pay more attention to the emotional aspects of interactions with lovers and spouses and hence should report more vivid memories of key past events in their relationships than should men. A strength of this study is that both members of 60 married couples participated in the research. The method involved asking spouses to tape-record de-

TABLE 3.3 Reports of Respondents to Vivid Memories of Loves Gone By

Beginnings

"The first time we slept together I was living alone in a little house in a tiny town in the middle of nowhere. We stayed in bed for fourteen hours—it was wonderful."

"Our first (almost) sexual encounter, we were at a retreat and in the kitchen, and people kept walking in. It was rather amusing; it was ludicrous."

"I met him at a small party given by our apartment manager . . . our eyes kept meeting across the room. . . . When the party was over, we both managed to saunter out the door at the same time. He invited me up to his apartment—I remember sitting in his bean bag chair and listening to the Eagles sing 'The Best of My Love.'"

Special occasions (both pleasant and painful)

"The first time he told me how much he loved me . . . considering he was a married man."

"Being raped by him when he was drunk."

"After seven years, he brought home yellow roses. Trips to New Orleans. Five wonderful days of being together, sightseeing, eating out. Time alone in the hotel room."

"August 15, 1984, the date we intended to marry."

Beginning of the end and endings

"Receiving the 'letter' January 21, 1978."

"Confrontation with girlfriend and husband. Stated he did not love me; that he loved her."

"I remember the time I caught him throwing rocks at my car."

"Our final interaction was an angry good-bye in the car when I was moving away. Time seemed to stand still for a long time."

SOURCE: Harvey, Flanary, and Morgan (1986).

scriptions of their first date together, a shared vacation, and an argument between them. They subsequently assessed the clarity of their own recall of each event. As expected, women reported more vivid memories than did their husbands. Women also attributed greater personal importance to the events, reported reminiscing about them more often, and expressed more affect in their event descriptions than did their husbands. Later, observers of each couple's reports also judged women's recall to be more vivid.

Overall, these two studies converge in suggesting that women report, and presumably remember, more intense, vivid, evocative memories of events in their past close relationships than do men. Why? Is it because, as Ross and Holmberg (1992) imply, women have learned to link critical relationship experiences with strong feelings? Is it because women pay more attention to critical events in relationships than do men? Or is this result mainly due to women's openness to recall and report such memories compared with men's openness? We do not know the answers to these questions. This area of work is fascinating in its implications about gender differences in close relationships and the role of emotion and imagery in the memory of relationships.

The Effects on Children

This topic is in the news regularly in the 1990s and has received much attention in the last two decades. It is also timely because in the 1990s, Census Bureau data indicate that 50% to 60% of the children in the United States will spend some period of time before they reach age 18 in a home in which a divorce is occurring. One-third of the children in this country will live in a blended family by the time they reach 18.

Research reports, such as those by Hetherington, Cox, and Cox (1982) and Wallerstein and Lewis (1998), and books, like Wallerstein and Kelly's (1980) *Surviving the Breakup* and Furstenberg and Cherlin's (1991) *Divided Families,* have provided data and perspective on the effects of divorce on children. Scholars and studies differ on the affect that divorce can have on children. Hetherington et al. (1982) found that although there was initial turmoil in the lives of the children, their lives had become more normal by the second year after divorce. Wallerstein and her colleagues (Wallerstein & Kelly, 1980; Wallerstein & Lewis, 1998) have found that as many as one-half of the young men and women they studied entered adulthood as worried, underachieving, self-deprecating, and sometimes angry people because of the divorces of their parents. Other scholars, including Furstenberg and Cherlin (1991), do not believe that the evidence is that clear regarding the potency of the effect on children. The latter scholars have argued that the people whose divorces have been studied may have had severe problems well before the divorce. Most of the people studied to date have been involved in counseling and have agreed to answer questionnaires and participate in research as part of the counseling process.

Scholars such as Furstenberg and Cherlin (1991) have suggested that stronger evidence exists to support the view that the long-term harmful effects of divorce occur only for a minority of the children involved. They have admitted that many young adults likely retain painful memories of their parents' divorce. It does not follow, however, that these memories will impair these adult children's marriages or lives in general. Such theorists have argued that if these children's parents had not divorced, they might have retained equally painful memories of their parents' conflict-ridden marriages. Furstenberg and Cherlin have proposed that whenever there is trouble in a marriage children will suffer and it is not particularly helpful for parents to stay together in order to alleviate their children's suffering. These researchers found that children who live with two parents who persistently quarrel over important areas of family life show higher levels of distress and behavior problems than do children from disrupted marriages.

Beyond this point about conflicted relationships, there is evidence that in comparison to their peers from intact families, *some* children show enhanced levels of functioning in areas such as maturity, self-esteem, and empathy following divorce (Gately & Schwebel, 1992). Why do some children blossom in these ways after their parents have divorced? Divorce may place responsibilities on the children (e.g., caretaking younger siblings) that they are experienced enough and otherwise ready to handle. Success in being responsible, in turn, may enhance their self-esteem, as well as sensitivity to the problems of others. Furthermore, children who learn that they can rise to the occasion during the adversity of divorce may develop a general kind of strength and courage that will assist them when they encounter problems later in life.

Young kids deserve to be listened to when adults are considering the effect of divorce on children. Consider what children told a reporter for *Parade Magazine.*[11] One 15-year-old said that when parents decide to get a divorce, they should be honest and definitely tell the kids. And they should tell the kids that they are not separating because of the kids. Kids often hold the belief that they are to blame for their parents' problems. Furthermore, parents should not use their child as a middleman by communicating through the child, saying things such as "Tell your dad that I say to send the child support right now." This child, as well as others, noted that kids need special attention and love during these tough times. The parents also need to work on not making their kids feel guilt about what the parents are doing with each other and to recognize that the other parent is still very much a full parent.

There are many other issues associated with the effect of divorce on children: Does the type of custody (joint or sole) make a difference in the child's adjustment? Does the type and quality of visitation for the noncustodial parent affect the children's progress? Do different blendings of stepfamilies help or hurt adjustment? The answers to such questions is inevitably "It depends." It depends on a host of factors such as whether the parents in a joint-custody or sole-custody situation have made arrangements to provide security, nurturance, and understanding for their children at the same time that they are dealing with their own postdivorce issues. It depends on how well-functioning blended families are and whether or not they have figured out ways to enhance both the group's as well as the individual's level of satisfaction in connection with the family experience. The recognition of children's feelings and their need to adjust and move on in new directions with their lives is an essential step in this process. As Wallerstein and Kelly (1980) said, "Even though the children may still regret the divorce and continue to wish that their parents had been able to love each other, some of these children may nevertheless grow in their capacity for compassion and psychological understanding" (p. 316).

Wallerstein and Kelly (1980) may have underestimated the growth that is possible for the children of divorce. Not only may the experience teach them about some of the issues of marriage and close relationships, but it also may give them insights about their own close relationships at that time and later in life. The evidence is unclear that children of divorce end up experiencing more debilitating marital problems themselves. If at a relatively early age, children are forced to witness destructive anger and hostility on the part of their parents for a substantial period—whether or not separation and divorce occur, they probably will be severely hurt. It is likely that, at minimum, they will be psychologically damaged by such experience. Then again, such children may recover over time with the help of good friends and confidants and counseling and may use their experience and perspective to contribute to stronger interpersonal relations on their own part. Many children will experience their parents' divorce at later ages when they can better assimilate the reasons, and many also will not be so adversely affected because the parents are thoughtful about their feelings and relatively civil in how they carry out the divorce. Parents and children alike should consider perusing this literature on the effects of divorce and be willing to seek counseling when necessary. Any way you look at it, divorce is a major loss for children, and parents should be alert to the need of the child to engage in the types of grieving and recovery steps associated with such losses.

Wallerstein's "Unexpected Legacy" Argument

A more recent presentation by Wallerstein, Lewis, and Blakeslee (2000) created quite a media frenzy. In this book, Wallerstein and colleagues reported on their three decades of research on children whose parents divorced in the 1970s. For these 131 children of 80 California families, a small and not-so-random sample of the 1 million children whose parents divorce each year, the data showed tremendous flux in their lives over the years from the point at which their parents divorced. Wallerstein et al. indicated that these individuals from divorced families spent much of their early adulthood negotiating relationships. Many were not married, nor interested in marrying. Many did not want children. But most important, Wallerstein and colleagues make the following argument: "The myth that if the parents have a poor marriage the children are going to be unhappy is not true" (p. 23). They argue that children do not care if parents sleep in separate beds if the household runs well and if the parenting holds up. A "good enough" marriage without violence or martyrdom or severe mental disorder will do for the children. That is, the children from such marriages will transit through their own adult relationships with much less turmoil than will children from even happily divorced families. Indeed, the divorce may be the solution for the couple's problems and the cause of the children's problems.

Of course, this evidence and the related argument stirred the passions of many critics. Writing in *Time,* author and columnist for the

Nation Katha Pollitt argued that this society does not need more "good enough" marriages full of depressed and bitter people.[12] She also asserted that America does not need more pundits blaming women for destroying "the family" with what are, after all, reasonable demands for equality and self-development. She argued that what we need to acknowledge is that there are lots of different ways to raise competent and well-adjusted children, which—according to virtually every family researcher who has worked with larger and more representative samples than what she termed Wallerstein's "small handful"—the vast majority of kids of divorce turn out to be. Pollitt argued that we have learned a lot about how to divorce since 1971. She suggested that when the ex-wife and mother has enough money and when the ex-husband and father stays connected, when parents stay civil and don't badmouth each other, kids do all right. In short, Pollitt asks, why isn't the "good enough" divorce ever the cover story?

Conclusion: The Future of Divorce and Dissolution

Unfortunately, no highly optimistic script can be written in the early 2000s for the future of divorce and dissolution. The evidence about the incidence of divorce suggests that no diminution of the high divorce rate of recent decades is on the horizon for the near future. Second and later marriages are no more apt to continue now than in any earlier period of history. All the factors that we recognize as potent in contributing to divorce and dissolution still are operative. Furthermore, other factors such as those associated with economic difficulties will also probably contribute to dissolution trends. People may be frustrated with their work opportunities or the lack thereof; they may move frequently to find work and may even leave their families behind to try to improve their work opportunities.

Robert Weiss has often eloquently addressed matters of dissolution. In a personal communication (November 2000), he suggested that in the dissolution form of loss, a person's sense of abandonment and isolation can be mitigated by new relationships. Nevertheless, this loss usually produces long-lasting self-doubt and possibly more pronounced forms of psychological distress. Weiss has also noted that because marriage plays such a major role in our lives, the breakup of a marriage is extraordinarily disruptive to a person's functioning and emotional life. For many, marriage is a way of fitting into society and a way of achieving status. When a marriage is over (including when a spouse dies), former spouses often speak of feeling like fifth wheels. In sum, with all the divorce and nonmarital dissolution occurring in so many lives, there is a huge reservoir of psychic pain and angst about relationship matters. We are, in short, too often confused and cynical people when it comes to making intimate relationships work.

A positive thread in this picture is the greater sophistication of the American people (and people in the Western World in general) in dealing with relational losses today. We have more support groups and counseling services available than ever before. These support activities stretch across socioeconomic levels. Divorce, separation, and death support groups, such as "Parents without Partners" that was established in 1957 and now has more than 300,000 members, contribute greatly to addressing people's social and practical problems. These support group activities do not make the hurt and damage go away. But they do allow the individual to vent, confide his or her hurt, and learn from and be supported by others who have survived similar circumstances.

Returning to the basic principles outlined in Chapter 1, the dissolution of close relationships illustrate each of these principles:

1. *Our major losses are relative.* They are relative to other losses we have experienced and to those experienced by others. We have seen that the dissolution of a relationship may vary in its effect on the individuals involved as well as their children. Some breakups are much more hurtful than others.

2. *Our major losses have cumulative effects.* For many of us, divorce and dissolution do not recede into meaninglessness. They continue to affect our feelings and thinking throughout our lives. Dissolution of marriages often has long-term adverse effects on children's lives.

3. *When major losses occur, they contribute to new aspects of our identity.* People often change in dramatic ways after dissolution of close relationships.

4. *Major losses involve adaptations related to our sense of control.* We experience a particularly painful lack of control when we lose an intimate relationship in a way that we did not expect. That loss may involve infidelity and feelings of betrayal.

5. *Valuable coping strategies for dealing with major losses include working on the meanings of the losses and learning how to give back to others based on our lessons of loss.* As before, these steps are central to dealing with the loss of a close relationship.

In returning to the questions I raised at the outset of this chapter, I must say that I believe that the evidence strongly suggests that young people in their early and late adolescence, as well as adults of all ages, are not learning enough about close relationships and how frail they are before commencing them. We still do not have enough relevant courses in grade school, high school, and even colleges on this topic. Nonetheless, these words on paper about divorce, common relationship problems, and scripts for problems have grown into the millions. However, the divorce rate continues to be exceedingly high with no likely reduction any time soon. So, maybe it is true that most of us will have to learn, if we learn much at all, via the "school of hard knocks." Maybe it is true that most of the readers of chapters such as the present one, who indeed do feel more enlightened by the information, already will have experienced enough major loss in the relationship arena that they truly understand the words.

Notes

1. From *USA TODAY*, April 5, 1993, p. 1.
2. From "Fresh Voices," *Parade Magazine*, April 25,1993, p. 21.
3. From Ann Landers column, *Los Angeles Times*, September 3, 1989.
4. From *Glamour*, January 1993, pp. 163, 180.
5. From *New York Post*, February 4, 1993.

6. From *Iowa City Press-Citizen,* October 4, 1989.
7. From *Chicago Tribune: Arts and Entertainment,* July 25, 1999, p. 18.
8. From an Associated Press news article.
9. As told to Jane Gross in an article in *Chicago Tribune,* December 20, 1992.
10. As told to Bethany Kandel, in *USA TODAY,* February 20, 1992.
11. From *Parade Magazine,* January 26, 1992, p. 5.
12. "Is Divorce Getting a Bum Rap?" Katha Pollitt, *Time,* September 25, 2000.

4 Loss Due to Illness and Injury

Life expectancy may drop to 30 in Africa.
—Headline from the AIDS Conference, July 2000

This headline reflects findings from a report given at the July 2000 AIDS Conference in South Africa. This report indicated that in sub-Saharan Africa, where three-quarters of all HIV-infected people live, 15 million people have died from the disease and 25 million more are infected.

In this chapter, I examine the special issues associated with aging, illness, and accidents occurring at relatively early points in a person's life. Aging is not a disease process. (In fact, as I argue, it may be viewed as a process leading to enhanced wisdom and ability to share stories of life with younger people.) Nonetheless, in our fast-paced Western world, we often stereotype older people as sick and dying. We also often relegate them to impoverished institutional living settings, which may constitute a major loss for them in terms of morale and the will to live.

Chronic Pain, Illness, and Disability

Jim Gennell, age 30, described his feelings after becoming a quadriplegic in a car accident. He was quoted in the *Chicago Tribune* as saying that the feelings come at you in no particular order—especially grief.

It's such a loss. He said that you feel like you're on your own island. You're by yourself. You can't hug anybody. He said that that was the first thought that hit him, he could not reach out and touch his family anymore.[1]

Whether by disease or accident, many people experience long-term chronic pain and/or disability. Millions of people spend a good portion of their lives as invalids or with significant handicaps that preclude normal movement about their environment.

Whether the chronic illness is associated with cancer, stroke, spinal cord injury, or whatever, Lyons and Sullivan (1998) provide a compelling argument that the person's success in adapting and having a fulfilling life will depend on mental and social adjustments. The mental adjustments have to do with work on personal identity ("Who am I now, and what value do I have for society?"), renewed motivation, will, and hope ("What keeps me going now and gives me a new spirit to accomplish or contribute?"). The development and acceptance of new plans that may violate long-term scripts for the way life was supposed to go is also important (see Chapter 2 discussion of Janoff-Bulman's 1992 ideas about how people can learn from "shattered assumptions" after major losses). Old plans may be unrealistic after an injury or illness occurs. Included in the new plans are often practical ideas about how to move about in one's immediate environment, how to deal with transportation in general, and how to conserve energy for daily tasks. Beyond the mundane activities, what about new scripts for leisure and sexual intimacy? Why shouldn't persons experiencing major disabilities or illnesses have these opportunities?

Since his debilitating spinal cord injury in 1995, actor Christopher Reeve has used his voice to empower disabled people throughout the world and to inform society about the need for research on spinal cord injury. His efforts, and those of his wife Dana, have led to dramatic increases in funding for spinal cord injury research and to increased interest in the welfare of spinal cord patients and the needs of the relevant funding agencies. This has been called the Christopher Reeve effect on funding by the *Wall Street Journal*. Reeve has created the Christopher Reeve Foundation to raise money for research on quality-of-life issues for the disabled. The efforts of this foundation include the following: lobbying for increased funding by the National Institute of Health, getting some states to use a portion of speeding ticket proceeds to support work on spinal cord injury, helping people get better wheelchairs, helping get better wheelchair access in buildings, and battling insurance companies—the foundation has influenced companies to raise funding caps from $1 million to $10 million dollars. As Reeve said in a speech at the 1996 Democratic Convention, "Either you vegetate and look out the window, or you get busy and affect change . . . and the second of course appeals to me a lot more."

Lyons and Sullivan (1998) suggest that social support is critical to renegotiating new personal relationships with spouses, lovers, family, and friends that will facilitate rather than hinder the survivor's adaptation. Having these vital others in your life and caring about you (and caring for you) can make all the difference in long-term adaptation and success in fulfilling one's hopes for work and family life. Christopher Reeve's wife Dana shows the critical contribution highly supportive loved ones can make to the lives of those who suffer from a life-threatening disease or injury. First, Dana had to help Christopher decide whether or not he wanted to die after sustaining one of the worst types of spinal cord injuries (called a "hangman's noose injury" because of the impact on the neck and spinal column—in which medical redress literally requires reattaching the head to the spine). Dana has contributed to his ongoing and agonizing rehabilitation program, and most important, she has been instrumental to his invaluable work to enhance funding for work on spinal cord injuries and find remedies for people who cannot walk or use their arms. Lyons and Sullivan (1998) also note the possibility that a disabling illness or accident may lead to relationship dysfunction and dissolution. For example, as people in brain injury support groups know, there is a greater than normal divorce rate associated with the occurrence of brain injuries. When a spouse incurs a brain injury that changes his or her personality and functional behavior, the effort required to deal with such an injury can really test a relationship. Lyons and Sullivan point to the following determinants of relationship adaptation after major illness or disability:

1. People need to be taught about illness and disabilities and their effect on quality of life.

2. There needs to be increased awareness about the linkages between relational well-being and the quality of life of persons with health problems.

3. There needs to be increased dialogue about personal and shared roles regarding the presence of disability in the family, workplace, and community.

4. There needs to be increased rational competence around illness and disability. Individuals need to know how to communicate more effectively with individuals with illness and disability.

5. Individuals with disabilities and their families need to discuss relationship issues, share strategies, and find models of successful relationship adjustment.

Lyons and Sullivan (1998) also alert us to the communication difficulties encountered by persons with disabling illnesses or injuries. A person with multiple sclerosis suggested that outsiders should have to spend just 1 hour in the shoes of someone who has the disease to know how difficult it is to make society understand the plight of the MS survivor: "The actual sensation that your body has or does not have is hard to explain" (Lyons & Sullivan, 1998, p. 143).

Kelley (1998) has also written about the losses associated with chronic pain and illness. She notes not only the potency of interpersonal losses but also the powerful existential and identity issues that influence adaptation and motivation. For example, there may be a loss or disruption of attachment both to close others and to one's body or to body parts and to a previous lifestyle. This existential loss may take the form of a chronic feeling of sorrow (see discussion later of Christopher Reeve's indication that he could have been swallowed up by depression after his spinal cord injury, but he chose not to let that happen).

Kelley (1998) estimates that chronic pain affects 6% of the population of North America, which would be approximately 20 million people. She describes how the symptoms of chronic pain, which may derive from major illness or disabling accidents, may include muscle aches and pains, sleep disturbance and fatigue, headaches, vascular reactivity, and urinary and bowel irritability.

The direct and more subtle losses associated with chronic pain connected with migraine headaches are suggested in the following account by a woman in her 40s who is a college professor:

> I began to get recurrent migraines out of the blue, about 8 years ago. Undertaking a major new project seemed to worsen their intensity and frequency, and I found myself turning from a normal, active person to a "disabled" individual. Worst of all, my headache pain was invisible to everyone around me, including my husband and my good friends. I know that almost all of them wondered, at least sometimes, whether I was faking it, or at least whether my pain was "all that bad."
>
> Thus, the pain is not only crippling, but the nature of the beast left me feeling isolated and resentful. This got worse when my doctors advised me to pull out of new work projects, since deadline pressure and stress triggered many headaches. This was a smart decision, but it essentially ended my career in those projects, and I had to tell my occasional employers [book publishers] that I was no longer reliable.
>
> In sum, the onset of this condition—which is a condition, chronic pain, and not a disease that might kill me—nonetheless left me with numerous losses: loss of comfort, mobility, visibility at work, social activity and involvement in work I love, and access to and trust in those closest to me. I may eventually find a solution to the pain, per se, or a way to manage it; but I won't find a resolution to those other losses in a pill, or a single new therapy. This will be a lifelong struggle, and I don't expect any neat, complete resolution.[2]

Losses Associated With Accidents and Diseases in Early and Midlife

I know a prominent scientist who experienced a brain hemorrhage in his 40s. The rapid bleeding in his left cerebral hemisphere resulted in the loss of much of his affective and memory functioning. Now he does not know what decade he lives in. He knows that he has experienced a tremendous loss—one that has also exacted a huge toll on his wife, children, and his extended family. But he cannot precisely understand what he has lost either physically or psychologically. As his wife suggested, he would not have wanted his life—maybe 40 plus more years—to slowly ebb away in this fashion, sitting in a nursing home wearing diapers because he cannot control his bowels. She would often say, "It would have been so much better if he had just died."

Yet that was not to be with this man, nor is it for millions of other brain-damaged individuals. As the acclaimed neurologist and writer Oliver Sacks (*The Man Who Mistook His Wife for a Hat*, 1970) wrote years ago, many people suffer brain injuries that transform their lives and the lives of their loved ones into something that is akin to constant sorrow. It is never the same as it was and will never be. Yet the patient may look totally normal and be in otherwise fine health. The adjustment process for all people concerned in these situations can be very difficult, and divorce is not uncommon.

Chwalisz (1998) writes eloquently about the many loss issues faced by persons who incur brain injuries. Frequently, these losses include the following: loss of purpose ("What value does my life have now?"), loss of personality (a wife may say, "I only rarely see in him the man I used to know and love"), and loss of intellectual capacity (where tests may show a loss of 50 or more IQ points in many cases). As Chwalisz notes, just as compelling may be the effects of other types of loss, such as sexual function, capacity to love, and family relationships. The scientist I knew whom I described earlier knew his two teen-aged children only as they existed 10 years earlier. And his children eventually gave up on him, after first viewing him as someone whom they hoped and believed would recover, then as someone whose injury had inflicted great discomfort in their lives, including embarrassment, and finally as someone for whom they could only feel sympathy. They seldom visited him because it seemed useless—"He always said the same things, and never seemed to feel any real love or care for us" (p. 190). The scientist could not change his reactions. His memory and intellect had been so severely damaged that his behavior was flat and usually lacking in clear feeling for anyone other than his spouse.

John Phillips (1998) describes how a stroke he had in 1995 at age 57 affected him and his family. At the time, Phillips was a high-ranking education expert working in Washington, D.C. His stroke was a hemorrhage in which blood vessels burst, sending blood out into and around his brain cells (which in time can die from a lack of fresh oxygen). Phillips was in an intensive care unit for 5 days before he started to become aware of his situation. His right side was paralyzed, and he had no control over his bodily functions. His right-side vision was impaired. He could hear but not comprehend very well early in his convalescence. Phillips did not suffer a completely devastating stroke (it was fairly average in the spectrum of possible strokes). Nonetheless, some of the effects he experienced deserve to be detailed, because they show how daunting any type of brain bleed may be.

Phillips sketches steps his family had to take to cope with his situation. They had to contact his employer and find a copy of his entire primary insurance policy. They also had to be with Phillips daily to help him exercise his limp body. He describes the subsequent period of rehabilitation as the "boot camp" for stroke patients. He was forced to use his moderately paralyzed hands to eat. He was helped into a wheelchair and later assisted for hours as he attempted to walk and move his limbs. Then he slept for a few hours and afterward worked with a physical therapist. The therapist helped him by pointing to pictures and asking him to answer questions, and later he worked with family members to say words such as "love." After 10 days in this rehabilitation setting, Phillips and his family were called together for a conference call to discuss his diagnosis. The attending physician said that his healing would be incomplete (not uncommon after a stroke). There would be losses of function. One such loss would be aphasia, or communication problems. In his case, he could not readily say the words that he wanted to say. At the same time, his wife was struggling with insurance forms and insurance companies to try to get the bills paid. Phillips, who was lucky to have good insurance benefits, notes that after the various disability settlements were reached, his income declined 75%. Phillips was finally released from the hospital after almost 2 months, but then he began a period of regular visits to physical therapists. In 1998, 3 years later, he indicated that his condition had improved to the point that communication difficulties were his most challenging ongoing problem. He indicates that in a blink, his high-powered job was gone and he was reduced to being an ordinary human, which he learned to appreciate a lot more than he did prior to the stroke. He says that he has gained a greater respect for the value of family and patience, which he must call upon daily in dealing with the effects of his stroke.

The following are some of the lessons Phillips offers based on his experience:

- Exercise can help reduce blood pressure and weight, as well as stress—all of which can be precipitating factors in a stroke. He exercised erratically and had problems with weight and cholesterol.

- Discuss with family issues that will need to be addressed if a family member has a stroke. Know the symptoms, such as shortness of breath, severe headache, and dizziness. Know the ambulance service you can rely on to be there within 10 minutes.

- Select the best disability, health, and medical insurance that you can afford; have entire medical policies available for emergencies.

- Ensure that your spouse or significant other has complete and immediate stand-by authority to obtain family financial resources, personal medical records, and blood-relation medical records.

- Have agreements in hand with your family regarding advance medical directives and codify them in some type of living will.

One of the most salutary developments in brain injury treatment is the growth of strong, active support groups. More than anything else, such groups can stand by members, especially spouses and family members, when others may dismiss them as whining about their loss. Outsiders may judge the lingering grief of survivors as an obsession about something small in the scheme of major losses that can confront people: "So he got hit on the head and is different now? Why is that so life shattering? How is that like getting cancer or something?" But a brain injury can literally change the whole interaction and emotional dynamics of the family. The brain-injured person may not be capable of the type of affective expression that he or she showed prior to the injury. With automobile accidents so common and major brain injuries also increasingly common, this area of work and public activism must be better recognized in our country, particularly among professionals concerned with loss, grief, and adaptation.

Losses Related to Major Accidents

Many other types of injuries and diseases can cripple the body, mind, and spirit at a relatively early point in one's life. Perhaps none is more devastating than those that clearly and fully knock out higher order mental functioning—a quintessential human quality. Some diseases, like Alzheimer's, destroy such functioning in a gradual way.

Accidents often lead to the same consequence without any preparation by the patient or her or his family. Approximately 1 fatality occurs every 13 minutes in the United States due to traffic accidents (Ehlers, Mayou, & Bryant, 1998). One alcohol-related automobile fatality occurs every 30 minutes. It has been estimated that each year as many as 10,000 Americans suffer serious brain or spinal cord injuries in accidents. Eighty percent are men, and most are between the ages of 15 and 35. A substantial percentage of persons involved in serious automobile accidents develop posttraumatic stress disorders (Kuch, Cox, & Evans, 1996). It is staggering to consider that every year in the United States approximately 50,000 people die in traffic accidents, nearly the number of U.S. personnel who died in the Vietnam War. These numbers are similar in Europe, where there are approximately 80,000 vehicle accident deaths per year.

Perhaps the most important loss issues associated with traffic accidents have to do with people's sense of control and justice. We want to control our environments to make them safer. State and federal governments often formulate laws designed to control speeding and unsafe driving practices on the highways. People purchase automobiles that supposedly give them more security in a traffic accident. Most citizens go to high school and other driving courses designed to enhance safety practices. However, as all experienced drivers know, we only have so much control. Even the most careful of us who have driven for a long time have had many close calls. We have learned to cherish caution, but we have also observed how frequently luck and chance seem to play a role in who lives and who dies in traffic accidents.

Too many people today feel like getting on the highway is like getting on a racetrack. This feeling presumably is leading thousands of people to enroll in racecar academies.[3] These people believe that they need to simulate real driving conditions much more closely than do driving schools. They feel the need to learn how to deal with other drivers speeding, driving while drunk, driving while enraged, and so on. People are paying up to $4,000 for a 4-day course that helps drivers learn how to stop quickly in difficult conditions, how to deal with skids in wet and unfavorable road conditions, how to drive defensively, and how to drive with varying road hazards.

The topic of drunk driving introduces both control and justice concepts. Again, society has imposed relatively harsh penalties for being caught by police while driving drunk (at the .10 or .08 levels in most states). Nevertheless, each year deaths and severe injuries result from drunk driving. Justice is in the minds of survivors and the families of victims. Mothers against drunk driving (MADD) was begun in the early 1980s after a woman lost her daughter because the daughter was struck and killed by a drunk driver. Many lawsuits have been successfully filed against bars and parents who have been alleged by claimants to have contributed to death and injuries by providing drivers with alcohol.

In addition to speeding and drunk driving, young people in the United States have recently invented what is called "car surfing," another form of deleterious driving behavior. According to Scott Bowles of USA TODAY, in such surfing, a "surfer" stands on the hood of a moving car. The driver builds speed, say to 20 mph, and then slams on the brakes, throwing the rider off. Those who say on their feet win points. Those who do not lose points. They also fairly frequently lose their lives or health. As one spokesman for the Ohio State Police said, "The kids are trying everything . . . sitting on the hood, standing on the roof. . . . Some of them seem bent on playing with their lives."[4]

Road rage is a behavior that started to occur in the 1980s on America's busy freeways. It has been carried out by persons of all ages and backgrounds. It may involve cutting people off at high speeds, giving people the finger (probably the most innocuous and common form of rage in the 80s and 90s), and even the use of guns and shootings by enraged drivers. Even the act of having a gun in a car is a potential act of road rage. But in some cities where safety is an issue (e.g., where automobile car-jackings have been reported), many people carry guns in their cars. The guns are then available when other events such as being cut off on the freeway on a crowded, humid day set the stage for an eruption of a person's aggression, even the most kindly and compassionate person in other circumstances.

Given the substantial losses associated with speeding, reckless driving, driving under the influence, and other destructive acts with motor vehicles, why do people continue to engage in this behavior? Do we not know that the consequences may be severe for ourselves and/or others? Do we not care about life? Do we not know that families may suffer pain and anguish the remainder of their lives after one of their own is killed in this way, or after we as members of these families have taken another's life with our driving behavior? The answers to these questions defy easy answers. So often careless driving reflects poor habits, a lack of alertness to the life-and-death nature of all driving, and a desire to show off for friends. Driving after drinking may be the result of similar factors, as well as inadequate planning with friends or others of how to handle transportation if drinking will occur. As with so many types of reckless behavior, young people are often involved as perpetrators and victims in driving fatalities and injuries. In my classes, I have encountered more than a few students who have become paraplegics or quadriplegics because of automobile accidents. It regularly occurs every school year, and in particular in the winter under adverse driving conditions or at holiday time when students are racing off to be with friends. It is as regular as the seasons. Schools often have customs of lowering the U.S. flag to half-staff after the death of a person affiliated with the university. The reader is invited to observe how frequently this index of loss and grief for many is associated with traffic accidents.

In the end, there really is no end to the losses associated with vehicular accidents. Fatalities and severe injuries are so common that we all will experience them in some way, even if only in knowing others well who experience them. The grief that follows is the like the grief of losses resulting from other types of events. It lasts a lifetime. In a guest column in the *Iowa City Press-Citizen,* Jane Heaton described her continuing grief on the 20-year anniversary of the loss of two friends in a car accident. Another driver killed them when he tried to pass a car on a hill. As she said, these victims who become statistics leave behind mothers and fathers, siblings, and friends who do not forget and whose grief may know no end.[5]

That certainly was the case for Mrs. Venita Kelley whose son David died in graduate school at the University of Missouri, Columbia in 1971. He died when he was hit by a drunk driver as he slept in a car his friend was driving back from a skiing holiday in Colorado. Dave had almost finished his Ph.D. in social psychology. He was a dear friend of mine. As I corresponded with his mother (usually at Christmastime) until her death she frequently wrote of the contributions Dave would have made and the successes he would have had if he had lived. She wanted the world to remember. I was a small window of such memory. I continue to be and continue to mourn the loss of Dave, who would have been a fine social psychologist and who might even have been writing in my stead this very minute.

"Marking" Persons Who Are Chronically Ill or Disabled

Our reactions to persons who are chronically ill or disabled too often reinforce cultural stereotypes. This process may involve what has been called "marking." In an important analysis of stigmatization, Edward Jones, Amerigo Farina, Albert Hastorf, Hazel Markus, Dale Miller, and Robert Scott published *Social Stigma: The Psychology of Marked Relationships* in 1984. This book is still one of the most comprehensive analyses of social stigma. In it, they cast social stigma in terms of "marks": "Mark is thus our generic term for perceived or inferred conditions of deviation from a prototype or norm that *might* initiate the stigmatizing process" (p. 8).

Marking, or labeling, which is a related process, is not done without consequence for the person who is marked. It usually results in some type of ostracization from a circle or community. As famed sociologist Erving Goffman (1963) eloquently argued, potentially every human being may be marked. It may occur because of physical features, physical functioning (e.g., disease processes), behavior, or presumed mental functioning (e.g., mental illness, mental retardation). More than three centuries ago, women who were labeled witches were burned at the stake in this country. That was a dreadful consequence associated with ill-conceived theorizing about other human beings. Yet such dire consequences associated with stigmatization have happened over and over again in human history.

Jones et al. (1984) provide the following story that tells of the psychological hurt that many people who are stigmatized suffer:

> November 26, 1981. A UPI report in the *Hartford Courant* is headlined "Teenager Describes How It Feels to Be Retarded." The article describes how the teacher of a trainable, mentally retarded 17-year-old transcribed his thoughts in a brief book: 'Sometimes it makes me want to cry inside because I am retarded, but sometimes other people may forget about me being retarded. I can't stand it if someone teases me, it makes me feel weird inside. I can't stand it! Nobody likes that. But when they realize that they are hurting my feelings sometimes they come over and apologize to me.' (p. 2)

Sometimes a loss that stigmatizes can serve as an explanation for a person's negative behavior. In 1994, Glenda Caldwell, who suffered from Huntington's disease and who had been in prison for 9 years after killing her teenage son, was finally given a new trial because of increased knowledge about the behavior that sometimes goes along with this disease. Doctors said that she suffered this disease at the time of her incarceration, but that fact had been minimized in her trial. Her new trial should help draw attention to Huntington's disease, but it also may stigmatize other sufferers as potentially violent. Philip Cohen, a spokesman for the Huntington's Disease Foundation of America in New York, made the following statements about this issue: "The sword is double-edged. Not every Huntington's person is violent. That would be a gross mischaracterization. . . . Being penalized for something you're not able to control seems to be inappropriate."[6]

In her acclaimed book titled *Shattered Assumptions* (1992), Ronnie Janoff-Bulman argues that victims are threatening to nonvictims because they are manifestations of a malevolent universe rather than a benevolent one. Janoff-Bulman suggests that most of us hold on to a set of assumptions, such as the world is benign, bad things happen to other people, and people get what they deserve and deserve what they get in life. Such assumptions do not help us when we ourselves suffer major losses and must deal with the reality that bad things happen to us too. But until we have had that experience and have empathy for others who suffer, we may regard them as deviants marked by misfortune. Their victim status sets them apart from ordinary folk, we may implicitly conclude, and in effect they are branded as somehow flawed or blemished. As an overall observation, Janoff-Bulman contends that victims are stigmatized because they violate the expectations established by people's illusions.

Aging and the Loss of Health

Closely related to the preceding discussion of marking and stigma is the issue of the perception of a loss of health that is linked to aging processes. Our bodies are dying a little bit each day of our lives. Furthermore, as discussed in Chapter 7, losses may be compounded (like the interest on a bank account), when an individual is contending with the ravages of aging. Such ravages may include deterioration of the body associated with life-threatening diseases, such as Alzheimer's and Huntington's (which assault selfhood in devastating ways), or relocation to a convalescent center. In addition, a person already suffering from health problems loses her or his support network of friends and close others. People in these situations are often quickly marginalized in our society.

A recent work that argues for a new appreciation of the value of age and its attendant wisdom is Pipher's (1999) *Another Country*. The idea of another country is a fitting metaphor for the isolation that many older people experience, as families frequently disperse and move away from senior family members, and families also increasingly fracture as a consequence of divorce. Pipher, a leading therapist and analyst of family issues, contends that we need more continuity in the interaction across ages. She mentions a residential care unit called Golden View, that is a nursing home for older adults and a day care center for 12 babies and 40 children. The kids, the elderly people, and the staff interact and play together (e.g., the kids like to help the elderly run their electric wheelchairs; the elderly like to have the kids sit on their laps and tell them stories).

The concepts of mutuality and interdependence are key elements of the new world Pipher advocates. She challenges our society to examine our biases and language about the elderly. A friendlier, more inclusive culture for them would involve such changes as a greater appreciation in families of the stories and wisdom that their elderly have to share with members at all ages; enhanced lighting in restaurants and larger print size in books; the building of housing to better accommodate the elderly; and the recognition of the value older couples may have as foster parents. Pipher advocates a medical system in which the elderly again have personal relationships with physicians and are treated as vital people with real needs, rather than as people who have already lived their lives and who only need drugs or some type of distraction from their ailments.

Caregivers

Family members or close others who care for persons suffering from serious illnesses or injuries often incur great losses themselves because of the demanding nature of their responsibilities. Many of these caregivers engage in this activity while at the same time carrying out family and work duties as well.

There is an emerging literature about the losses of caregivers. For example, a general finding is that caregivers are at risk for poorer mental health outcomes compared with their noncaregiver peers (see Schulz, O'Brien, Bookwala, & Fleissner, 1995; Williamson & Shaffer, 1998). Also, caregivers whose relationship with the recipients of their care before the onset of their illness was closer and more affectionate report experiencing less burden and depressed affect (Uchino, Kiecolt-Glaser, & Cacioppo, 1994).

There are frequent stories in the media about family and caregivers of persons with Alzheimer's disease. These stories often speak of the loving sacrifices of spouses, who for years tend to their invalid partner who may not even recognize them anymore. In an article titled "Consuming Love," Chicago Tribune writer Barbara Brotman chronicled

the devotion of a retired physician, age 76, who did everything to reduce the devastation of Alzheimer's disease on his wife (through intensive rehabilitation to maintain her walking skill) and to take care of her
in a high-quality way without putting her in a convalescent center, despite his own frequent exhaustion. They had been married more than
50 years and his wife was everything to him. Brotman quotes him as
saying, "I'm always afraid something will happen. . . . I don't know what
I would do if something happened to her and I was gone. I would go out
of my mind" (p. 6). His son added, "At this point, he doesn't care about
anything but her. He doesn't want to take time to do anything else. He
has become withdrawn from the other people he knows. Everyone is
aware that it's just him and her right now, and that's it."[7]

This man also made a 90-minute video of his wife's life and had one
of her poems printed in a vanity book. He had 500 postage-size stamps
printed with her picture on them, sent 10 each to 50 friends and asked
them to use them on their holiday mailings so that even more people
would see how lovely she was. These were his ways of honoring and
paying tribute to his wife and trying to make sure people did not forget
her. His son and other family members wondered if the husband's efforts would make the wife's eventual death that much harder—delay it
and make it impossible for the husband to adapt to life without her. I
would say that the husband's efforts to care for his wife should be respected. It gives his life meaning and very likely makes life much more
comfortable for her. Yet this story highlights the dilemma faced by families with persons suffering from serious progressive mental diseases
such as Alzheimer's disease.

Courage in Dealing With Loss
Due to Injury or Disease

One of the most uplifting stories I have heard from a survivor of
traumatic injury is Bob Wieland's story. Wieland was a medic in the
Vietnam War and in 1969 stepped on a booby-trapped shell that actually blew off both of his legs. This fact did not stop Wieland from ac-
complishing these achievements during the next three decades: He be-

came a world-class weight lifter, benching more than 500 pounds. He worked for the Green Bay Packers as a strength and conditioning coach. He has traveled extensively and speaks as a motivational speaker. Incredibly, he gained national attention starting in 1982 by walking on his hands, one yard at a time, from Los Angeles to Washington, D.C. It took him more than 4 years, as he traversed deserts and mountains and endured horrible weather and pain from the struggle. His journey raised more than $315,000 in pledges for disabled veterans. In a motivational talk to the Green Bay Packers football team before a game, he said of his rare trip,

> I lifted myself 2 inches off the ground and moved ahead 3 feet. I did that 4,900,016 times. I know because I counted. . . . If you guys can't run up and down a football field for 60 minutes, you ought to be ashamed of yourselves.

Wieland added that "players don't often look at things that way. They take their God-given ability for granted." Wieland's message from his arduous trip was simple: "You're alive, so use your life to the fullest."[8]

Conclusions

As noted at the outset, in no way could I thoroughly document the breadth and depth of loss issues associated with diseases and accidents. A topic that deserves a chapter in its own right is the continuing plague of AIDS in the world. Although so-called AIDS cocktail medicines appear to be having a positive effect on lengthening the lives of many people who are HIV-positive, there are and will continue to be millions of people dying of AIDS throughout the world well into the 21st century. This disease continues to affect African Americans more than any other group in the United States, accounting for approximately 57% of all new infections each year.[9]

Furthermore, in Africa AIDS infections are increasing each year at astronomical rates in many countries, with children and women at the top of the list of victims. Poverty and a lack of access to the best medical care are factors in these drastic rates of infection in Africa, as well as parts of the United States. And the sharing of dirty needles among drug users is a huge factor in the continued AIDS epidemic in America.

Princess Diana's death in 1997 in an automobile accident made us all aware of how quickly any person, regardless of their fame or stature, can die on the world's roadways. Similarly and unfortunately, most of us who have been around very long know people like the former scientist I described who was struck down by a brain aneurysm at midlife. The quality of this man's life and that of his family were drastically diminished for at least the remainder of his life—which may well be until he is quite old because other bodily difficulties do not necessarily accompany a brain injury.

A major emphasis in this chapter and throughout this book is one losses that reduce our mental capacity. If we cannot think and feel in a normal manner, our human capacities are greatly reduced. Many events can lead to this diminishment, including problems created by humans such as prejudice and genocide. So often, though, diseases and accidents that lead to mental impairment are beyond our control and invoke our most strenuous efforts to reestablish some degree of control and meaning in our lives so that we can make sense of the resulting suffering of our loved ones. Through new techniques in neurology such as brain imaging, we are learning more each year about how the brain, brain trauma, and behavior are related. As a society, we need to embrace ways to help everyone struggling with chronic illness. As John Bland's (1997) empowering work on aging and his own life makes clear, this enhancement can be done and is being done by many older persons, as models of positive thinking and behavior for persons of all ages. In the end, the message of this chapter is that there is a lot out there that can whack us in potent ways. Yet we can find ways to go on and achieve meaning again. As one person in a family beset by cancer through many generations (with 40 known deaths from breast or ovarian cancer among 600 family members) said,

> The legacy our mother left us is the understanding that this is life—you're dealt a hand and you have to deal with it as best you can. Everyone has problems. Ours just happen to be cancer. And, believe me, there are a lot worse things in this world than the cancer that's affecting my family.[10]

Finally, Christopher Reeve's battle against his own spinal cord injury and on behalf of persons fighting similar bodily difficulties suggests the healing power of this type of battle. He says that he could readily be swallowed up in the memories of his former life of fame, wealth, and vibrant physical activity and the depression those memories evoke everyday. But he has decided to let go of those memories and to dedicate himself to his new work. He sees his former life as preparation for his current campaign. Reeve defines "hero" in the following way: "I think a hero is an ordinary individual who finds the strength to persevere . . . in spite of overwhelming obstacles."[11]

Notes

1. From the *Chicago Tribune,* November 17, 1996, sec. 4, p. 4.
2. Account supplied by Dr. Ann Weber.
3. From an article by Scott Bowles, *USA TODAY,* November 28-30, 1997, pp. 1, 2.
4. From *USA TODAY,* December 22, 1998, p. 4A.
5. From the *Iowa City Press-Citizen,* April 11, 1997, pp. 11A.
6. AP news release, *Cedar Rapids Gazette,* September 29, 1994.
7. From the *Chicago Tribune,* January 24, 1998, p. 6.
8. "Pack Strength Coach a Perfect Example," Ray Didinger, *Chicago Tribune,* December 16, 1990, p. 6C.
9. From an article by Sheryl Stolberg in the *New York Times,* June 28, 1998, p. 1.
10. From an article by Barbara Mahany in the *Chicago Tribune Magazine,* June 28, 1998, p. 17.
11. CNN-*People Magazine* Special, May 16, 1999.

5 Unemployment and Homelessness

In 1998, 1.2 billion people were in dire poverty throughout the world. This is the same number, though, a slightly smaller proportion of the world's population, as were poor in 1990.

The poor still account for nearly half of all sub-Saharan Africans. . . . This dilemma is further reflected in the high levels of unemployment and homelessness in places where such poverty abounds.[1]

This chapter focuses on loss of employment and the loss of a home, or homelessness. It is interesting to note that many of the major losses discussed in this book can be related to unemployment and homelessness. For example, I note in the chapter on violence and war that a significant percentage of Vietnam veterans have experienced posttraumatic stress disorder, and because of this they often have trouble holding jobs. Thousands of veterans find themselves homeless off and on during their lives. Loss events such as divorce and the death of loved ones play a role in the evolution of job difficulties and homelessness for many, including veterans of wars (Brende & Parson, 1985). Thus, a theme sounded at various points in this book is found in the present material, namely: Major losses may pile up and accumulate, with the result being a reverberating sense of distress that causes its own secondary losses in a person's life.

Related questions that will not be answered in any full way in this chapter include the following: How much is homelessness an adaptive strategy for dealing with loss and trauma? How much is homelessness a sign of the failure of society to head off loss and trauma and to help people experiencing major loss deal with their difficulties? How often are people's job performance and career changes linked to loss and trauma?

As noted in the opening quote, worldwide poverty associated with unemployment and homelessness affects a huge number of people. In 2000, 6,000 people living in barely habitable shanty huts were killed in the Philippines when heavy rains associated with a typhoon hit the country and weakened the earth around the shanty village. This kind of tragedy occurs regularly in different places around the world, as the billion-plus very poor people suffer enormous daily losses in their lives as they try to survive.

Unemployment and homelessness are types of loss that may be connected, as when people lose their home or valued possessions due to the loss of a job. They also may be quite separate phenomena. Homelessness may be the result of mental illness in conjunction with major loss events in a person's life. This chapter highlights some of the key loss ideas associated with becoming unemployed and becoming homeless. The reader is referred to Price, Friedland, and Vinokur (1998) and Morse (1998, 2000) for recent in-depth reviews on loss aspects of job loss and homelessness, respectively.

Loss of Employment

Nanette Bellefleur, age 48, told the *Chicago Tribune* what it was like to be unemployed and to search almost indefinitely for another reasonable position.[2] A former account executive for Sears, she said that she felt so low, she really did not care what she did. Then she thought about how she had wanted to study law when she was younger, but she didn't because of finances. She figured that she still did not have any money, but that her situation couldn't get any worse. So she applied to law school and got in. She said that unemployment was hanging over her head every minute of every day. She indicated that she would wake up in the middle of the night and the recognition would confront her; she could not get away from it until the law school admissions letter arrived.

In early and mid-2000, the U.S. economy contributed to a surfeit of jobs of varying types and levels of income. However, job creation has been cyclic in this country and around the world. We certainly have lots of experience with loss of employment and to some degree with the psychological effect of such losses. The loss of employment can be just as devastating as any other kind of loss. The focus here is on the experience of people who are involuntarily laid off from permanent jobs. Something vast in scope is sweeping the world of work. A combination of automation, instant communications, globalization, standardization, and cheap means of transport is creating changes unseen since the Industrial Revolution. Everywhere, businesses are seeking the cheapest costs and lowest wages. Technology lets them cut costs without sacrificing quality. Jobs can now be moved all over the world at will, from suburban Chicago to Mexico to Sri Lanka. Yet people, especially those with families, do not move as readily around the globe to keep their jobs or find new employment. Seldom is there any warning about the layoffs that have swept major corporations in this country, with 265,000 in 1994 alone (according to news reports). Layoffs can leave careers and families in turmoil. Again, again, and again.

One typical sequence for many people is the loss of a high-paying salaried job and then an inability to find work beyond that of a temporary $5- to $6-an-hour job. As one Detroit worker said about her quest to find a job that paid a reasonable salary,

> I've seen all the help wanted signs, but it's crazy to think that I'll work for minimum wage. How can I ever think about buying a house on those wages? I don't care what work I do, as long as I get what I deserve.[3]

U.S. Secretary of Labor Robert Reich said in 1994 that people must become accustomed to the fact that job security is a thing of the past. The tens of thousands of secure, high-paying manufacturing, factory-type jobs of decades past are not going to return to the U.S. job scene. He said that people need to stop fooling themselves about the possibility that such jobs will return. People at all levels of employment have been the target of job cuts during the past decade. Mid-level management has become a particularly prominent target for retrenchment in the 1990s because companies have been trying to cut their expenses significantly and make themselves more competitive. Hardly a week goes by that another major company does not engage in a major job reduction. For decades, the employees of major corporations such as IBM and Sears were employed throughout their careers and then retired under outstanding pension programs. Although some employees still hold on to long-term jobs, many other people have been let go in recent years by employers who previously had not engaged in such reductions. Many current employees cannot count on these major corporations to be immune to employee reductions. Increasingly, companies are making their supervisory levels leaner and looking to computers to monitor performance. Another new trend is for employees to work out of automobiles or hotels using computers, phones, and FAX machines. In some cases these people do not even have offices per se. Such arrangements cut down on the overhead companies have to pay to carry on their business.

For better or worse, many of us define ourselves and our value to a considerable degree in terms of our occupations. "I'm a professor." "I'm a nurse." "I'm a writer." Such self-descriptions are loaded with meaning about our experiences and the work that we have done and continue to do in our lives. They may connote something about our ego and our expectations regarding how others will respond to us. Practically, jobs feed and clothe us. Psychologically, jobs give us pride and add to the meaning of our lives. Thus, when our job is taken away or we are forced to retire, our sense of value and self-worth are very much on the line, and we may suffer for a long period of time. As one recently unemployed person said, "The hardest part is the mental aspect. I know I can't sell myself to anyone if my spirits are down."[4]

In recent years, we have often heard of people becoming violent after they have been fired. In fact, persons who have been fired have killed many people in acts of revenge. When fired, people reasonably ask questions such as: Was my work that bad even after years of success and pay raises? How do I start over at this late age? How do I tell my family and friends that I have lost my job? How can I assure my family that their needs will be taken care of now when I retire? How can I meet the bill for my children's college tuition and help them as they try to get started in their adult lives?

A secondary dilemma associated with the massive cutbacks is the tendency for some workers to push themselves beyond their natural limits. They sometimes fear their company's impending downsizing and want to position themselves to try to survive. Eugene Griessman, a commentator on work tendencies, suggests that the rubber band is being stretched for many of these workaholics and that a price is going to be paid before too long.[5] For the purposes of this analysis, even if the person keeps his or her job, such a person may experience grief later in life about losing out on central aspects of life, such as being with his or her children during vital parts of their growing-up years. In this type of situation, there may be a latent sense of loss that the workaholic person does not allow himself or herself to feel. Beyond this issue of the number of hours one puts into a job is the contemporary problem of a slide in wages in some job areas, with smaller annual increases if any at all, and an erosion in health and other benefits. Overall, therefore, the accumulation of job-relevant uncertainties and hardships facing many individuals in our world may be associated with many of the problems in a person's domestic life and with drug addiction and mental health difficulties as well.

In the 1990s, U.S. Secretary of Labor Reich estimated that a young person entering the workforce would change careers, not just jobs, two to three times in her or his life. He also stated that an individual might change positions within a particular profession, on average, six to seven times. That is a lot of movement and potentially a lot of disappointment, dashed hopes, and derailed plans. It is unfortunate that our understanding of the psychology of job loss is embryonic at best. One finds many magazines devoting stories to this type of loss and what to do to get a new job. However, there have been few systematic programs of research devoted to the psychology of job loss. Leading textbooks in industrial psychology and organizational behavior seldom if ever contain material on the loss to self-worth and the grief that may accompany job loss.

To illustrate what many workers fear in the 1990s, consider the following excerpts from a letter from George Kaforski, chairman of

Ameritech Downsized Employees, to John McCarron, a business columnist for the *Chicago Tribune.* Kaforski was in his 40s when he was "downsized" out of a major position at Ameritech. He had this to say about his experience:

> We are composed primarily of former Ameritech employees who were "downsized" out of employment during the previous couple of years. Until recent years, downsizings were done by corporations in financial trouble, and were needed as a matter of survival, to reduce huge overheads.
>
> However, during the past few years a very disturbing trend has been taking place. Many very solvent and prosperous companies have jumped on the downsizing bandwagon. The real goal is to rid these corporations of larger numbers of employees who have 15 to 30 years of service and replace them with employees who are better educated, younger, and willing to work for a much lower salary. This is done to obtain huge amounts of cash that can be used to boost stock price, to expand or do whatever the corporation deems appropriate, including large bonuses and stock option plans for senior officers.... In a number of these downsizings, the real goal is to rid these major corporations of employees who have worked themselves up to good salaries, have obtained a number of good benefits, and are close to good pensions.
>
> What is lost in all this rush for money is the social responsibility these companies should practice toward their employees and their communities. Instead they have chosen to turn their backs on a large number of middle-aged Americans who unfortunately believed what these companies told them when they were working.[6]

As is true with so many life-span losses or potential losses, at any point in time any person, however wealthy or otherwise secure, may be only a bare margin away from economic disaster. Jack Beatty, a senior editor at *Atlantic Monthly,* said as much regarding the job climate of the 1990s: "Most of us are only a restructuring, a re-engineering, a firing, a major illness, or a divorce away from joining [the ranks of the working poor]."[7]

What do we do when we are fired? We need to take time to grieve. We also need to carefully consider our options. Many former salaried workers have created successful small businesses after being fired and then finding no reasonable comparable job. In the following, I have paraphrased some steps to recovery from the previously cited article by John Ehrlichman:[8]

1. Process what has happened as carefully as possible. Don't try to cover up anger about the firing. Be open to mourning and willing

to talk to close friends and professional counselors about your feelings and future plans.

2. Assess yourself and try to identify your strengths that may facilitate your movement to another type of field or the creation of your own business.

3. Create a first-class resumé and write an effective cover letter when mailing out new job applications.

4. Network by contacting friends, colleagues, and acquaintances and telling them about your interests in certain types of jobs of which they may become aware.

5. Market yourself. Remember that perseverance in finding new possibilities and then pursuing them with vigor often pays off. (p. 4)

Other Work-Related Loss Issues

Before leaving the topic of unemployment, other work-related losses should be mentioned. Some of these were discussed earlier in this chapter. There have been many instances of disgruntled, former employees returning to kill a supervisor involved in the firing as well as other employees. This situation became so salient to the U.S. Postal Service in the 1990s that it led to a special investigation of violence by former Postal Service employees. This investigation indicated that violence was no more common in the Postal Service than in many other types of occupations.

Sometimes unemployment occurs as a response to a loss in another area of one's life. Many employees change careers or give up prosperous careers when major loss events occur in their lives. This issue is illustrated by a January 20, 1998, AP wire story that told the story of how Saul Bennett, who headed a communications firm in New York, quit his job when his daughter died of a brain aneurysm. At the time of her sudden death she was a healthy 24-year-old journalist. The shock was so great that it motivated Bennett to change his career. After his daughter died, he stopped working as a communications executive and began writing poetry and consulting.

Bennett's change of career is not that uncommon, coming as it did on the heels of a huge personal tragedy. Candy Lightner started Mothers Against Drunk Drivers (MADD) in 1980 after her 13-year-old daughter was killed by a drunk driver. She gave up a thriving real estate career to found and lead this important organization. There are countless examples of people who leave their careers in the context of devastating personal losses that change their whole lives. In many cases, these losses lead them to leave a highly profitable profession and move to one in which they feel they would be making more of a contribution to others.

The Impoverished and the Homeless

One of the most interesting and revealing instances of homelessness was discussed by writer Evelyn Nieves in the *New York Times*.[9] Nieves reported on the new, urban homeless in the Silicon Valley and the San Francisco Bay Area. These people often worked during the day but did not make enough money to afford the average rent of $1,000 per month in the area—much less the $350,000 average price of a home in the Silicon Valley. Some lived at shelters or missions, but some also lived in their cars or rode the buses and overnight transit system, using them as places to sleep when they were not at work. Some were dealing with recent traumas, such as divorce and the death of loved ones (such as parents). Some had been hampered because they were experiencing mental illness. But some were having no such mental difficulties. It is a new reality for shelters to have more than 50% of their residents working, but that was the case in the Silicon Valley. Such a fact did nothing to help these people deal with the costs of securing their own apartments or homes. Such was the world of homelessness in the early 21st century in a locale where 20-something computer and Internet specialists were sometimes becoming multimillionaires virtually overnight.

As Morse (2000) notes, homelessness has become all too commonplace within contemporary American culture and throughout the world as well. In the United States, it has been estimated that more than 13.5 million people (7.4% of the U.S. population) have been homeless at one point or another in their lives.

All over the globe millions of people are significantly impoverished and malnourished. Some of them are also homeless. There are so many who fall into this vast chasm that such a state may be close to representing a "frequent life span loss." Maybe the state is not so frequent as to be considered "normal," thus meeting one of the chief characteristics noted in the introduction, but it happens frequently enough to be considered close to normal. In fact, it is uncanny how many fairly well-to-do people describe events in their lives by saying something like "Were it not for the grace of God, I too would be homeless or destitute."

In the United States, the Great Depression of the 1930s showed how quickly any human being, however wealthy, can lose every physical resource. In preparation for the Jewish High Holy Days in 1994, Rabbi Gordon Tucker of Temple Israel in White Plains, New York, commented on the frailty of all our lives and our constant vulnerability to loss: "There's a sense we increasingly have in this world of a very thin line that we're all up against that separates us from very different kinds of fate."[10]

Although there is not much government funding available to study homelessness, the social and behavioral science community has awakened somewhat to the need to study homelessness. In *Homelessness: A National Perspective* edited by Robertson and Greenblatt (1992), a group of scholars analyze the many facets of homelessness in the United States. Some of the problems and needs of the homeless addressed by these scholars include the following: the need for temporary shelter (because many homeless people suffer from exposure to the weather each year); inadequate food and nutrition; a shortage of clothing; sexual victimization, especially among homeless women and young people; criminal and legal problems, including police harassment; poverty and inadequate financial assistance; poor physical health and inadequate medical service; drinking problems and alcoholism; social isolation and the absence of a supportive social network; an absence of leisure, recreation opportunities, and day activities and programs; and mental health problems.

These losses associated with being homeless are staggering. Many of them have ended up homeless because of their inability to cope with catastrophic losses. An interesting aspect of this long and still partial list of problems faced by the homeless is that grief is not on the list! Such an exclusion probably means that the question has not been asked explicitly enough in research done with homeless respondents. The sense of loss and grief clearly are there. Consider the following story of a young man, age 15, who was interviewed in a New York shelter and discussed by Petry and Avent (1992) in Robertson and Greenblatt's book on homelessness:

> What comes to mind is running from home, where I experienced a lot of abuse. Without asking any questions at all, my mother would beat me, either with her hands, her fists, a belt, belt buckle, stick, frying pan, or spatula. . . . She once came to school with a tree branch, took down my clothes in front of my whole class, and beat me.
>
> My mother grew up in a home in which, if she did something wrong, she would get beaten by one of her parents. . . . My mother had a cousin who she never got along with. This cousin stole nail polish one day and said that my mother did it. My mother got stripped and tied to her bed and beaten by her father and grandfather. So when I was growing up my mother thought that that was the way a child should be raised.
>
> When I visited my uncle, he would ask me if I would watch him masturbate . . . it was a regular thing. . . . The abuse also happened with my two male cousins. . . . Yes, I do feel pushed out by the fact that my mother did not give me an opportunity to be a kid. . . . One time she told me to get out of the house and never come back. If I had said I'm not sure I want to date girls, or I want to talk to you about the abuse that I experienced while I was growing up, she would have said, "I'm tired of this, get out of here." (pp. 303-304)

After a period of time in his adolescence in which he worked as a prostitute and was virtually on the street, this young man returned home and tried to kill himself and then took to the road completely.

As Morse (2000) has documented, homelessness is often associated with serious mental illness. People who experience both conditions are probably prone to suffer greater levels of despair and more serious losses related to functioning, social roles, meaning, hope, and personal identity. Identity is a particularly difficult issue for a person grappling with mental illness and an uncertain home situation. This person may feel as if he or she is persecuted by some people (as in some cases of paranoid schizophrenia) and unwanted by others with whom he or she is in contact. Furthermore, it has been estimated that 50% or more of people who are homeless and mentally ill abuse alcohol and drugs (Drake, Osher, & Wallach, 1991).

In an invaluable study of homelessness and mental illness, Baxter and Hopper (1981) reported that people experiencing these conditions use a number of creative strategies to survive. For example, loud talking that may be thought of as psychotic by some, actually may be a defense tactic used to protect oneself. The same may be true for "bag ladies," who literally use bad hygiene and foul smells to ward off persons inclined to attack or steal from them while they are on the streets.

Fort Worth Star-Telegram staff writer Yvette Craig documented the plight of mentally ill homeless people in a Fort Worth shelter in late 2000.[11] She said that a frail woman paced the hallways. Blackened calluses the size of apricots covered the bottom of her bare feet. Craig reported that a bloodcurdling scream echoed from the hall: "Why, God? Why me?" Craig observed that a few people stared at a TV set tuned to 1980s reruns. These were homeless people suffering from the most severe types of mental illness. As Craig reported, these people found a refuge at Safe Haven, a mental health facility for homeless people, operated by the Presbyterian Night Shelter. Tucked away on East Presidio Street near downtown, the 7,600-square-foot refuge sits about a half-block from the night shelter, near a shelter for homeless women and children and another for homeless veterans. It has 20 beds. Safe Haven provides three square meals, access to mental and physical health care, and a warm place to stay 24 hours a day, 7 days a week.

The director of Safe Haven contended that there is no shame in being mentally ill. Yet many suffer unwanted discrimination due to the myth that somehow mental illness makes people violent and evil monsters.

Craig said that the director alternated between being a drill sergeant—once staring down a combative man twice her size—and a caring mother. The director said that the job is all about the heart, not the number of degrees you have.

Morse (2000) recommends that service providers help the homeless and mentally ill by doing the following:

- Instilling hope by helping the individual remember better times and how he or she coped with life's dilemmas
- Imagining and planning for recovery: assisting clients in visualizing work settings in which they may work and succeed, perhaps envisioning a recovery

roadmap with problem-solving suggestions for likely roadblocks in work and domestic settings

- Developing social resources: finding ongoing work, low-rent housing, furniture, utilities, and the like

- Accepting limitations: accepting how the person's illness affects his or her daily life and being patient in accommodating that illness and its effect.

- Helping to foster a positive sense of self apart from the illness and a recognition of values the self possesses, perhaps using narrative therapy to help instill a sense of self in these situations (Parry & Doan, 1994)

- Fostering symptom management skills: training the person in how to control or manage his or her illness symptoms (e.g., practicing self-instruction, self-talk, and self-direction)

- Building additional client skills: developing skills such as how to relate to people interpersonally (especially helpful for younger mentally ill and homeless persons)

- Building meaning, perhaps facilitated by narrative therapy, and helping the person build a social network that is constructive and assists the other forms of recovery

- Helping to prevent relapses in regard to addiction, which is critical to all the other steps and may involve crisis or relapse prevention plans (e.g., whom to call, what to watch for, how to cope under frustrating, trying conditions as when all does not go well at work or in personal relationships); teaching clients to notice early warning signals and how to respond

Of course, there probably are as many stories of loss experience among the homeless as there are homeless people in this country. An extremely valuable book containing stories of homeless persons and an analysis of policy issues involved in homelessness is Baum and Burnes's (1993) *A Nation in Denial.* Their book presents a powerful portrait of this country's homelessness problem and our collective denial of it. They contend that it was only in the late 1970s that this country began to recognize the problem. Baum and Burnes argue that only by overcoming the denial we are in about homelessness will we be able to offer help and hope to the homeless. According to these authors, it is our failure to see the roles that alcoholism, mental illness, and drug addiction play in the homelessness situation that is especially problematic. They suggest that there is a huge class prejudice and stigma that operates against the homeless receiving the type of public empathy and aid that they need.

One final story about homelessness is necessary to reinforce Baum and Burnes's denial argument. In December 1993, Yetta Adams, age 43, froze to death on a bench in a bus shelter across the street from the U.S. Department of Housing and Urban Development. This death coincided with a battle in the federal government over the annual budget for the homeless. Department of Housing and Urban Development Secretary Henry Cisneros said at that time,

> You could describe me as a secretary who's shamelessly describing the death of this woman while talking about budget increases, but I'm told there were homeless people outside who knelt in prayer at this woman's body. So when I raise my voice in search of funds, I know I'm not alone.[12]

Adams was a single mother. She suffered from depression and had experienced a series of major losses prior to becoming essentially a "street person." It is estimated that at least a third of the homeless in this country suffer from serious mental health problems. Where Yetta Adams died is a fitting testimony to a gigantic social welfare system that has many holes in its safety net. *USA TODAY* writer Mimi Hall reported that Adams's stepmother Geraldine Adams said, "She [Yetta] would never lie down on a grate. She was too proud for that."[13]

Conclusions

Compared with other types of loss that have more immediate and direct effects, losses related to becoming unemployed or homeless are more subtle and deserve greater attention in the loss and trauma literature. The early 2000s reflect a period of relative prosperity in the United States. Broadly speaking, work conditions (e.g., sweat shop labor or the exploitation of children in manufacturing clothing and various products), rather than job loss per se, are of more concern to the public and advocates of impoverished, mistreated workers throughout the world. When the American economy hits hard times, as it always has, our concern with job loss and its effects may be revitalized and there may be more research on this topic in the scholarly and scientific literature. At that point, we may also become concerned again about ageism and other forms of discrimination in work hiring situations and job issues that contribute to human loss.

As Morse (2000) has noted, the topic of homelessness has waned in importance in the relatively affluent prosperity of the United States in the early 2000s. There is relatively little government and media concern with homelessness at the present time. This paucity of attention is unfortunate because of the multitude of loss problems experienced by the homeless. These problems are also often associated with mental illness. The issues of loss and recovery among the homeless, many of whom are seriously mentally ill, are poorly understood.

Notes

1. From *The Economist,* July 31, 2000.
2. From *Chicago Tribune,* January 24, 1994, sec. 1, p. 10.
3. "Help Wanted: Metro Detroit Jobs Unfilled," by Joel Smith, *Detroit News,* September 4, 1994, p. 6C.
4. From an article by John Ehrlichman in *Parade Magazine,* August 29, 1993, p. 4.
5. From National Public Radio News, November 14, 1999.
6. From *Chicago Tribune,* August 28, 1994, sec. 7, p. 2.
7. From *Chicago Tribune,* September 25, 1994.
8. *Parade Magazine,* August 29, 1993, p. 4.
9. From an article in *New York Times,* December 19, 1999, p. 25.
10. From *New York Times,* September 1, 1994, p. B8.
11. From *Fort Worth Star-Telegram,* December 14, 2000, pp. 1-4.
12. From *New York Times,* November 30, 1993, p. A1.
13. From *USA TODAY,* December 9, 1993, p. 8A.

6 Suicide

"It's the gray eyes," he says.

I see his mother laying her head on his chest and just sobbing, sobbing her heart out.

—Les Franklin, commenting on the suicides of his children[1]

The Pervasiveness of Suicide

The preceding quotes come from the story of Les Franklin and his family, told in *People* in 2000. Two of Franklin's sons killed themselves. Ironically, Franklin, a successful businessman, has devoted much of the past decade to helping kids who are depressed and suicidal in the Denver area. He began this work after his son Shaka's death. During the same period, Franklin's wife, Cherllyn, learned she had cancer. Then a few years later, Jamon, apparently unable to find hope in his grieving for his brother and mother, took his own life. As is true with many suicides, there was a layering of loss and pain involved in these suicides. Not only was Shaka and Jamon's mother's battle with cancer a loss that devastated them, but Les Franklin and his wife Cherllyn divorced in the late 1980s. During the divorce Cherllyn chose not to seek custody of the boys. Thus, they were feeling a doubled sense of loss at the point that Shaka shot himself, sending Jamon into a period of depression, drugs, and hesitancy about his life, culminating in his suicide.

These tragedies have left Les Franklin reeling, but ever more devoted to his work with kids. The suicides of these two boys also speak to the powerful sense of loss that often underlies this ultimate act. This sense of loss creates a hopelessness that cannot be assuaged and that cripples one's ability to discern ways out of the unfolding mental drama.

Those who end their lives by suicide leave a legacy that is indelible and profound for their survivors, whose own chances of taking their lives by suicide are then enhanced dramatically. Suicide leaves a legacy of pain, guilt, and long-term questions of "why" in families. As described in detail in this chapter, the act of taking one's life can involve the usual means such as taking a drug overdose, or some form of physical violence, or it could involve the intentional decision not to go on life support when key organs such as the heart fail.

What is suicide? As Maltsberger (1998) has shown, developers of dictionaries, professional scholars and therapists have had considerable difficulty defining suicide. A brief definition is "the act or an instance of taking one's own life voluntarily and intentionally" (*Webster's Third New International Dictionary*). Probably every human being has thought about suicide at one time or another. Often, this thinking emerges in the context of great loss. Often, it is situational. We frequently hear of murder-suicides, which involve one person killing another, usually a close relation, then killing him- or herself. Murder-suicides occur in the contexts of terminal illness, when the caregiver may want to end the ill person's suffering then his or her own life as well. Murder-suicides also occur when one person is leaving a close relationship and his or her partner is unhappy about the departure. In an act of desperation or impulse, the partner being left kills the departing partner and then him- or herself.

Suicidal behavior can accompany many types of emotional disturbance, including depression, schizophrenia, and other psychotic illnesses. In fact, more than 90% of all suicides are related to an emotional or psychiatric illness (Shneidman, 1996). Suicidal behaviors occur as a response to a situation that the person views as overwhelming, such as social isolation, the death of a loved one, an emotional trauma, a serious physical illness, old age, unemployment or financial problems, guilt feelings, drug abuse, and alcohol abuse. Suicidal activity is quite common. Lifetime ideation of suicide is common among approximately 13.5% and attempts by approximately 4.6% of the population (Shneidman, 1996).

In the United States, suicide now accounts for more than 1% of all deaths each year (Murphy, 2000). However, there are many unclear cases of death. Shneidman (1996) suggests that 10% of all deaths are equivocal in terms of whether there were lethal intentions on the part of the victim. Suicide is now the third leading cause of death for those 15 to 19 years old (after accidents and homicide). The incidence of reported suicides varies widely from country to country; however, this may in part be related to reporting (especially in cultures where suicide is considered sinful or shameful). Suicide attempts (where the person tries to harm him- or herself but the attempt does not result in death) far outnumber actual suicides. Shneidman (1996) reports that only 2% to 3% of threatened suicides are carried out.

The method of suicide attempt varies from relatively nonviolent methods (such as poisoning, overdose, or inhaling car exhaust) to violent methods (such as shooting or cutting oneself). Males are more likely to choose violent methods, which probably accounts for the fact that suicide attempts by males are more likely to be successful (Shneidman, 1996). Many unsuccessful suicide attempts are carried out in a manner or setting that makes rescue possible; they must be viewed as a cry for help.

Institutional suicide is a special form of suicide. The 900 Americans who followed Jim Jones to the jungles of Guyana and who committed mass suicide represent an example of a cult-type institutional suicide. In such cases, "group mind" (Janis, 1982) predominates. Groups of people believe that they know the answers, and individuals have been indoctrinated to follow the group leaders. The group's will is superior to that of the individual's will, and so the individual does not ask questions or challenge the group (or challenges too late). Ritual suicide was illustrated by Japanese kamikaze pilots who gave their lives in their attempts to destroy American ships during World War II. The self-destruction is demanded by their society. The same is true for the ship captain who goes down with the vessel instead of trying to save his life.

Suicidal thoughts may cross people's minds in times of crises: when a valued close relationship has ended; when valued possessions have been lost (e.g., the loss of one's home because of bankruptcy or a natural disaster); when a person discovers that he or she has a terminal illness; when a loved one has a terminal illness; when a person has experienced a particularly hurtful humiliation in interpersonal relations; or when a person has lost a large amount of money.

In cases in which suicide or attempted suicide involves psychological and/or physical illness and incapacity, a person may spend a lot of energy planning and obsessing about suicidal acts. Each suicide is determined by the interaction of several motives. Suicide is hardly a simple or unitary piece of human behavior. Rather, the impulse to commit suicide grows out of a variety of feelings and behaviors with many important aspects—historical, legal, medical, psychological, philosophical, and social.

More generally, for definitional purposes, suicide may be conceived on a continuum from the obvious final act of taking one's life to avoid pain to acts such as "base jumping" with a parachute from a tall building or mountain such as El Capitan in the Yellowstone Canyon or taking up a lifetime habit of smoking in youth. Parachuting from the top of a mountain is an act that has a significant probability of death because of the need to open the chute relatively soon and the fact that only one chute is used. And there is overwhelming evidence that smoking causes disease and death, and yet people knowingly continue to smoke. Suicide, then, is not always such a clear-cut act as we might think. We might even consider a range of acts that communicate a lack of will to continue life as reflecting a behavioral pattern almost tantamount to suicide. (See later discussion of Ross's thesis in her 1997 book *Ray of Hope.*)

Historical Notes

Suicide has been a topic of study in the social, behavioral, and medical sciences since the 18th century. As discussed by Maltsberger and Goldblatt (1996), Jean Esquirol (1772-1840), psychiatrist of the French Revolution, led the way in early efforts to medicalize insanity. He devised a classification of mental disorders, and suicide had a prominent place in his studies. Sociologist Emile Durkheim (1858-1917) gave the study of suicide a sociological orientation. He explained suicide in terms of the integration of individuals into society. Durkheim (1951) described a state called "anomie," a condition in which a person lacks meaning and hope and experiences a sense of alienation from society.

A short time after Durkheim's work appeared, Freud's (1923/1961) work "Mourning and Melancholia" was published and became an influential foundation statement about the nature of suicide (see Shneidman, 1996). Another view of this paper, however, is that it deals more with depression than with aggression against the self (Weiss, personal communication, December 2000). This paper was based on the Vienna Psychoanalytic Society's 1910 discussions of suicides by students. According to Freud (1923/1961), the melancholic person who either in reality or in fantasy has suffered the loss of a beloved object is unable to free his libido (loosely translated as "life energy") from the object and its associations. Regression often occurs, such that ambivalence and sadism are evident. The aggression directed toward the original object becomes directed toward the individual's self. The patient, therefore, is forced to destroy himself.

A more recent development in the study of suicide was the formal organization of the American Association of Suicidology in 1968. This association publishes a journal (*Suicide and Life Threatening Behavior*) and holds regular meetings. There are many centers studying suicide, but the most prominent early center was developed by Edwin Shneidman, Norman Farberow, and Robert Litman who established the Los Angeles Suicide Prevention Center in 1958. Also, in 1987, the American Suicide Foundation was developed to fund suicide research across the United States.

A Cry for Help

Suicidal behavior may be engaged in as a form of communication known as a cry for help. This situation emerges when the person's normal avenues for expressing feelings are blocked. Many suicides by young people are of this variety. There may be no history of suicidal behavior. The purpose of the behavior seems to be to make significant others aware of how desperate or unhappy the person feels (DeSpelder

& Strickland, 1992). Many suicidologists believe that two fairly distinct populations of individuals engage in suicidal behavior: (a) attempters, who tend toward repeated but not lethal attempts, and (b) completers, whose first attempt typically results in death (Evans & Farberow, 1988). Thus, in this view, the attempters are more likely to be engaging in cries for help via their attempts; however, completers may have cried out for help before their act of suicide. As we will see in many of the examples in this chapter, for both attempters and completers, most people who attempt to take their own lives probably believe that their attempts will be found out and stopped. Unfortunately, many are not.

Shneidman (1996) indicates that for unequivocal suicides, where there is clear evidence of intention, such as a suicide note, 90% had given verbal or behavioral cues within the week or so before they committed suicide. With only 2% to 3% of those giving clues actually committing suicide, the problem becomes how to identify people who will go all the way. I agree with Shneidman that we should err on the side of caution and consider all indications of possible self-destruction as serious and worthy of some type of intervention. Shneidman argues cogently that those that go all the way are often skillful at wearing "masks" and hiding their true feelings. They are essentially people who have undisclosed lives. Here is a relevant quote from the writer William Styron who has written about his struggle with life-long depression (Styron, 1990) and who has contemplated suicide:

> My wife and I had been invited to dinner with half-a-dozen friends at a fine Italian restaurant in New York. I very much feared the hour . . . by dinnertime I felt virtually suffocated by psychic discomfort. . . . For no particular reason, the sense of encroaching doom was especially powerful that night. . . . I chatted with my companions, nodded amiably, made the appropriate frowns and smiles. The restroom was nearby down a flight of carpeted stairs. On the way there the fantasies of suicide, which had been embedded in my thoughts daily for several weeks and which I had kept at bay during the dinner conversation, returned in a flood. To rid myself of this torment (but how? and when?) becomes the paramount need. . . . I wondered desperately if I could make it through the rest of the evening without betraying my condition. On my return to the floor above I astounded myself by expressing my misery aloud in a spontaneous utterance which my normal self would have rejected in shame. "I'm dying," I groaned, to the obvious dismay of a man passing down the stairway. The blurted words were one of the most fearsome auguries of my will to self-destruction; within a week I would be writing, in a stupor of disbelief, suicide notes.

Some months later . . . my two table companions reflected that I had appeared to be behaving normally.[2]

What to Do If Confronted With a Friend's Thoughts of Suicide

The most powerful antidote to suicidal thinking is talk. If we have a friend who indicates he or she is contemplating suicide, we should take the matter seriously. Talking with the person about his or her problems and feelings may help, as may direct steps to ensure that the person seeks professional counseling. Suicidal threats must be taken seriously. Friends need to *engage* anyone close to them who indicates that they are thinking about suicide. Get them talking and considering options and implications. Challenge the tunnel vision of reality that a suicidal person will emphasize. Be there, and do not make jokes about the person's reported thoughts or feelings.

Contemporary Issues in Suicide

In the United States over the last four decades of the 20th century, teens and young people ended their lives by suicide at ever-increasing rates. Each year, suicide kills more young people than any other cause, except automobile accidents and the head trauma resulting from them. According to data from the National Center for Health Statistics, suicides per 100,000 for children age 5 to 19 increased from 1.26 in 1962 to 2.50 in 1972 to 3.57 in 1982 and to 3.97 in 1995.[3] Experts often argue that the great flux in the American family (divorcing parents, chaos and conflict in the home, children's depression stemming from home and school problems, drug use by children, early sexual experimentation, etc.) is a central factor in this increasing rate of suicide (see Popenoe, 1993).

It has been estimated that about 30,000 Americans commit suicide every year (Jamison, 1999). That number is greater than any other type of death, except death by traffic accident. Jamison (1999) estimated that 500,000 Americans go to the emergency room every year after attempting suicide and that another quarter of a million people attempt suicide but do not succeed or seek medical care. In 1996, the greatest number of suicides were carried out by people between the ages of 10 and 50, with the greatest concentrations in the teen years and the 20s.

Teen suicide has soared since 1956. Table 6.1 shows suicides per 100,000 for persons 15 to 19 years of age compared with the rate for the entire U.S. population.

It is unclear why teen suicides have increased, especially during the 1980s. We might guess that there was a slight decrease in teen suicides in the 1990s relative to the 1980s because so much attention began to be focused on teen suicide by the media, schools, and parents. Outreach activities became more prominent, as did understanding of some of the dynamics of suicide among young persons.

Meanings of Suicide

Psychological autopsies of suicides and suicide notes (e.g., Shneidman's, 1996) have greatly improved the accuracy of death classification in general and the depth of our understanding of the meanings of suicide. Suicide has many meanings in American society. Kastenbaum (1981) identified some of these meaning: Suicide is sinful; suicide is criminal; suicide is the rational alternative; suicide is a reunion with a departed loved one; suicide is rest and peace; suicide is getting at back others— revenge; suicide is the penalty for failure (as in not living up to expectations or in letting others or self down); and suicide is a mistake, starting with a cry for help that was not heeded (but that was meant to be heeded, thus stopping the behavior).

Etiology: "Psychache" and Depressed Anguish

There have been many analyses of the etiology, or study of causes, of suicide. An important analysis of suicide is provided by Shneidman (1996) in his book *The Suicidal Mind*. In this book, Shneidman uses case studies and his extensive experience with persons attempting or

TABLE 6.1 Teen Suicide Rate Since 1956

Year	Age 15-19	All
1956	2.3	10.0
1961	3.4	10.4
1966	4.3	10.9
1971	6.5	11.8
1976	7.3	12.1
1981	8.6	11.5
1986	10.1	11.9
1991	11.1	11.3
1996	9.7	10.8
1997	9.5	10.6

SOURCE: National Center for Health Statistics (1998). See *USA TODAY,* November 30, 1999, pp. 1A-2A.

actually committing suicide to suggest that an internal, subjective state referred to as "psychache" goes along with most suicides. This state is characterized by depression, despair, and strong feelings of hopelessness and helplessness. As Shneidman argues, psychache is the drama of the mind of the suicidal person that is played out in private, usually over an extended period of time. It is the compelling background force that pushes the individual to take the actions required to kill his or her self. Preventing suicide requires mollification of psychache. Similar to the concept of psychache, Maltsberger and Goldblatt (1996) argue that "depressive anguish" is at the core of many suicides. Depressive anguish, like psychache, is not a concept to be found in the standard nomenclature of the American Psychiatric Association (or the *DSM*). Shneidman (1996) describes several principal components in people's progression toward suicide:

1. The vicissitudes of life, such as stresses, failures, rejections, and insults are omnipresent by virtue of just living.

2. The individual treats these vicissitudes in a funneled perceptual way, such that a conclusion, "I hurt too much," is made when the psychache is unbearable.

3. The individual also concludes, "I won't put up with this pain."

4. Cessation of consciousness becomes the option of choice, and termination of life, rather than sleep, is the preferred mode. Death is preferable to life, and the person realizes, "I can kill myself."

5. A lowered threshold for enduring or sustaining the crippling psychache occurs—the final step before the act of committing suicide.

6. The suicide outcome. "I hurt too much to live."

Based on his research and clinical case studies, Shneidman indicated that there are ten commonalties of suicide. These commonalties are listed in Table 6.2.

Etiology: The Biological Case

Kay Jamison is a psychiatrist at Johns Hopkins School of Medicine. Jamison also suffered from manic-depressive illness and attempted to kill herself by ingesting an overdose of drugs. Jamison (1999) wrote a memoir and analysis of suicide that discusses the prominence of mental illness as a determinant of suicide. Jamison stresses the role of biology and genetics in contributing to the type of mental illness that typically culminates in suicide. She argues that as many as 90% of all suicides involve mental illness and/or the abuse of alcohol, drugs, or a combination of alcohol and drugs. She states that a majority of people who are depressed will not kill themselves. However, combining their depression with alcohol is particularly lethal.

Jamison (1999) asserts that we know a lot about the underlying biology of suicide and that a genetic component exists that can interact dangerously with other biological factors involved in mental illness. Scientists have isolated neurotransmitters that along with stress hormones are involved in the volatility, impetuousness, and violence that

TABLE 6.2 Commonalties of Suicide

1. The common purpose of suicide is to seek a solution.
2. The common goal of suicide is cessation of consciousness.
3. The common stimulus of suicide is unbearable psychological pain.
4. The common stressor in suicide is frustrated psychological needs.
5. The common emotion in suicide is hopelessness.
6. The common cognitive state in suicide is ambivalence.
7. The common perceptual state in suicide is constriction.
8. The common action in suicide is escape.
9. The common interpersonal act in suicide is communication of intention.
10. The common pattern in suicide is consistency of lifelong styles.

SOURCE: Shneidman (1996).

characterize the moody temperaments often associated with suicide. Another powerful interaction is the triggering force of a major loss (such as an interpersonal humiliation), the presence of a gun, and this backdrop of genes and personality.

Jamison stresses that we have ways to help people fight depressive tendencies. Antidepressant medications, anticonvulsant medications, drugs that treat anxiety and ameliorate or prevent psychosis, and psychotherapy all have been used with varying degrees of success. She argues that too many people remain undiagnosed and untreated, with the profile of persons who commit suicide turning more and more toward that of teenagers, young African American males, and elderly men.

The Dynamics of Suicide: Clues to Intentions

In the formal assessment work of psychologists and psychiatrists, the formulation of suicide risk typically involves assessing (a) the patient's past responses to stress, especially losses; (b) the patient's vulnerability to loneliness, self-contempt, and murderous rage; (c) the nature and availability of the patient's exterior sustaining resources; (d) the patient's death fantasies; and (e) the patient's capacity for reality testing (Maltsberger, 1988).

In an article in *Chicago Tribune Magazine*,[4] The Reverend Charles Rubey of Catholic Charities in Chicago argued that when dealing with a suicidal person, one must "Take their pain seriously." This article documented the double suicide of a young man and his girlfriend, who spread their bodies out in front of a train. Their suicides seemed senseless to outsiders. A baby girl had been born to the couple a short time before their suicides, and it was believed they loved her very much. But the young man, age 20, was facing a period of confinement in a "boot camp" for convictions related to multiple crimes. He was an effective manipulator of the young woman. He didn't want to go the camp and somehow influenced his girlfriend to join him in taking her life too.

Reverend Rubey continued with this advice to parents: "Take the pain of your children seriously. That doesn't mean you have to cart them off to a clinic or a social worker, but so often the idea is that 'Oh, well, you'll get over this.' It's important not to downplay but to take their pain seriously and to listen to them" (p. 14). Teens can be especially vulnerable if they're exposed to peers or lovers who manipulate their emotions. In the same *Chicago Tribune Magazine* article, Dr. Alan Berman, executive director of the American Association of Suicidology, made the following comments: "In this kind of case, typically the male is suicidal and in effect convinces his female partner to go with him. It's almost the equivalent of a homicide. She has no developed ego and they share some romanticized notions, sort of like Romeo and Juliet, of dying together" (p. 14).

This dual suicide continued to have major effects on the families of the two young people over a year after the event. The young woman's mother indicated (in a follow-up article nearly a year later) that she coped with her daughter's death by finding as many ways as possible to remember her life. "I talk about her so much that people think I have a daughter who's alive. I still keep a journal and I write down what's happening in my day and address it to her."[5]

Suicide expert Frederick Goodwin suggested in a *USA TODAY* article[6] that parents, teachers, and adult friends should beware of certain signs that may indicate a young person is contemplating suicide. These signs (derived from Fassler, 1999) include the following:

- Drop in grades or behavior problems at school
- Fatigue; sleep pattern changes
- Social isolation; antisocial or delinquent behavior
- Feelings/expressions of sadness; suicidal thoughts or actions
- Inattention to appearance
- Extreme sensitivity to rejection or failure; low self-esteem
- Eating-related problems
- Loss of enjoyment of previously pleasurable activities
- Unprovoked hostility or aggressive behavior

Consistent with the earlier argument about what to do when suicidal thoughts are noted by a friend, Evans and Farberow (1988) suggest that the cardinal rule in suicide intervention is to do something (pp. 171-173). Take the threat seriously. Watch for clues to suicidal intentions and behaviors. Answer cries for help by offering support, understanding, and compassion. Confront the problem and don't be afraid to ask questions and discuss suicide with the person in crisis. Talking is a positive step toward resolution.

DeSpelder and Strickland (1992) note that the highest risk factors for suicide among young persons are early separation from one's parents, family dissolution, pressure for achievement and success—especially based on parental expectations, low self-esteem, and lack of effective relationships with peers. Also contributing to suicidality are family-related factors, such as hardship, mobility, or a high level of conflict in the family.

Suicide and the Elderly

Increased risk of suicide as a function of age is one of the most well-recognized statistics in the suicide area. Elderly men show a marked increase in suicide incidence, with 80-year-old men twice as likely as 20-year-old men to take their own lives (Valliant & Blumenthal, 1990).

DeSpelder and Strickland (1992) identified the following factors as influencing suicide in later adulthood: social isolation and loneliness; boredom and depression; loss of purpose and meaning; financial hardship; multiple losses of loved ones; chronic pain and illness; alcohol and drug abuse; and the desire to avoid being a burden.

Often, suicide in the elderly is as much related to isolation, meager social support, and related depression as it is to declining health and related depression. Interpersonal networks may provide the social support that offers assistance and encouragement to persons with physical and emotional problems to help them cope. There is considerable evidence that social support systems have disintegrated among suicide attempters compared with nonsuicidal individuals (e.g., Veiel, Brill, Hafner, & Welz, 1988).

Suicidal behavior in the elderly can be prevented through provision of increased resources, particularly enhanced opportunities for independent living and psychotherapy and other modes of psychological intervention among depressed older adults. As a society, we need to have more sensitivity to the issue of morale and well-being in later life. It is imperative that physicians and the various professionals who attend to the elderly devote more effort to understanding their unique needs and feelings of loss. There are too few health care professionals trained adequately to work with the elderly and to appreciate the profound nature of their diverse losses and feelings of isolation and despair.

Suicide and Mental Illness

Suicide may be associated with mental illness. Fawcett et al. (1990) conducted an important prospective study of suicide. In this research, 954 patients with major affective disorders were followed over a 3-year period. Thirty-two of these patients committed suicide during this 3-year period. Increased suicide risk among the 32 patients who killed themselves was associated with the following disorders: panic attacks, severe psychic anxiety, diminished concentration, global insomnia, moderate alcohol abuse, and severe loss of interest or pleasure. Three other features noted at admission were associated with suicide at the 1-year mark: severe hopelessness, suicidal ideation, and a history of previous suicide attempts.

Beck, Steer, Kovacs, and Garrison (1985) found that the seriousness of suicidal intent was correlated less with the degree of depression than with one particular aspect of depression, namely, hopelessness about the future. These investigators observed high suicidal intent in some patients who had minimal depression but whose expectations for the future were also minimal. A total of 89 of 207 patients hospitalized because they were contemplating suicide had high ratings on a measure of hopelessness from the Beck Depression Inventory. In the subsequent 5 years, 14 of the 207 patients committed suicide. Of the 14 who committed suicide, 13 were from the group of 89 who had the high ratings on the hopelessness scale. A variety of diagnoses were given for the patients who ranked high on hopelessness, but one-half were diagnosed as having some form of depression.

Myths About Suicide

There are a number of myths about suicide (DeSpelder & Strickland, 1992). Each of the following is a false statement. Believing that these statements are true can interfere with one's ability to cope with the possibility of suicide:

1. People who talk about suicide don't commit suicide.
2. Improvement in a suicidal person means the risk of suicide has passed.
3. Suicide is inherited (it runs in families).
4. Suicidal individuals are necessarily insane.
5. Suicidal individuals are intent on dying, and the motive is clearly apparent.

These myths relate to the complexity of suicide and that simple truths about it and its causes are not tenable.

Rational Suicide

There are two general categories of suicide: suicide that involves an attempt to end a state of suffering associated with a terminal or life-threatening illness (rational suicide) and suicide not associated with terminal or life-threatening illness. The category of suicide known as rational suicide is quite controversial. Can suicide ever be rational? This is the type of suicide that is usually associated with a person's decision to end the suffering connected with a terminal illness. Jack Kevorkian is a Michigan pathologist who became famous for assisting scores of persons who felt that their suffering was so great that they had to end their lives. Oregon was the first state in the United States to make physician-assisted suicide legal under certain conditions. However, as Jack Kevorkian has repeatedly argued, in quiet, discreet ways physicians have been assisting patients and families make decisions about how to terminate life under conditions of hopelessness and suffering since the beginning of medicine.

As Lokhandwala and Westefeld (1998) have argued, the person deciding on a rational suicide course of action may be electing not to live a certain way, as opposed to deciding to take his or her own life. Lokhandwala and Westefeld were especially concerned about the role of the mental health professional in contributing to a person's decision to commit rational suicide. They argued that to err on the side of a pro-life choice during assessment and treatment would not be unethical. In fact, they suggested that such a contribution would give the client more time to decide, which would be beneficial in the long run.

Mayo (1998), a philosopher, suggested that most suicides are irrational but also said that suicide may sometimes be a rational option. Suicide is irrational in the sense that usually the person is in great despair, possibly suffering from a debilitating terminal illness, and sees suicide as a viable option. Feelings of despair, depression, and hopelessness may influence most people in this situation when suicide is contemplated, even if sound psychological and pain-reduction treatment is being offered.

In October 1999, Oregon was under attack in the U.S. House of Representatives because in 1994 Oregon passed the first state law in the

United States legalizing physician-assisted suicide. Oregon's law survived the 1999 House debate, but it is likely to come up again in future U.S. legislative sessions. In 1999, only a few people had taken advantage of the law, and physicians in the state tended to support the law's existence even if they did not personally endorse physician-assisted suicide.

Coping With the Suicide of a Loved One

In her book, *Life After Suicide,* Ross (1997) tells the story of her husband's suicide and provides insights from her three decades of work with suicide survivors that involved creation of the international support organization "Ray of Hope." Ross suggests that we sensationalize and glorify death in this society. At the same time, she believes that we deny the reality of death. This denial becomes an emotional load when a loved one commits suicide.

Denial is often illustrated in the notes left by persons who commit suicide. As Ross (1997) has noted, especially when written by young persons, these notes sound as if the person believes he or she will simply depart and come back to earth in a matter of minutes. The permanency of death is not recognized. In a 1995 *Chicago Tribune Magazine* story, Annie Gowen documented the double suicide of two 16-year-old girls who were best friends. They both hated school and particularly so after returning from a wonderful 2-week study trip to Italy. Each had the world in front of them. They came from good, middle-class families, had lots of friends, did relatively well in school, and were healthy. But in the case of one, her father had died earlier in her life, and it became clear later that her pain about this loss was still profound. The girls influenced one another, and it may be the case that the girl who had lost her father convinced her best friend to join her in the act of suicide. But we will never know—as is so often the case with the suicides of the young. The note left by one of the girls, however, spoke to the naïveté and denial that Ross (1997) discusses: "I hate school. I don't want to go to college. I know these aren't good reasons to take my own life . . . but I can't think about this right now." As her father said, the note read as if she were saying "I'll get back to you in ten minutes."[7]

Ross (1997) argues that suicide attempts are calls for help and that people in most situations can be helped to avoid taking this final step. She also recognizes the breadth of possible definitions of nonviolent suicide as including people's willful decision not to continue living, as in an ultimate stage of terminal illness. Ross argues that when suicide occurs, it often brings to the surface a survivor's career of major, unresolved losses. To successfully deal with this culmination of unresolved loss, Ross believes that the survivor must address the suicide, its personal meaning, and the other unresolved losses.

Ross (1997) encourages people close to individuals who talk about suicide to take the threat seriously. She stresses the need to watch for clues such as protracted depression related to some major loss event or events. These losses may have built up and reverberated over the years, and it may be difficult for the individual to readily tell a confidant about the extent of his or her feelings of loss. The individual may only be able to describe something like Shneidman's idea of "psychache"— the feeling of hopeless and helpless despair.

Ross (1997) describes a number of possible reactions by a survivor to a loved one's suicide. These include PTSD (posttraumatic stress disorder) symptoms, such as shock and denial, anger, shame and guilt, withdrawal, depression, self-destruction, and a search for meaning. She suggests that frequently all members of a surviving family will be wrapped up in these emotions, and each member will need to work on a personal plan of healing. Ross notes Shneidman's (1996) powerful point that the person committing suicide sentences the survivor to an emotional burden of great proportions. In dealing with the suicide, the survivor must deal with any guilt he or she may feel about his or her possible role in this event. Ross indicates that survey data show that children of persons who end their lives by suicide have a 300% increased likelihood of also ending their lives by suicide.

In the end, Ross's message is one of hope. She contends that used constructively, fear can be a positive, energizing emotion. She points to her own spiritual beliefs and the emphasis other experts place on inner peace, hope, and family support as keys to the empowerment of the survivor. She stresses the need for the survivor to arrive at a point at which he or she can forgive the loved one who committed suicide. Such forgiveness helps alleviate shame and guilt.

The Internet and Support Groups

By the late 1990s, the Internet had emerged as one of the main sources of support for survivors of suicide. Web sites such as www.1000deaths.com serve as central clearinghouses for memorials to victims of suicide and links to many related Web sites. "Listservs" enable survivors of suicide to seek support or conversation or to compare experiences or get advice from fellow survivors. Some memorial Web sites are quite elaborate, running many pages in length, featuring music, photographs, art, memorabilia, and links to other sites including suicide prevention sites or information on addictions, depression, bipolar disorder, and the like (see Hollander's, in press, study of Internet support for survivors of suicide).

As Hollander (in press) argues, for survivors of suicide it is important to be linked to a community of people who are tolerant of talk of loss and grief, and who are experts via their own experience in the area of suicide. Hollander reports that one Internet respondent reported, "I think we are all still grappling with being left with silence," and another said, "I have no real answer to how we make others understand our need to talk and cry" (p. 10).

In Hollander's (in press) study, one respondent speaks of the disenfranchised grief often experienced by survivors of suicide victims:

> When my son committed suicide, I experienced the same things that all other suicide families experience—friends avoiding us, people judging us, little "pep talks" from clueless coworkers about "moving on" and maintaining a "professional attitude" at work (which, I found, means never cry, never appear to be having a bad day, at least after six months).... The grief sites on the Internet ... are open 24/7 so you can dump what you need to dump when you need to dump it.... Practically everyone who comes to these sites has been through it, and has some idea how bad we feel (unlike the rest of this culture).... It certainly helps us feel less freakish, and that reduces stigma.... I don't think I could have survived my son's suicide without the Web.... Without the Web, I would have sucked it up and toughed it out the way my coworkers wanted me to, and I would have stayed in my high-powered career as an

engineer for Sun Microsystems, and I would have stopped talking about Billy, and then one day I know I would have bought a gun and followed him to the next world. I can't prove this, but believe me, I know this. (p. 8)

Conclusions: Legacies

So often suicide seems meaningless and senseless to us on the outside. But as the thrust of the material in this chapter suggests, it is difficult to know the drama of other people's minds from the outside. If we live long lives, we all will know people who seemingly have perfect lives but who, like Richard Cory, in the poem by Edward Arlington Robinson, kill themselves. A couple of years ago, I heard of the suicide of a psychologist with whom I had worked when the psychologist was a doctoral student in counseling psychology. The psychologist, in his 40s, had battled depression for decades. Like the writer William Styron (1990), he had fought his depression with courage, and yet had sunk deeper and deeper into its clutches, despite years of therapy, becoming a marathon runner, and achieving reasonable success as a practitioner and college teacher.

What apparently no one outside this person's mind could appreciate was the powerful sense of loss that pervaded him from his childhood to his death. His suicide letter suggested as much, indicating that his loved ones would be better off without him. It also mentioned a few loss experiences that were especially galling (e.g., the potential loss of insurance benefits and a humiliating interaction with an agent in that context). His "psychache," to use Shneidman's (1996) term for the internal pain that energizes many suicides, apparently had become unbearable. Why did this psychologist conclude that he could not go on when others who have had greater histories of loss decide to fight on? Why did he choose to overlook the support of his family and loved ones, or the appreciation of his students and clients?

I do not know the answers to these questions about this psychologist. Only he could address why the end had to come then. One can only conclude that the struggle had come to a head. He had "tunneled" down to this as the only remaining possibility. Whether he considered the grave effects on his family, we do not know. But the long-term effects of his acts are fairly clear. The substantial and lingering effect of suicide on families and survivors cannot be overstated. As one of the parents in the preceding story of teens taking their lives at the same time said, "I don't know if the grief [after 4 years] is as intense anymore. . . . In some ways it's even worse because it's been so long. . . . You miss her more and more as the years pass" (Gowen, 1995, p. 120). The writer noted that this person's eyes and voice reflected a sense of hollowness as she spoke.

Families and survivors are often confronted with years of uncertainty and questioning about a loved one's suicide. "Why" becomes their lifelong question, a legacy of the person's decision to commit suicide. Ironically, as we have seen in this chapter, the person committing this act may view it as a way of alleviating a burden for loved ones. But it may lead to an even bigger burden for those who remain, a burden of guilt and anger.

Ross (1997) alerts us to the possibility that other types of death, such as heart seizures or car accidents, may actually be forms of suicide. Suicide in these cases may occur when people are faced with what they see as insurmountable odds, so they just give up and in so doing end their lives.

In the *Des Moines Register,* Ken Fuson reported a story about a farmer who because of inadequate income and poor crops soon would lose his farm—a 40-year passion to him and his family.[8] In the months before the farm was to go back to the lender, this 58-year-old farmer began to lose his health. He lost weight, his asthma attacks were more frequent, and he developed pneumonia several times. At the same time, he continued to anguish about bills. For hours, he sat in his chair at the kitchen table and searched for an answer. He scribbled numbers—what if he sold the big tractor or the dairy cows? The economic and health pressures were unrelenting. Then, one early morning, his wife found him in this very chair, slumped over and dead, his billfold on the table in front of him.

Thanks to this farmer's life insurance, his widow was able to pay the farm bills, although she was unclear whether she could save and work the farm in the future. His widow said, "This farm killed him" (p. 4A). The writer noted that something still puzzled the widow:

What was Gerald doing with his billfold on the table that morning? He always kept it in the kitchen cabinet. When Roberta opened it, she cried. It struck her as such a pathetic symbol of Gerald's life in trying to save the farm. It bothered her more than selling his John Deere tractors, more than battling the farm agency, more than living in a house with peeling paint. Gerald Farrington, an Iowa farmer, died with six bucks in his billfold. (p. 4A)

The dead have nothing except the memory they've left. (Ferenc Molnár, Hungarian playwright and novelist)

Notes

1. Quoted in *People,* December 4, 2000, p. 166.
2. "An Interior Pain That Is All But Indescribable," by William Styron, *Newsweek,* April 18, 1994, p. 52.
3. See *USA TODAY,* November 30, 1999, pp. 1-2A.
4. "She Loved Him to Death," by Meg M. Breslin and Todd Lighty, *Chicago Tribune Magazine,* February 7, 1999, pp. 10-15.
5. *Chicago Tribune Magazine,* December 19, 1999, p. 16.
6. "Children Don't Have the Anchors, the Emotional Support They Used to Have in Growing Up," by Fredrick Goodwin, *USA TODAY,* November 20, 1999, pp. 1-2A.
7. "Fatal Secret," by Annie Gowen, *Chicago Tribune Magazine,* October 25, 1995, pp. 80-122.
8. "Death Saves the Farm He Loved," by Ken Fuson, *Des Moines Register,* August 29, 1999, p. 1A, 4A.

7 Life Span Losses and Aging

All things must change to something new, to something strange.
—Henry Wadsworth Longfellow

The Normality of Frequent Life Span Losses

This chapter is about losses associated with aging that occur across the human life span, but particularly after midlife (with midlife representing a period that now, with increasing life spans, is often conceived to be from the 30s to 50s). There are many kinds of losses that occur over the course of a normal lengthy life span that wound us in ways that are similar to the loss of close relationships. They may include the death of parents and other loved ones, divorce, financial difficulties, alienation from some family members—even children—and the emergence of various types of health problems. Some losses are more subtle than others. Aging, and the diminution of certain cognitive and motor abilities usually, comes about in gradual, subtle ways.

Although age may be correlated with a pileup of major losses over time, every developmental stage has its own types of major losses that make it a highly vulnerable time (Robert Weiss, personal communication, December 7, 2000). The young may be devastated by the loss of parents. Middle-aged persons may be wiped out by divorce. Those in later life may experience both the failing of their bodies and the deaths of close others. Aging sometimes creeps up on us, but eventually its potency is undeniable. Losses that may be associated with aging include the loss of health, which may occur slowly or in major developments; these developments might involve the onset of a life-threatening disease such as the development of emphysema or Alzheimer's disease.

Selectivity is essential in discussing life span loss topics. As Viorst (1986) contends in her book *Necessary Losses,* there are many kinds of losses that simply come with the normal passage of time. Everything from the loss of one's pets to the loss of one's sexual virginity and eventually to the loss of health and loved ones to death may be construed as falling within this large and diverse universe. The key, as has been argued repeatedly in this book, is the *psychological sense of loss* on the part of the person experiencing the loss event. In many instances, more subtle kinds of losses are just as daunting to the spirit as is the loss of a close relationship.

Each life span loss probably has its own constellation of dynamics, some of which are more straightforward than others. The loss associated with relocation, as an example, is getting more attention as people live longer. There is increasing societal recognition that millions of us will end our lives living in institutions called nursing homes or convalescent centers. Giving up long-term homes can represent a huge loss, especially for people who value what they have created in their home and its ambience. Perhaps it is less well recognized that relocations may occur often earlier in people's lives and also constitute experiences of loss.

People often move from city to city in order to ascend the ranks of their profession. Some national and international companies require this type of movement from one place to another, and usually military personnel cannot expect to be at any one installation very long. The resulting loss of support and friendship networks, not to mention the sheer fatigue of packing and unpacking boxes, can be defeating and can accumulate, leading to a vast sense of loneliness and alienation over many moves. Whenever we leave a home or a city or region in which we have experienced important events, we lose something that we value. We may gain a new home and "place of the heart" (to borrow a term

from a movie of that name about a small farm in North Texas). But nostalgia and feelings of regret are common when we think back about past homes and places. So often these past "places of moment" are meaningful because they are associated with people and events that help define who we are and have been.

One of the principal features of "frequent life span losses" is that they are normal. They may not seem that way. They may, in fact, seem quite particular in their perils and debilitations. Yet by definition, many people experience them at various points in their lives. All of us will experience some of these losses, such as aging and the deterioration of health. They are not "frequent," rather they are "absolute." That is just the way it is; it is a life span progression that can traumatize, humble, and/or be faced with courage and grace, but that takes a toll on both the body and the mind.

Is Aging Just About Loss?

It is essential at the outset to recognize that aging is not just about loss. Eastern cultures have embraced aging as the conduit to wisdom that should lead to veneration. Western cultures have typically not been as generous, with a prevalence of negative stereotypes about the elderly or older very sick persons. Yet through the experience and maturity that occur over time, people may grow tremendously in their knowledge and what they have to offer others. This reality may continue virtually until death in the lives of those who are lucky enough to have good mental health until the point of death. This chapter not only examines many of the losses associated with aging, but it also explores such positive aspects of aging—*how aging can be a significant human gain.*

Actor and director Robert Redford said as much in commenting on what it felt like to be 56:

> It's not much longer I'm going to be able to do things I've loved so much—skiing, horseback riding, all the physical things. I've just enjoyed having my body be able to pretty much do anything I wanted it to. But that time is being diminished. . . .

[The best part about being 56 is] the wisdom, the perspective you gain that allows you to be more compassionate, more forgiving about some of your hostilities and anger.[1]

Themes in Life Review

The themes that older persons emphasize as they review their lives link loss issues to aging in interesting ways. O'Connor (1994) provided evidence about salient themes in the life review of a sample of older respondents in London. These reviews indicated that loss issues figured prominently in this sample of 142 people all over 65 years of age and living alone. A semistructured taped interview invited respondents to discuss and review central areas of their lives. Coders then analyzed major themes that occurred in the discussions.

Themes indicative of loss included the following: past relational losses, current relational separations and/or inadequacies, issues related to health loss and ability to look after oneself, issues associated with adequacy of material or financial resources, and feelings of loss of control and/or mastery. All these themes were mentioned by significant percentages of the respondents. O'Connor (1994) suggests that there was a strong feeling of long-term unresolved grief in all these interviews. As Wortman and Silver (1989) have argued, people may feel pressure to show others that they have "moved on" in their grief about the loss of loved ones. Thus, this life review technique may be a useful way of eliciting true unextinguished grief among people who have experienced years of bereavement and who may continue to do so until they die.

The Experience of Aging

Our perception of the aging process in ourselves or in those we love can be a difficult experience. It can be terribly demoralizing to begin to turn gray or to learn that you cannot do physical tasks that you could do before. Successful aging requires flexibility in exercising cognitive control strategies in navigating the challenges of daily life in a body that is increasingly limited in potential (Schulz & Heckhausen, 1996).

Perhaps the most dispiriting aspect of life for many elderly people is the disproportionate emphases in all areas of society on younger people and their activities and interests. Such an emphasis is clearly seen in the media, particularly in advertising, movies, television programs, and newscasts. As a society, we could benefit greatly from being exposed to more movies such as *On Golden Pond,* which was aimed at showing the bridges that can and need to be made among people at different stages in their lives. "Being old" is such a relative matter in society. As a college teacher who has spent more than 30 years around people who are in their late teens to early 20s, it still shocks me to hear students in their casual comments refer to people over 30 as "old." At the same time, in visiting nursing homes, a visitor readily hears comments that reflect a more refined analysis of "oldness" from residents who span the 60s to 90s continuum. "Old" to them is usually a lot farther down the road than 30.

As the huge baby boom generation bubbles along toward their 60s, a vast literature on aging is developing. This literature on aging and gerontology (a synonymous term for the study of aging) covers a range of topics, including the following issues (from a leading textbook by Aiken, 1995): illness and health care, cognitive abilities, personality and problems of adjustment, sex and marital relations, employment and retirement, economics, living arrangements and activities, crime and law, and death and bereavement. Loss and aging issues connect with this set of topics at various points, but most particularly in areas such as problems of adjustment, cognitive abilities, retirement, marital relations (especially the death or divorce of a partner), discrimination (that pertains to crime and law), and death and bereavement.

Selective Review of
Loss-Related Aging Evidence

Fatal diseases and chronic disorders such as arthritis are common plights of aging. If we live long enough, we are apt to encounter clogged arteries, and on autopsy many older persons are found to have cancers of various types, even though they did not die of cancer! It is a blessing to live a long life. But it is likely that all who do will encounter life-threatening illnesses or chronic, major disorders during some period in life. Table 7.1 provides age-specific rates per 100,000 people in three age groups for the 10 most common fatal diseases in Americans 65 years and older in 1991.

Arthritis does not directly kill many people but is a huge loss issue for many older persons. It is the leading disorder of Americans over 65, having a slight lead over hypertension and a large lead over hearing impairment, the third-ranked disorder (Aiken, 1995). Arthritis, or inflammation of the joints accompanied by pain, stiffness, and movement difficulties, affects everything from mood and self-esteem to participation in activities (including walking, driving, exercising, and sex). There are many levels of impact for different types of arthritis, and there are different treatments for arthritis, including drug therapy, exercise programs, orthopedic devices, and surgery.

There is a general stereotype that older people suffer from declining mental abilities. Such a stereotype is offset by evidence that older persons show great variability in mental abilities and modifiability in such abilities (Schaie, 1983). Extant research showing the vast superiority of younger over older persons on memory tasks has often involved laboratory memory tasks that are adapted from nondevelopmental cognitive psychology studies (Aiken, 1995).

In general, however, motor abilities, short-term memory, and technological skills often decline as a person becomes older (Aiken, 1995). Nevertheless, these limitations may be overcome to a considerable degree by learning new ways to address skill tasks (e.g., making lists to help with memory, taking computer courses, and practicing computing procedures). As the media now communicate in advertising for Viagra and other performance-enhancing drugs, even sexual performance may be modified in positive directions.

One of the most difficult circumstances facing many older persons is that of economic survival. In particular, individuals who suffer from major illnesses (e.g., those requiring expensive medical services) may face the daunting task of trying to living out their final days without

TABLE 7.1 Leading Fatal Diseases in Older Americans

Cause of death	65-74	75-84	85+
Heart disease	872.0	2,219.1	6,673.4
Cancer	871.6	1,351.6	1,773.9
Cerebrovascular disease (e.g., strokes)	139.6	479.4	1,587.7
Chronic obstructive pulmonary disease (e.g., emphysema)	153.3	327.0	446.9
Pneumonia and influenza	156.3	238.5	1,080.5

SOURCE: Adapted from Aiken (1995); taken from National Center for Health Statistics (1991).

becoming totally destitute. A major study at the University of Michigan led by economist Robert Willis found that older couples in the United States who are in poor health have a net household worth of only $31,000 versus the average net worth for couples in their age group of $417,000.[2]

Bereavement and Aging

The loss of loved ones to death is common for persons in their 70s and beyond. The most frequent death of a close family member in later years is the death of a sibling. More than two-fifths of elderly persons experience the death of a sibling after the age of 60, and nearly 10% of persons over 65 have had a sibling die in the previous year (Aiken, 1995).

The most significant literature on bereavement and aging has focused on the lives of widows at different ages and stages after the loss of their husbands. A variety of factors can influence adaptation among older widowed persons (Lopata, 1996). There are more than 13 million widows over 65 in the United States alone (O'Bryant & Hansson, 1995). There also are more than 1 million new widows in the 35 to 54 age range in the United States *every year* (Levinson, 1997). Also, according to the latest census data, in the age range of 65 and above, men still die, on average, 7 years earlier than women. Thus, one can easily see the major health and policy issues related to our understanding of widowhood and women's coping with the loss of spouses. These statistics do not include women who lose romantic, nonmarital partners, including those in homosexual relationships.

Lund, Caserta, and Dimond (1989) reported that early after the loss of a spouse, older women (average age in their 60s) showed greater depression than similarly aged men and that both bereaved women and men exhibited greater depression than similarly aged nonbereaved control groups. The preponderance of findings on age as a vulnerability factor for grieving widows suggests that younger widows (Stroebe & Stroebe, 1987) and younger families (Hansson, Fairchild, Vanzetti, & Harris, 1992) are at greater risk for negative outcomes than are older individuals and families. This pattern of evidence may reflect several dynamics, including the following: the greater anticipation of and preparation for death later in life, the greater acceptance of death later in life, and the greater feeling of injustice if death occurs relatively early in life. Consistent with findings reported by Barnes, Harvey, Carlson, and Haig (1996), this evidence may also be partially explained by the greater experience most older people have in telling their stories of loss and gaining solace as a consequence of their account-making and confiding activities compared with younger people.

O'Bryant and Hansson (1995) reported that given reasonable social support networks, both younger and older women adapt relatively well to widowhood over time. In a longitudinal study of persons over 65, McCrae and Costa (1988) found that widows did not differ from married people in a control group at a 10-year follow-up on measures of depression and general well-being.

The concept of disenfranchised grief is particularly relevant to older persons who have lost a spouse to death. Disenfranchised grief pertains to grief that is not widely recognized in society and for which there is a limited support system (Doka, 1989). Because it is assumed that older persons die more often than do younger persons, the grief of elderly women and men who lose spouses and romantic others may be given little due by others, especially younger persons and even family members.

When older persons evidence normal responses to bereavement such as lack of energy, confusion, loneliness, and social withdrawal, these behaviors sometimes are interpreted as problems reflective of old age (Moss & Moss, 1995).

One investigation that compared grief experiences of persons who had lost spouses to death with grief experiences of persons who had lost spouses to divorce was carried out by Farnsworth, Lund, and Pett (1989). A sample of 110 widowed persons was compared with a sample of 109 divorced persons. All respondents were older than 50 (although the divorced persons were slightly younger on the average) and had been widowed or divorced within the past 2 years. Farnsworth et al. found that widowed and divorced respondents experienced similar feelings of emotional shock, helplessness, avoidance, and grief. Both samples felt relatively positive about their psychological strength and coping ability and were similar in terms of their overall life satisfaction. Divorced participants had significantly more difficulty with anger, guilt, and confusion, and widowed participants were significantly more depressed.

Farnsworth et al. offered several explanations for the differences between widowed and divorced persons. The greater anger, guilt, and confusion of the divorced persons may have been caused by stigmatization of their experience and ongoing discussions involving blame and rebuke in their families. Farnsworth et al. also felt that the depression of the somewhat older widowed respondents may have reflected a "generation effect." The widowed group may have been less socialized to express their grief, may actually have had more physical ailments associated with their circumstances, and may have had less helpful support networks than the divorced group. The reactions to loss of divorced persons who have dependent children are also strongly influenced by the effectiveness and perceived fairness of the custody arrangements (Ahrons, 1994).

Farnsworth et al.'s study shows the difficulty of comparing samples on criteria of loss that are aggregations of diverse experiences, as is true with divorce and death. At minimum, care needs to be taken to ensure control or comparability of general physical, familial support, and socioeconomic conditions across such groups.

In the previously mentioned study by Barnes et al. (1996), the grief and coping responses of persons over 65 and persons in their 20s were compared. The grief and coping responses of both groups occurred after the loss of a loved one (usually a spouse for the older respondents, and a combination of siblings and romantic close others for the younger respondents). The losses had occurred in the past year. Barnes et al. found that on a variety of adaptation measures (e.g., resolution, anger, guilt), the older respondents showed more positive steps toward adaptation than did the younger respondents. Furthermore, consistent with Harvey et al.'s (1990) account-making and confiding model of coping with severe stressors, older persons, who were presumably more experienced in dealing with loss than were younger persons, reported more account making and confiding in others as ways of coping.

The Dialectic of Loss and the Quest
for Romance in the Golden Years

Harvey and Hansen (2000) examined the contradictory goals of persons over age 65 who had divorced or lost spouses to death and were looking for new romantic partners. At a later point in their lives, these individuals were facing the dilemma of simultaneously addressing loss and love.

The dialectic conception of relationships (Baxter & Montgomery, 1996) is an interesting perspective from which to explore the relationship between loss and love. Baxter and Montgomery provide a fascinating analysis of the extent to which every close relationship involves a "ceaseless interplay between contrary or opposing tendencies" (p. 3). Dialectics may help us understand how people in close relationships may be simultaneously moving closer together and separating psychologically. As implied by Baxter and Montgomery, this dialectic tendency may or may not be recognized by the couple. To the extent that such a tendency exists, part of the dialectic tension arises from people's continued bereavement and sense of being incomplete, which is associated with past close relationships and possibly past major losses in general. Baxter and Montgomery argue that dialectic tension is natural in its evolution in relationships and helps the couple achieve a type of equilibrium.

Extrapolating from the dialectic logic, it might be expected that people who explicitly recognize the role of past relationship losses in their lives while working on finding a new romantic relationship would be more persistent in searching for such a relationship. Based on the account-making and confiding approach (Harvey et al., 1990) outlined in Chapter 1 and the dialectic argument, Harvey and Hansen (2000) predicted that persistence in pursuing romance would be particularly strong when people were able to engage in confiding about previous losses with their new partners.

Harvey and Hansen's (2000) study involved administering a questionnaire that included structured and narrative items to 90 individuals over 60 years of age (58 women and 32 men) living in Arizona and Iowa, all of whom were dating or had been engaging in dating behavior since the loss of their previous partner. The average age of the women was 68.5, and the average age of the men was 69.7. All these individuals had been single for at least a year, and all were heterosexual in sexual orientation. All were reasonably healthy such that they could be involved in the pursuit of social relationships. Of the 90 participants, 70 were widows or widowers, 16 were divorced, and 4 had been in long-term nonmarital relationships that had ended. Of the sample, 75% were currently involved in dating behavior (defined as at least occasionally going on "dates") or had been involved at one time after the loss of their spouse or previous romantic partner.

A questionnaire was created to investigate individuals' persistence in pursuing romantic relationships. It contained questions about the loss of spouses to death or divorce, how they had coped with the loss, their present quest for new romantic partners, and how they balanced this quest with continued adaptation to the loss of their spouse.

Responses were coded concerning whether respondents were continuing or had given up the pursuit of romantic relationships; respondents were defined as giving up if they indicated that they had dated to some degree after the loss of a primary close relationship, but now no longer desired to have such relationships—for whatever reasons. Also, responses were coded concerning whether respondents indicated that they had engaged in account making and confiding regarding their relationship losses; respondents were defined as having engaged in account making and confiding if they indicated that they had worked to develop a personal understanding of their loss and had confided part of that understanding to others. They were also asked to indicate who those others were.

It was found that 28 of 58 women fell into the "giving up" category, whereas 5 of 32 men fell into this category. All respondents who were inactive at the time of the study indicated that they had engaged in some degree of dating and romantic relationship-seeking behavior after the loss of their previous romantic relationship. Inactive women and men indicated in their responses that their lack of pursuit or interest was related to the loss of a spouse or lover with whom they had been in a highly satisfying long-term relationship.

Excerpts of explanations for lack of dating persistence are listed here:

I've looked around and tried [dating] a bit, but I'm devoted to his memory. He meant everything to me.

I would like to find someone, but no one can compare to her.

I've discovered that all the good ones are taken already.

I'd like to fall in love again, but I never want to care for an invalid husband again—it is too draining.

I still have an appetite, and my health is good for my age, but most men my age are too frail to engage in active dating lives.

Partial excerpts for those indicating they were very active included the following:

I take advantage of meeting every man I can. I meet them in organizations, at my temple, on AOL [America Online Internet Web site].

I take out a different woman every third night. I'm dating and having more fun than I did when I was a teenager dating.

I'm in a singles organization that has dances, socials, and the like—it keeps me busy a few days a week and fulfills my dating needs.

Following is a more in-depth excerpt for the "giving up" category from the narrative of a woman, age 65. She discusses why she was no longer dating; she also projects a theme of not expecting to date much in the future and to focus social and emotional interests on close friends and family members, especially grandchildren:

> [For the first two years since my husband's death] I tried going out occasionally. I was fixed up by friends and met people in support groups. But I soon discovered how difficult it would be to find any one who could fill my husband's shoes. He was such a wonderful person and we had such a good relationship [for 38 years].
>
> I always compared each new person to him, none came close. . . . I now have a circle of close female friends, and I dote on my grandchildren. I often keep them for my children and they bring me such pleasure. . . . I would like to be in love and married again, but the older I get I doubt very much that it is possible.

In further narratives, however, many of the women in the giving-up category noted that another reason for their unwillingness to continue searching for romantic partners was the relative scarcity of available men (i.e., either in their age range, "interested," or with the requisite qualities). Most of these women were in their late 60s or 70s.

Interestingly, neither the 5 men who were classified as having given up nor the 27 who were classified as active noted availability as an issue. A few of the men and women who were classified as having given up reported that they were haunted by memories of past close relationships. The following excerpt from a 62-year-old man is illustrative:

> For the first two years [since my wife's death] she was constantly on my mind. I know that bothered women when I would go out on dates. I was in such a fog that I don't even remember what I did at work—it could not have been very good work. Going out socially became impossible for my partners and myself. For them, I was no fun and I could not even make small talk. For me, it was agonizing. My wife meant the world to me and these relationships were meaningless. I've stopped dating at this time [5 years after my wife's death].

Of 58 women in the study, the narratives of 40 were coded as showing signs of having engaged in account making and confiding. This proportion compares with 14 of 32 men whose narratives showed activity in account making and confiding. Partial excerpts from narratives showing account making and confiding included the following:

I frequently go to divorced and widowed support group meetings. I'm not afraid to tell my story. I talk about my wife and how I feel being a widower [for 4 years].

I've learned over and over in life the value of close friends being there to listen and talk with you about your losses—I've got some of the best close friends in the world.

I cry, pray, talk about, and mourn the loss of my husband of 55 years just about every other day. But I know that that is good, and even the men I go out with have accepted my strong feelings not to let his memory die and often want to hear about what made my husband so special.

Partial excerpts from narratives not showing much account making and confiding included the following:

I believe grief is a private matter.

No, I haven't talked much and don't really have any close friends.

I think that my friends and family would get tired of my whining over why she's not with me at the best time in my life.

I don't want to think about her death—it's too distressing.

What's past is past, and I've tried to move on in my thoughts. I do cry a lot about why he had to die so young.

As noted previously, 28 of 58 women respondents had given up their romantic quests. Of the 30 who remained active, 28 indicated that they had spent considerable time and energy in account making and confiding regarding their losses of past close relationships. If they commented on the effect of such thinking, feeling, and behavior in their lives, they emphasized its positive effect.

Regarding the question of the identity of the confidants with whom they discussed their losses, 22 of the 28 women noted that their account making and confiding about past relationships occurred in discussions with current romantic partners. Following is an excerpt from the narrative of a woman, age 63, outlining this position:

[After my husband's death] I had to help myself. . . . I worked on myself. I privately reflected long and hard about our life together. But I joined support groups (e.g., Young Energetic Widowed Singles) and met the man I intend to marry in one of them. He had lost his wife in 1989, about the same time I lost my husband. We have been dating about 2 years. We have recovered from our grief and have a happy relationship. It's a real blessing. We talk often about our deceased spouses and how they would approve of our new relationship. We have shared our grief and stories, and are not afraid to shed tears. . . . But we go on and appreciate each day in our new life. You have a right to have and express your memories of your former life. You have to talk, talk, talk—never stop. We are now sharing our experiences with other widows and widowers. We hope to help them in their grief and help them be successful in making their new lives.

As for the men's account making and confiding, there was less evidence that they had engaged in such activity or that it was related to their current dating. Twenty-seven were judged not to have given up in their dating pursuits. Of these 27 men, 14 noted that they had engaged in regular account making and confiding, and each also mentioned that it had been done both with close friends and new romantic partners. All 14 also noted the positive influence of the discussions of their losses with others.

As has been noted in reviews of account making and confiding as a way of coping with loss (e.g., Orbuch, 1997), women tend to show a stronger inclination to use this approach than do men. The present evidence also suggests that women are more active account makers and confiders. Even among the 28 women who were inactive in dating, 12 indicated that they had engaged in account making and confiding. The 5 men who had given up did not indicate that they engaged in account making and confiding.

We also asked questions about future plans for closeness and relations with family and friends. Most respondents indicated that they had and expected to continue to have relations with some group of friends and family members that were close and supportive. Such relations were emphasized more by persons who were classified as giving up on dating and romantic relationships. Some women said they had no choice but to revert to close relationships with other women because so few men were in their networks.

Overall, Harvey and Hansen's (2000) research provides information about singles over 60 years of age and how their romantic quests are intertwined with their resolution of past losses of close relationships. The data are supportive of the extrapolations from the account making and confiding and dialectic positions on grief and persistence in romantic pursuits.

The evidence also strongly points to the different situations encountered by females and males seeking romantic partners. Our results suggest that compared with males, many females give up their quest for a new relationship because of the low numbers of available men and/or their conclusion that those men available do not compare well with their previous husband or lover. Men in this age range generally do not perceive availability to be an issue. Women also showed a tendency to be more involved in account making and confiding regarding their losses than were men (Simpson, 1994).

Stigmatization and the Elderly

Nowhere are stereotypes more widespread, entrenched, and ruinous than in the area of older adults. The negative ideas linked to later life cut a wide swath, minimizing every aspect of humanity: in health ("Older people are disabled" or "Typically, they are in nursing homes"); in thinking ("Their mind goes"); and in personality ("Older people are depressed, childish, set in their ways"). These stereotypes apply to the main transitions in later life, too—retirement and widowhood. Each event oozes with connotations of unmitigated loss.

This quote is from a chapter by Janet Belsky (1994), "Aging in Later Life," in *Counseling Approaches Throughout the Life Span.* Belsky's observations are touching and perceptive. There is, perhaps, no group that is as regularly (almost automatically) stigmatized as the very old in our culture. Instead of honoring them, as some other cultures do, we relegate them to "old folks homes." Too often, the elderly—especially those whose spouses and friends have died—suffer from loneliness, anxiety, low self-esteem, and low morale. They frequently have little will to continue to live. It is immensely difficult for them to construct new meanings for their lives, particularly if their bodies are adversely affected by disease and normal aging processes. Macdonald (1983) comments on this experience for elderly women:

The process of aging has been hidden from us all our lives. We are told with the help of modern medicine and technology old age isn't really necessary. One can have an active life right up to the "end." You are as young as you think you are. There are hair dyes to make your hair look its "natural color," with creams to remove the wrinkles and brown spots, and with all of these no woman should look as though she is "failing"—she should look "well-preserved." (p. 99)

Lisel Mueller's (1986) poem "Face Lift" raises related questions about a newly face-lifted woman. The first line asks the question of how old someone really is if she has been altered to appear younger. Spotted by an acquaintance in the grocery store, this woman's new appearance suggests a set of questions to her acquaintance: How many years that had been indelibly sculpted on her face had been magically removed—the lines, bags, crinkles, crow's feet? Where were the remnants of smiles, the looks of dread, the expressions of sadness and grief? Now, her face "has retracted sleepless nights, denies any knowledge of pain," (p. 21) along with the dark eyes left by mourning someone she loved. Memories etched into her face are gone, and the onlooker wonders how it feels to remember, "under the skin of a thirty-year-old, something that happened at forty" (p. 21).

In this regard, it should be noted that French futurist Gerard Delteil has predicted that in 100 years, through advances in cosmetic surgery, 60-year-olds can be made to look indistinguishable from teenagers (Bland, 1997). Would most of us want that fate? Is aging so stigmatized that we want to totally wipe away those thousands of experiences that stand behind the lines on our faces? As I suggest at the end of this chapter, maybe there is something to be said for accepting the slings and arrows of living with grace and recognizing that death itself is a natural experience—one like so many others that deserves honor, not avoidance and denigration.

The Loss of Health, Hope, and Meaning

The worst fear of people who are at risk for Huntington's disease is that they will eventually get the disease and life will become meaningless for them . . . [the meaning of life] varies from day to day, even from hour to hour. The meaning of life constantly changes but *never ceases to exist.*

The preceding quote appears in Dennis H. Phillips's *Living With Huntington's Disease.* In a speech to AFL-CIO leaders in 1994, Senator Jay Rockefeller of West Virginia talked about the 1992 death of his mother from Alzheimer's disease:

> It isn't painful in the way cancer is, but even as you are watching yourself, your brain cells begin to die, you lose control of yourself, you lose control over your actions, and you become somebody else. . . . And I watched this over a period of six or eight years with my mother. And it got to the point where she would get up at 2 a.m. and put on two dresses and go down for breakfast. And then somebody would take her back to bed. And she'd be up an hour later and she'd do the same thing. . . . She knew what was happening to her and was humiliated because she knew she was a different person and she was ashamed.[3]

The aging process certainly does not have to involve the loss of health, hope, and meaning. But sometimes it does. It does usually when an individual also is contending with other battles, such as a quickly deteriorating body, a life-threatening disease such as Alzheimer's and Huntington's, or relocation to a convalescent center. These struggles are compounded when a person already suffering from health problems loses her or his support network of friends and close relatives. People in these situations are quickly marginalized in our society.

As suggested in the chapter on stigmatization, part of the loss associated with aging occurs as a result of being stereotyped. Both in the minds of younger persons and in the minds of older persons too, there is often a minimization of the value of the older person: "Older people usually are childish and set in their ways." "Older people are disabled and have to be in nursing homes." "Older people are often depressed and noncommunicative. Their brains do not think straight." Such ideas may even have a self-fulfilling effect on the elderly, moving them in the direction of the frequently heard stereotype. The "loss" that results from such sequences is grave for society. There is no necessary reason why people beyond the age of 80 must exhibit the behavior associated with such stereotypes. Furthermore, to unconsciously push them in that direction through our casual commentary and other ill-conceived behavior means that we begin to lose them as functioning citizens. Finally, just as important, judging older people in such simplistic ways may represent an enormous loss to younger people. It reflects a process of rigid thinking that in itself is a loss of the proper perspective. It reflects an inability or unwillingness to look closely at the great diversity exhibited by older people, what they really are like, and what they really can do. It reflects a failure to let the "evidence" determine the type of judgment that is formed about a given individual. It reflects a glossing over of many people with a broad stroke of the perceptual brush—the real senility here is in the judgment, not in the target!

In an article in *Parade Magazine,* Hugh Downs addressed the theories of Leonard Hayflick, a cell biologist and founding member of the Council of the National Institute on Aging.[4] Hayflick contends that having a long life is no more important than having a life that does not involve considerable suffering and anguish at its end. He said that we may imagine that the perfect life is one that is long, full, happy, and devoid of the losses that often go along with aging. But then, healthy people would not want to die at all. Hayflick also points out that a "generally happy life" is a recent development and that life in the Middle Ages was a terrible ordeal—except for the rich and powerful. Most people then probably would not have wished to live more than 20 or 30 years.

The unfortunate state of affairs for many senior citizens today is an institutionalized life that ultimately leads to anguish or depression and meaninglessness. Consider these comments from persons contributing to Gubrium's (1993) provocative book *Speaking of Life,* which involved interviews with people living in nursing homes:

I have wanted to die ever since I went in that home. . . . I have thought of taking my life. I don't want to be in the shape I see these people [other residents of the home]. I just wish I could die today. (Roland Synder, age 78, 3 months before he died, p. 31)

I lived with my daughter for a while when she decided, well . . . she met this gentleman who was going to marry again. She decided I guess there wasn't room for mother. So from then on I got thrown out, lived here and there. . . . I tell you, life looks pretty empty. I feel really unwanted. I am trying to overcome that now. For some reason, the good Lord leaves me here. I have almost died from my breath. . . . Mainly, life's dull, just dull. I just sit there and think and wonder how it all come to this. (Mary Stern, age 80, a heavy smoker suffering from emphysema, pp. 61-67)

Well, life looks to me like a big blob! . . . I've often wondered why the Lord lets me live on, because what good am I to anybody. I'm a burden, you see. . . . I'm a bump on a log. I'm absolute useless.... Just sitting here, and I have to be cared for. I'm not able to contribute to anything. I hope I don't live the rest of the year out because there's no point in it. There would just be more worry and more trouble on my son and his wife.... Life don't mean anything now. There's nothing to look forward to. All you've got is your memories to look back on. (Myrtle Johnson, age 94, suffering from Parkinson's disease, pp. 55-57).

The reader who has experience with institutionalized older adults "under the care of others" will find these comments to be on the mark for many adults in these settings. How do we as a society reconstruct these institutions and the people who come to inhabit them (most of us if we live that long) to help them be more "empowering"? This question is daunting, particularly as we, on average, live longer and have enough medical technology available to move the average life span ever closer to the 100-year mark. What good will it do if typically our last 15 years are lived in a vegetative condition?

Not only do the individuals faced with this final stage of life often experience despair, so do their children and caretakers. Kim Painter of *USA TODAY* described how Ginger McCray took care of her mother Dorothy Allen, who was suffering from Alzheimer's disease, until her death at age 63 in 1993.[5] Alzheimer's disease is a degenerative brain disorder that causes memory loss and sometimes an inability to control emotions. Dorothy Allen's struggle with Alzheimer's disease lasted more than 5 years, but Ginger still viewed her opportunity to help her mother as a labor of love.

Ginger said that she had never prepared herself to take care of a parent. But she did it, and she was glad to do it. She said that there were times when her mother made it hard for her. Her mother would reject her, and her mother would not allow shows of affection. Ginger said that she knew that this was not her mom—it was the sickness. She concluded by noting that when they were just sitting together, her mother would reach out and just start touching Ginger. Her mother would start feeling her face or just touch her hand or just start putting her hands in Ginger's hair. Ginger knew that her mother knew her, even if she didn't know what day it was. She said that she still had her mother's spirit with her every day.

There are many other conditions associated with the aging process that may dampen a person's spirit and that reduce people's ability to find meaning in their lives. Some are individual, whereas others are societal. Many older people live on very modest means. They can be wiped out financially and emotionally when major health care needs develop.

At the individual level, there are many physical and psychological conditions that seem to go with aging. Columnist and comedian Art Buchwald's 1994 autobiography, *Leaving Home,* poignantly describes his battle with depression that lasted more than four decades. Buchwald, now 68, said that he came very close to committing suicide on two occasions, in 1962 and 1987. He finally got psychological help and feels that he has licked his severe case of depression. Interestingly, he said that he decided not to kill himself one time because his now deceased wife Ann had strategically put up a photograph of his children to remind him that he was not alone—and in effect to quell his urge to kill himself.

Buchwald's "coming out" about his depression is a valuable contribution to the estimated 17 million or more Americans who suffer from clinical depression. Many of them are between 65 and 90 years of age—a span of time when the suicide rate is the highest for any group in the United States. "Clinical" depression means that the condition is deep and durable, not the moderate and occasional depression we all probably experience. It also has been estimated by the National Institute of Aging that more than 50% of this group do not receive treatment.

In the discussion that follows are examples of people living their final years with zest and, most important, living the way they want to live. But to end the foregoing discussion of nursing or convalescent homes on an upbeat and amusing note, writer David Greenberger has created an industry of books, compact disc recordings, and newsletters that pertain to the funny and wise sayings of persons who live in these institutions. His book, *Duplex Planet* (Greenberger, 1993), has revealed a whole new way of seeing nursing home residents, who in general are usually viewed as having little left to offer and as suffering from old age dementia. Greenberger perceptively discovered the underrecognized talent of nursing home residents to tell amusing tales while he worked as an activities director for Duplex Nursing Home in the Boston area. He wanted to help the residents create a collective memoir of their community, so he started asking them questions and recording their answers. (He often asked strange questions such as "Do apes have picnics?" to which Ernie Bookings replied, "I don't know, my dictionary's too small," p. 45.) Greenberger said that despite the various "old age" diseases and mental conditions of many of the residents his interactions with them were very meaningful. In describing his experience of the older people, Greenberger said, "The names of their conditions of deterioration mattered little to me; what did matter was that this was someone still very much alive, very interested in conversing, in entertaining or being entertained, in connecting with someone else" (p. 7).

Examples of the gems of logic reported to Greenberger include the following:

> I can't complain too much. I've been to California. (Ed Poindexter, p. 47)

> I got eighty-six hours of sleep since last Friday. Fifty-six hours of sleep is a good amount of sleep for a week and I had thirty extra hours of sleep. And I have another business, I'm starting to sell cigarettes to my friends. (Henry Turner, p. 80)

> Everybody's askin' who I was. (Charlie Johanson, p. 9)

> In answer to the question "Can you tell me what a compact disc is?" "Who the hell knows?! Write this down: Where do you get all these stupid questions? What's a compact disc?! Where do you think we went to school anyway? That's like asking why doesn't snow fall up instead of down. If you look at it long enough it does fall up." (Frank Kanslasky, p. 138)

Via his different publications, Greenberger continues to report what residents in different nursing homes say in answer to his "stupid" questions. These publications have been praised and referenced by famous people such as comedian George Carlin, who have indicated their appreciation of the wisdom often displayed by the respondents. The *New York Times* has likened these gems of logic to modern-day versions of Chaucer's reports from the road to Canterbury.

Life's Final Season: Going Out With Pride and Dignity

Ernest Hemingway's famous story, *The Old Man and the Sea,* embodies a spirit of finishing one's life with as much daring and self-reliance as a person can muster. This story of an older man's relentless pursuit of a fish symbolizes the quest of many elderly people to battle old age and death with valor and dignity until their final breath. That is the message that I hope the reader will get about all the aspects of loss discussed in this book. With aging losses, for ourselves or our loved ones, it may be that keeping the faith, maintaining our spirit, and trying to conquer obstacles will be extraordinarily difficult. As discussed in the chapter on the experience of dying, there likely is a point at which each of us—if we have the choice—will need to let go of life. But until that point, the charge issued by many courageous people, some of whom are discussed later, is that we should "never quit."

Many older individuals who still have their health intact are shining examples of generativity—giving back to other generations (a topic expanded on in the final two chapters of the book). For example, in 1990, Paul Reese, age 73, ran across the United States from California to South Carolina and plunged into the Atlantic Ocean at Hilton Head with the television cameras recording his historic moment. It took 5 months for him to make the journey with the help of his wife who drove a van along to accompany and assist him. His feat could be compared with running a marathon for 124 consecutive days! In 1993, Reese published *Ten Million Steps,* a chronicle of his run.

In describing what he felt about his accomplishment, Reese told Bard Lindeman of the *Chicago Tribune* that it was sad to see so many homes with older people just sitting in a chair on the front porch or in the yard watching the world go by.[6] He said that this should be "their" day. To sit there, hour after hour, seemed a waste of body and brain. He considered himself fortunate to be able to experience this run, especially at his age. Yes, fortunate to be able to handle it physically and financially (it cost him about $45 a day), fortunate to have the time, and blessed to have his wife's help.

Reese, an ex-Marine, had also suffered prostate cancer only 3 years prior to his run. He continued to train right through the period of his treatment. In the end, Reese did what he did to heighten the sense of possibilities of later life—a noble achievement that can give new meaning to many senior citizens who still believe that they too can in some way reach possibilities that they otherwise might not have entertained.

In August 1994, 84-year-old Virginia Eddy of Middlebury, Vermont, who had been very sick, died. Why was her death so special that it was reported by the Associated Press and picked up by the *New York Times* and other newspapers? Because she too lived her life to the end in an exemplary fashion. Her death was both planned and peaceful. This little old lady was described by her physician-son David Eddy as being like the proverbial "little old lady in sneakers." She faced a number of health problems toward the end of her life, but she did not want to die in a nursing home—"declining with little more than a blank stare," as she told her son.[7] Nor did Ms. Eddy want to die after a protracted period of grave illness, being cared for by others. As she said of her life and death,

> I've lived a wonderful life, but it has to end sometime. And this is the right time for me. I don't want to spoil the wonder of my life by dragging it out in years of decay. I want to go now, while the good memories are still fresh. (p. 8F)

So with the consultation of her son and family, Ms. Eddy celebrated her 85th birthday in a rousing party atmosphere. Then she stopped eating and drinking. That did it. On the sixth day of fasting, with a relaxed, natural smile, she died. That's not all. She requested that her son tell others about her decision. So he wrote about her death in an issue of the *Journal of the American Medical Association,* and her story was then picked up on the wire services. Indeed, Ms. Eddy had lived a life of vigor and accomplishment, one that had involved traveling across Africa at age 70 and surviving a river rafting accident at age 82. She offered this question to all of us who may face her situation in the end: "Is the quality of life defined by its duration? Or does life have a purpose so large that it doesn't have to be prolonged at any cost to preserve its meaning?"

Finding Will and Hope
Despite the Frequency of Loss

The frequent life span losses described in this chapter often require great effort and willpower to transcend. There are good examples in every area of loss of people rising to the occasion to deal with loss and anguish with grace and courage. Perhaps if nothing else, the material in this chapter suggests the value of taking a minute to reflect on the many different ways people lose, and yet also cope—taking a day at a time. Perhaps we would all be stronger if each day we took time to try to understand how someone else is dealing with life's stressors. Consider what one woman and her husband discovered when they spontaneously decided to stop their trip to the beach and talk with a stranger, an elderly woman whom they observed waving from the front porch of a nursing home.[8] The elderly woman told the couple that she was so glad they had stopped. She said that she had prayed that they would stop a few minutes to sit and chat. The elderly woman said that many people pass by the facility, especially in the summer, and peer from their car windows and see nothing more than an old building that houses old people. But this couple saw her and took time to stop. The woman said that some people believe that old people are senile. But the truth is that they are just plain lonely. The elderly woman later wrote to the couple and said that the past few days (since they stopped in) had been the happiest ones in her life since Henry, her beloved husband, died 2 years before. She said that she felt that once more she had a family who cared about her. She also gave the couple the cameo brooch that she wore on her wedding day, June 30, 1939. Three days after their visit, the elderly woman died peacefully in her sleep. Little things mean so much to the old and lonely.

John Bland is a physician in his 80s who has written a marvelous book, *Live Long, Die Fast* (1997). This book offers an uplifting message about the challenges of aging that each of us will face. The title of Bland's book sums up his powerful thesis that it is possible to live long and die fast, an outcome many if not most of us would prefer to be our fates.

In his argument, Bland takes issue with the idea that the elderly must be reduced to living a life characterized by passivity, boredom, and meaninglessness. He contends that society is wasting 25% of the population by treating them as disposable, and this attitude creates a self-fulfilling prophecy with the elderly. He argues that retirement is a curse and that work is as important as water and sex. Of sex, he says, "Use it or lose it." Bland advocates activity (more than rest), physical fitness (along with the avoidance of smoking, which, as only one outcome, reduces lung breathing capacity by as much as 25% after 5 years of regular smoking), a positive attitude (avoid the negative self-talk that is common among the elderly), and contributing to others as antidotes to dying in a protracted way. In the end, however, Bland is espousing a package of attitudes and behavior that must start early in people's lives to be effective. Let's hope his message is received by persons who think that aging is something that is a long way off in their lives.

"The true way to render age vigorous is to prolong the youth of the mind." (Mortimer Callius)

Notes

1. From the "Tempo" section of *Chicago Tribune*, May 15, 1994, p. 4.
2. From an AP wire story. See also this Web site: www.umich.edu/~hrswww
3. "The Heartbreak of Alzheimer's," by James Gannon, *Des Moines Register*, April 28, 1994, p. 9A.
4. From *Parade Magazine*, August 21, 1994.
5. From *USA TODAY*, May 6, 1994, p. 6A.
6. From the *Chicago Tribune*, July 31, 1994, p. 6F.
7. From an article by Bard Lindeman, *Chicago Tribune* Media Services, in *Cedar Rapids Gazette*, September 4, 1994, p. 8F. Also see Eddy (1994) and the following Web address for a reprint of the article by David Eddy: www.mcn.org/c/irapilgrim/death05.html
8. From Beverly K. Fine's column in *Baltimore Sun*; reprinted in *Cedar Rapids Gazette*, August 28, 1994.

8 Violence and War

At the bottom of the trenches there lay frozen green Germans and frozen gray Russians and frozen fragments of human shapes . . . how anyone could have survived was hard to imagine. But now everything was silent in this fossilized hell, as though a raving lunatic had suddenly died of heart failure.

—Alexander Werth (Overy, 1997, p. 21)

In February 1943, at the end of the critical World War II battle at Stalingrad, Alexander Werth offered this grim commentary. This chapter focuses on the many losses and the grief resulting from violence and war. It overlaps with Chapter 9, which addresses the Holocaust and genocide. Violence and war usually have an effect on many people over an extended period of time, and unfortunately they are quite common in our world. The focus of work in this field is as much on the perpetrators of acts of violence as it is on the victims of such acts. In the discussion that follows, I consider some of the basic and classic literature on violence and aggression. Then, specific types of violence are discussed. The concluding section focuses on war and especially wars that have led to long-term trauma in American history.

The Basic Literature on Violence and Aggression

In this discussion, some of the vast literature on the determinants of violence and aggression is reviewed. A definition of aggression is "any sequence of behavior, the goal response to which is the injury of the person toward whom it is directed" (Dollard, Doob, Miller, Mowrer, & Sears, 1939). Most subsequent analyses adopted "injurious intent" as an essential aspect of aggression; otherwise, any unintentional act that accidentally harms another person could be construed as aggression or violence. Classic treatments of violence and aggression (e.g., Bandura, 1973) analyze the determinants of violence and aggression as involving both social-environmental and biological factors. They also distinguish between instrumental aggression and hostile aggression. Instrumental aggression is aimed at securing extraneous rewards other than the suffering of victims. Hostile aggression is focused on inflicting injury.

For example, the act of Paul Tibbets and his crew in dropping the atomic bomb over Japan in 1945 was an act of instrumental aggression. This act, which killed 70,000 initially and thousands others later is often explained, or rationalized, as having shortened the war, saving millions of lives.[1]

Bandura (1973) believes that a more complex definition of aggression is necessary in light of the varied forms that these behaviors take and the fact that cultural labeling of the behaviors as aggression or violence is essential. He offers this definition: "injurious and destructive behavior that is socially defined as aggressive on the basis of a variety of factors, some of which reside in the evaluator rather than in the performer" (p. 8).

Environmental Factors

Most of the events that evoke aggressive behavior in humans are energized by learning and environmental stimuli rather than by genetic endowment (Bandura, 1973). Prominent elicitors of aggression are personal insults, verbal challenges, status threats, unjust treatment, and provocative aggressive displays. Engaging in harmful but acceptable violence such as in boxing may also provoke an aggressive response. Although so-called cathartic aggression may distill aggressive tendencies, researchers such as Feshbach (1956) have shown that it may also enhance subsequent instances of unacceptable aggression. The modeling of aggression and nonaggression is considered to be a major factor in how children learn to be aggressive or to refrain from aggression (Baron, 1971). The model may be another child, an adult, or someone observed on television.

A provocative but controversial finding on the dynamics of aggression has been presented by Roy Baumeister, Brad Bushman, and their colleagues (Baumeister, 1997; Baumeister, Bushman, & Campbell, 2000; Bushman & Baumeister, 1998). It is that villains, bullies, criminals, killers, and other evildoers have high self-esteem and engage in violence to serve their egotistical view of themselves. These investigators suggest that the evidence supports the idea that violent men, and possibly violent women too, have a strong sense of personal superiority, and their violence often seems to stem from wounded pride or a need for revenge. Baumeister and his colleagues, however, believe that those most susceptible to violence are the individuals prone to ego threat who have inflated, exalted opinions of themselves or whose normally high self-esteem does occasionally take a nosedive. Baumeister and colleagues would like to dismantle the school self-esteem movement that he believes takes the form of uncritical celebration, as an entitlement of being a human.

Baumeister and colleagues believe that violence is usually directed at the sources of the ego threat or substitutes for such threats. Baumeister and his associates might argue that the two teens who were members of the so-called Trench Coat Mafia in Littleton, Colorado, who killed 13 of their fellow students in a shooting rampage in April 1999 are examples of this exalted self-esteem. These two young men killed themselves too, but they presumably hated minorities and athletes who were included among their victims.

Bushman and Baumeister (1998) conducted an experimental study involving an insulting provocation and how it affected persons whose self-esteem and other personality qualities had been measured. They found that it is not necessarily the narcissistic aspect of self-regard that is connected to violence. In their work, persons scoring in the high range of the personality variable of narcissism did not differ from other participants in showing aggressive behavior, as long as there was no insulting provocation.

The self-exalted statements and apparent arrogant egos of serial killers such as Ted Bundy and John Gacy are consistent with this line of
reasoning. This exaltation can be seen in Kenneth McDuff, who was executed in Texas in 1999 for a series of brutal murders of women with
whom he had had sex. He bragged of his killings, saying that he "used
them up and blew more than one away who were begging for their
lives."

Baumeister and colleagues' view on self-esteem is controversial because therapists and corrections system officials often have stressed the
probable role of low self-esteem in aggression and violence. Baumeister
debated Ervin Staub, another well-known researcher of violence, in
"point-counterpoint" columns in the *APA Monitor* (Baumeister & Staub,
1999). Staub took the position that young boys' acts of aggression are
often associated with harsh punitive parenting, poor social skills, and
poor performance in school. He contends that level of self-esteem may
be less important than what self-esteem is based on. Children and
youth will attempt to gain a positive image of themselves, and many
boys resort to aggression because they have no socially valued means to
gain a positive image, competence, and social skills. He believes they
also turn to gangs in those contexts because gangs focus on boosting
the self-esteem of members.

Biological Factors

In terms of biological influences, James Dabbs and colleagues (e.g.,
Dabbs, Frady, Carr, & Buesch, 1987) have examined the relationship
between testosterone and criminal behavior. They determined that inmates with the highest testosterone concentrations had often been
convicted of violent crimes. The relationship between testosterone and
violence was most notable at the extremes of the testosterone distribu-
tion, where 9 of 11 inmates with the lowest testosterone had committed
nonviolent crimes and 10 of 11 inmates with the highest testosterone
had committed violent crimes. Of course, correlation does not prove

causality, and this work on testosterone does not preclude the possibility that early learning experiences are important determinants of aggressive behavior.

Other research with persons convicted of criminal activity points to the role of early training and overall socialization in contributing to a life of crime. Gottfredson and Hirschi (1990) showed that habitual criminals tend to lack inner discipline and restraint. The thinking of such criminals exemplifies a short-term focus and a simplistic value system geared toward finding easy ways of getting desired outcomes.

Maintaining Aggression

Some of the factors that presumably contribute to the maintenance of aggression include the following:

1. Justification of aggression in terms of higher principles. An example is instrumental aggression such as that carried out in dropping the atomic bomb on Japan.
2. Displacement of responsibility. This involves attributing hurtful actions to a legitimate higher authority. Consider, for example, the findings of Milgram's (1963) famous work showing how readily people will obey authority figures and harm others; they often said that the university sponsoring the research was responsible for their aggression and its harmful consequences.
3. Diffusion of responsibility. This is similar to displacement and involves attributing one's hurtful actions to the collective organization in which one is operating. For example, U.S. troops claimed that their atrocities at My Lai in Vietnam were part of the way war had to be carried out and no different from the behavior of the enemy.
4. Dehumanization of victims. This involves stereotyping the victims of one's aggression. U.S. troops called the Viet Cong and North Vietnamese "Gooks" in the Vietnam War.

5. Attribution of blame to the victims. For example, according to Lerner's (1980) "just world" theory, people who are victimized must have done something to deserve it.

6. Graduated desensitization. This involves the slow process of turning a person who otherwise may be compassionate into someone who could under some circumstances be cruel or brutal or engage in unjustified aggression against another person. Presumably, the Nazi's activities in the 1930s may be seen as desensitization of well-meaning Germans, which turned them into persons who either could engage in unjustified aggression or who could readily stand by and let such aggression occur. (Baumeister, 1997; Fromm, 1941)

Every war in history most likely has involved too many examples of dehumanization to begin to list. One that stands out, however, came from the invasion of China by Japan in the late 1930s. The Japanese had begun a campaign of imperialism aimed at expanding their territory and dominating Asia and the Pacific, which later led to their attack on the United States at Pearl Harbor. As part of this campaign, the Japanese attacked and killed hundreds of thousands of Chinese civilians beginning in 1937. More than 300,000 Chinese civilians were killed in the ancient Chinese city of Nanking. Iris Chang (1997) documents this atrocity in *The Rape of Nanking*. She reports what one Japanese soldier said, that he and his associates became involved in raping and killing thousands of Chinese women:

At first we used some kinky words like "Pikankan." "Pi" means "hip," "kankan" means "look." "Pikankan" means, "Let's see a woman open up her legs." Chinese women didn't wear underpants. Instead, they wore trousers tied with a string. There was no belt. As we pulled the string, the buttocks were exposed, we "pikankan." We looked. After a while we would say something like, "It's my day to take a bath," and we took turns raping them. It would be all right if we only raped them. I shouldn't say all right. But we always stabbed and killed them. Because dead bodies don't talk. (p. 49)

Research Evidence on Domestic Violence

A very substantial literature exists on the dynamics of domestic and relationship violence. This discussion only touches on some of the findings that illustrate the major dynamics of such violence. A constellation of factors has been consistently associated with rape in general (including research in a number of countries around the world; Walker, 1999). According to Malamuth (1989), this constellation includes the following:

1. Rapists have a need for control and dominance. The rapist wishes to dominate women or the particular woman whom he has selected as a target.

2. As a related point, rapists often have enduring hostility toward women. These are the angry rapists. For these men, the victim's suffering and resistance are not respected and may intensify the attack.

3. A percentage of men who rape women may have antisocial personalities. However, Koss and Leonard (1984) suggest that this relationship between personality type and rape is weak.

4. More sexually aggressive men are likely to be highly experienced sexually and to view sexuality as a means of establishing their self-worth and as an arena of conquest (see also the preceding discussion of Baumeister's 1997 argument about high self-esteem contribution to violence). These men take advantage of opportunities in being with women to try to seduce them and thereby achieve consensual relationships. They may, however, encounter resistance, in which case they may resort to nonconsensual sexual behavior.

Across a variety of situations, it appears that men misinterpret women's interest in sexual behavior (Muehlenhard, Friedman, & Thomas, 1985). For example, men are likely to think the woman wants sex if the couple goes to the man's apartment "to talk." They are likely to think that the woman wants sex if she asks the man out rather than if he asks her out. Men are more likely to think the woman wants sex if she allows the man to pay all the dating expenses.

In a classic investigation of men's tendency to misread signals about sexuality, Abbey (1982) conducted a study in which female and male strangers talked for a few minutes in an unstructured "get to know others" situation. Later, the men's and women's attributions about friendliness and sexual interest were measured. It was found that males interpreted females' behavior as inviting sexual interest, even though females interpreted their own behavior as simply showing friendliness.

A Real-World Example of Dating Violence

Unfortunately, there are countless stories of real-world dating violence and death. Victoria Crompton has a story to tell and at the same time a crusade to conduct. Years after the event, she tells audiences around the country the story of her daughter Jenny's death. Victoria Crompton's daughter died at age 15 at the hands of her 19-year-old boyfriend, Mark. I first became aware of Victoria's story when she took a graduate class with me.

The story of Jenny's death is a story of a tragic early ending to a very promising life in 1986. It is the story of a first romance—in this case Jenny's and Mark's. It is the story of Mark's attempts to control most parts of Jenny's life—from what she did and how she spent her time to her network of friends. It is the story of Mark's physical and verbal abuse of Jenny, both in private and in public. Ultimately, it is the story of Jenny's attempts to break away from the relationship and Mark's dogged refusal to let her go. Such refusal included Mark's obsessive behavior. He followed Jenny, surreptitiously watched her, broke into her house and school locker, and finally broke into her house and waited there to kill her. His dazed reasoning must have been that if he couldn't have her, no one would. He now serves a life sentence for murder in an Iowa prison. Victoria, Jenny's mother, continues to feel her grief, as do her relatives and her best friend—a young woman who recently got married. Their lives all changed that day in 1986.

Victoria's grief and her resolve to give greater meaning to Jenny's life and death have led her to spend years of her life making presentations about teen dating violence. She said the following in a paper presented in my class:

> My life, since 1986, has been taken over by the topic of Teen Dating Violence. I give approximately 500 speeches per year to high schools, church groups and parent groups. After every speech I am approached by teens who tell me they, too, are being abused. I tell them what signs to look for, how to get out safely, and whom to contact for help. I can sense when a school has a problem, and I can usually identify the victims in the audience. (Crompton, 1993, p. 7)

Sexual Abuse and Revictimization

In no way can this chapter cover in depth the many forms of violence that are pervasive in the world as we enter the 21st century. One topic, however, that is recurrent over time and that requires discussion is sexual abuse and revictimization. Hundreds of thousands of individuals—mostly women but many men, too—currently suffer from the effects of sexual abuse. The revictimization idea is that people who are sexually abused early in their lives may have a strong tendency to be abused later in life.

Krahe' (2000) provides a thorough review of this topic. She notes that the research evidence strongly suggests that women who have been sexually abused as children are also likely to become victims of sexual aggression in later life, relative to women who have not experienced early sexual abuse. Krahe' reports that some of the psychological effects of being sexually molested are depression, loneliness, and suicidal ideation. Many victims show symptoms of posttraumatic stress disorder (PTSD). Behavioral problems, such as sleep disturbances, hyperactivity, and aggression, as well as low self-esteem and feelings of worthlessness or even hopelessness, also are commonly displayed. Victims often attempt to dissociate themselves from the experience of abuse and deny feelings of shame and anger, a coping strategy that makes them susceptible to the development of dissociative personality disorders. Without a lot of work and/or intervention, it has been found that many of these difficulties may extend late into a person's life.

As Barnett, Miller-Perrin, and Perrin (1987) show, the adverse effects of childhood sexual abuse frequently extend into adolescence and adulthood. These effects include depression, interpersonal difficulties, and PTSD symptoms. Sexual revictimization has been studied by Messman and Long (1996), who reviewed 18 studies showing considerable revictimization across college student samples, clinical samples, and community samples.

Why does revictimization occur? As Krahe' (2000) discusses, learning theory would suggest that people learn to associate aggression or satisfaction of an aggressor's needs with sexuality. In the context of abuse in early life and adolescence, women may not learn to take charge of their own sexuality; indeed, they may have no resources or incentives to act for their own good and reject aggression by relatives or close others. A second explanation is that women may become dependent on these types of relationships for affection. Finally, women may show learned helplessness—any way they turn is unsuccessful in removing themselves from the situation or the abuser.

Krahe' (2000) also reviews evidence that indicates that victims of sexual abuse differ from nonvictims in that they tend to be more sexually active. She also found that high levels of sexual activity are associated with an increased risk of sexual victimization. So the victim often becomes embedded in a vicious cycle of abuse that defines her and her life more than any other event or factor. This revictimization also may derive from other harsh circumstances of childhood such as physical and emotional abuse.

Sexual Stigmatization and Violence

Other forms of sexual stigmatization and violence also are evident in our society in the early 21st century. Herek (2000) defines sexual prejudice as all negative attitudes based on sexual orientation, whether the target is homosexual, bisexual, or heterosexual. In general, though, such prejudice is almost always directed at people who engage in homosexual behavior or who label themselves as gay, lesbian, or bisexual. *Homophobia* is the term coined in the 1960s to refer to this type of attitude.

Herek (1997) notes that as of 1996, survey data showed that about 56% of adults sampled in the United States regard homosexual behavior as always wrong. This view often is correlated with fundamentalist religious orientations and with conservative political views. Explanations for sexual prejudice include the following factors: unpleasant (though often brief) interactions with gays; in-group norms and attitudes that have been inculcated by the individual; and the view that gay behavior and communities are in direct conflict with one's personal value system.

In the late 1990s, the topic of sexual prejudice and hatred became quite prominent in the United States after the brutal killing of gay college student Matthew Shephard in Wyoming. Hate crime laws now have been enacted in some states and cities in the United States. However, as Herek (1997) suggests, there is reason to believe that anti-gay feeling is so deep in the United States that lives of gay people may still be endangered in certain regions and in certain types of situations.

Incest: A Fundamental Assault on the Self

As my colleagues and I showed in the 1990s, incest represents a powerful form of sexual violence and stigmatization. There can be no greater stigma associated with the loss of trust in close relationships and the sense of a violated self than that experienced by incest survivors. Over the past few years, Terri Orbuch, Kathleen Chwalisz, Garil Garwood, Susan Davis, Nancy Merbach, and I studied the feelings of more than 100 incest survivors in a series of questionnaire and interview studies conducted in Iowa, Illinois, Michigan, and Colorado. The survivors we interviewed were both females and males, and all had experienced years of sexual abuse by family members, including fathers, mothers, brothers, stepfathers, stepmothers, grandfathers, and uncles. In a few cases, the offending family member also invited outsiders to participate in the sexual abuse. Our respondents were provided with complete anonymity. Their only reason for participating was to provide information that might be of use to other survivors, scholars, and counselors.

Orbuch, Harvey, Davis, and Merbach (1994) reported a study with male survivors of incest that also revealed major psychological dysfunctionality over an extended period on the part of survivors. Shame and deep embarrassment was a theme of these male survivors. A 31-year-old man who had been assaulted by his father and a family friend between the ages of 3 and 7 said, "I suffer from depression constantly, and feel deep inside that I am damaged goods" (p. 260). A man, age 47, told of the damage to his close relationships from incest perpetrated by his father and mother:

> It has affected every portion of my external and internal life. Close relationships? I don't have any, and never have had.... And I've been married for 25 years now! But it is not close, personal or intimate. If anything, it is abusive to me. I don't trust anyone. (p. 260)

A 31-year-old man who had been repeatedly raped by his mother said, "It hurts like hell . . . it's easier to stay sick, stay in denial, commit suicide, stay drunk, or perpetrate the crime onto another victim for relief [than to have to confront it]" (Orbuch et al., 1994, p. 249). A major controversy has developed regarding the so-called false memory accounts of persons who report having been sexually abused by a member of their families. This controversy has pitted supporters of persons making these claims (e.g., Bass & Davis, 1988, in *The Courage to Heal*) against the scholars, attorneys, and defendants contesting them. Psychologist Carol Tavris provided examples of the typical counterarguments in the lead review in the January 3, 1993, *New York Times Book Review*. In this piece, she challenged the claims of therapists and clients about sudden recall of past incest experiences. The sudden recall of incest events occurring many years earlier is sometimes brought about by the use of a controversial technique called regression. Tavris argued that there are strong reasons to believe that people often make up stories (many times unintentionally) as they try to conjure up the past. She reviewed evidence of distortion and false reconstruction in retrospective memory research. She also suggested that the profile of "typical incest survivor" provided by therapists such as Bass and Davis (1988) could apply to almost anyone. In the 1990s, there was at least one civil law suit settled on behalf of the defendant against his daughter and her therapist on the ground that the memories of incest were not real and were induced by the therapist.

I mention the controversy regarding false memory in incest reports in part to distinguish the following reports of stigmatization by incest survivors from this contemporary debate. The names of our respondents were not known, and they were not involved in legal actions concerning their reports. They had to go to great lengths and summon considerable courage just to provide these anonymous reports. These facts make us believe the general details provided by the survivors, although we did not have the ability to try to verify them.

Why do incest survivors frequently feel terribly violated and stigmatized? They often feel this way because the incest occurred when they were quite young and could not talk about it. Beyond that, sometimes persons in their families to whom they attempted to confide shut them out and told them that breathing a word to anyone would destroy the family. Thus, they had to go into a shell for sometimes decades before they found the courage—usually through therapy—to begin to discuss the incest and confront their perpetrators, if the perpetrators were still alive. Following is what one female survivor in her 30s told the research team of Harvey, Orbuch, Chwalisz, and Garwood (1991):

> The first time I revealed the abuse [by her brother between the ages of 8 to 18] was to a state agency and my parents when I was 12. The agency concluded it was normal sibling curiosity. My parents reacted with anger towards me, yelling about my brother's reputation if it should get around town. Their reactions left me feeling totally isolated and alone. Forcing me to be victimized for another four years. (p. 526)

Thus, having to "keep the secret" can literally be deadly to survivors. In *The Helper's Journey,* Dale Larson (1993) provides a detailed discussion of the long-term consequences of keeping dark secrets. He argues that people who avoid coming out for a long period after the loss often show high negative self-images and use words such as "weak," "frightened," and "shameful" to describe their behavior and self-concept. Avoidance and denial are natural strategies that may have short-run effectiveness, as when the individual simply cannot bear to confront reality in any way. Avoidance and denial can also be unconscious process that, by definition, occur outside a person's awareness. Over the long run, however, such strategies appear to be far less effective than actively working through the secret's meaning. Even if it hurts like hell and it feels like it is easier to commit suicide, as suggested in a quote in this section, the only way to heal and relieve one's pain is through the active process of opening up and confronting one's experiences in the context of caring interaction with others. Over time, the survivor usually tries to create meaning and develops a story in her or his mind. Then the critical step is talking about that story and confiding in caring others.

What came through in a profound way in the Harvey et al. (1991) incest study was the importance of caring empathy on the part of the person or persons in whom a survivor attempts to confide. When the confiding attempt occurred relatively soon after the event and when it was met with empathy, the survivor was able to begin the healing process and usually suffered far less psychologically in subsequent years. When there was little empathy, the burden of the secret and associated stigma could not be confronted and hence continued to take its toll on the survivor. For example, another woman survivor in her 40s who had been sworn to secrecy said of her life after being raped by her father, stepfather, and uncles when she was between 5 and 10 years of age,

> I cannot have a close relationship with a man only as a friend, because I hate to be touched sometimes. And they think I'm having sex with another man because I get this way. I try to explain about my past, but they say that's over. It shouldn't bother me anymore. If only it was them instead of me. . . . I often cannot sleep and when I do I have dreams [of the rape events] and wake up in a cold sweat. (Harvey et al., 1991, p. 527)

Violence Perpetrated by Children

The United States made news internationally in 1998 and 1999 after several schoolyard shootings publicized the fact that guns are very common in America. Kids have access to them (and sometimes are well practiced in using them), and kids often use guns to kill other kids, even in the schools. Interestingly, the killings that made headlines were not in urban areas or on the streets of America where gang warfare and drive-by shootings are seen as endemic to areas of urban impoverishment.

Killings occurred in 1998 in school settings in Jonesboro, Arkansas; Pearl, Mississippi; Springfield, Oregon; and Paducah, Kentucky. In April 1999, the most deadly of the shootings (involving a variety of types of weapons and 30 bombs and in which 15 people were killed, including the perpetrators) occurred in Littleton, Colorado. The Colorado killings were followed by "copycat" threats in several schools and the wounding of several students in a school in Georgia 1 month after the Littleton killings. The copycat incidents (e.g., calling in bomb threats, kids caught bringing guns to school apparently with the intent of using them) were particularly worrisome because they occurred throughout the country. In Michigan, less than 1 month after the Colorado killings, four 12- to 14-year-old boys were charged with plotting a shooting at their middle school. They apparently had planned a massacre of students that would top the death toll of the April massacre in Littleton, Colorado.

The killings in Oregon involved a 15-year-old boy who walked into the school cafeteria in May 1998 and opened fire on his fellow students, murdering two of them and injuring many others. Later that day, police went to this boy's home and found his parents lying dead on the floor— they were also victims of his violence. An investigation of the 15-year-old killer's background showed that he had an obsession with guns and explosives, a history of abusing animals (a trait that scholars in the domestic abuse area have found to be correlated with abuse of humans), and a nasty temper when crossed. When police examined his room, they found two pipe bombs, three larger bombs, and bomb-making recipes that he had downloaded from the Internet. Clearly, some signs were present in this young person's life to suggest serious problems, but how can we predict that the person will act on his anger and commit murder? Could his parents or teachers have taken some steps to prevent these drastic actions?

Much speculation has been made about the "whys" of this phenomenon. Do the kids lack a moral conscience ("Moral Poverty," as one headline said)? Do their parents teach them right from wrong? (Quite often the parents have been regular church attendees and have claimed they imparted religious wisdom to their children.) Is it revenge for lost love or striking back against bullies (as was suggested in a couple of the killings)? Is it an act of high or low self-esteem (see earlier debate between Baumeister and Staub about the role of self-esteem in violence)? Gary Melton, in a report in the *APA Monitor* noted that "one in five gun owners say they use [guns] to get respect or to instill fear."[2] Such attitudes may be readily transmitted from the adult gun owner to a child who lives in the house and sees the owner use and store the weapon.

Kathleen Heide (1995, 1999), a criminologist at the University of South Florida who has studied 100 young murderers, stresses the role of children's rage over everyday conflicts as a central dynamic in their violence. She believes that the signs of building hatred or a desire for revenge on the part of kids can be readily spotted and encourages teachers, parents, and caretakers to intervene and help children learn the arts of discussion, negotiation, and reconciliation as ways of dealing with conflict. Of course, no one believes that guns will go away in this country. Thus, this criminologist's recommendations may be the best we have for now.

According to news reports, the two teenage killers in the Littleton Colorado shootings were possibly reacting to a long-simmering feud.[3] They supposedly traveled in a small group ("the Trench Coat Mafia"), idolized Adolf Hitler, and were in a war of words and acts (name-calling that had occurred for years before the violence) with some of the school's athletes. Experts on school violence indicate that as a step toward prevention, family and school personnel should be alert to the following warning signs of imminent major violence: lack of remorse (no expression of regret for harmful acts), sudden secrecy, cruelty to animals, a "need to win" (see Baumeister's argument), defiance and combativeness, and changes in friends.

Loss and Grief Resulting From War

Wars do not end when the shooting stops. They live on in the lives of those who are veterans of those wars. They live on in the lives of those who are the survivors and the dependents of those who lost their lives in war. (Clelland, 1982, p. 3)

The preceding quote is from Max Clelland's book, *Strong at the Broken Places.* Loss and grief resulting from war are experiences that can traumatize survivors, both those involved directly and families who lose loved ones in war. In the wake of serving in combat, soldiers frequently experience posttraumatic stress disorder (PTSD). The symptoms of this disorder are numerous but include feelings, thoughts, and behavior that are similar to those shown by persons exhibiting signs of serious bereavement (Kuenning, 1990). Specifically, persons showing PTSD symptoms often report the following problems:

- Depression
- Anger
- Anxiety
- Sleep disturbances
- Tendency to react under stress with survival tactics
- Psychic or emotional numbing
- Emotional constriction
- Loss of interest in work and activities
- Survivor guilt
- Hyperalertness
- Avoidance of activities that arouse trauma memories
- Suicidal feelings and thoughts
- Flashbacks of war or death scenes
- Interpersonal difficulties

Of these symptoms, the "cardinal symptom domains of PTSD" are reexperiencing the traumatic event, numbing, avoidance, and hyperarousal. Such symptoms have been related to reports of greater health impairment; that is, PTSD core symptoms may mediate reports of poor health (Kimerling, Clum, & Wolfe, 2000).

General symptoms of PTSD may continue for years. These symptoms also may not begin to appear for months, or even years, after the traumatic event. For some, the memories will never fade in their lifetime. These types of experiences associated with PTSD sometimes involve such great trauma that one cannot imagine anyone surviving it.

When Y. C. Lindsay, now 73, was a young soldier in 1941 he was captured by the Japanese when 20,000 American troops defending Bataan Island were overwhelmed by 150,000 Japanese troops. He then survived the 1942 Bataan Death March, a forced march of prisoners involving thousands of deaths in the Philippines. Later he and thousands of other prisoners were shipped to Japan. The trauma he experienced could be compared with that of Holocaust survivors.

In May 1994, he described part of his experience to reporter Mike Patty of the *Rocky Mountain News*.[4] Lindsay said that the Japanese troops loaded 1,200 of the U.S. prisoners in the hold of a ship. They were packed in so tight that one man could not sit down unless another man stood up. They were in that hold for 39 days. Eventually enough people died so that everybody could sit down, but there never was enough room to lie down during the whole 39 days. He said that an American torpedo missed their ship by about 9 feet, but the prisoners just didn't care. At night, it was totally black down in the hold, and they could hear the sonar ping against the hull, the torpedoes going off, and the Japanese dropping depth charges. They were only getting about a cup of water a day to drink. Lindsay said that he hoped a torpedo would hit them so the cool water would come in. As an example of the possible long-term effect of traumatic wartime experiences and the way that environmental cues can trigger traumatic reactions, Tick (1991) told of a client who had not heard a Joe Cocker love song with the lyric "the great relief of having you to talk to" since his service in Vietnam. But 20 years later while he was driving down the road, he had a dramatic reaction to hearing that song. He pulled over and started to cry. Then that night, many aspects of his Vietnam experience came back rushing to him, as he explained, "It was everything—the guys I left behind, the brothers I had over there who were the only people in the world I could talk to because the others would never understand" (p. 30).

It appears that the individuals who are most susceptible to PTSD symptoms have often been involved in the most gruesome experiences that can be encountered in war (Sutker, Uddo, Brailey, Vasterling, & Errera, 1994). For example, as reported later, a significant experience for many combat troops landing at Normandy on D-Day, 1944, was the sight of countless corpses littering the beach accompanied by the cries of men in agony because of injuries. These macabre experiences were vividly recalled 50 years later, and the veterans reporting them indicated that they had spent a lifetime trying to deal with such sights and sounds—whether by trying to suppress them, getting counseling, or talking about their experience with other veterans and confidants. Another example studied by Sutker et al. (1994) was the PTSD displayed by troops assigned grave registration duties (which involved the intimate handling of bodies of dead soldiers) during the Gulf War of 1991. They found PTSD rates of 48% among those who had such duties compared with no PTSD among soldiers in a sample of veterans who were not deployed to combat.

Vietnam

There were more than 58,000 American casualties and more than 2 million Vietnamese casualties in the Vietnam War. The losses and grief resulting from the Vietnam War are particularly daunting because of the magnitude of these losses but also because of the very particular characteristics of that war. These characteristics combined to make the losses and grief resulting from Vietnam greater than most people recognized for many years after the end of combat in the mid-1970s. Not until the mid-1980s, at least a decade after the formal cease-fire and 20 years after the intense period of combat, did the American public begin to give proper credence to the losses of Vietnam veterans. Then, many of them, as well as many of us, began to come out and grieve openly. The catalysts for this development were the creation of the Vietnam Wall in the early 1980s and mid-1980s movies such as Oliver Stone's *Platoon,* which displayed the terror of the combat and death in the Vietnam War.

As Kuenning (1990) contends, the Vietnam War was different for a number of reasons, including the following:

- The average age of soldiers was 19, compared with 26 in World War II.
- The largest segment of troops who served in Vietnam came from working-class and poor backgrounds; African Americans served in Vietnam in disproportionate numbers.

- Compared with motivation for serving in previous wars, motivations for serving in Vietnam varied but often did not involve patriotism. It was unclear to many there and in the United States why the war was being fought.
- There were few if any front lines in Vietnam. Guerrilla warfare, battling Viet Cong and civilians, in miserable weather under extraordinarily difficult conditions characterized much of the war.
- A tour of duty in Vietnam was set at 1 year. This shorter length of time than in previous wars was designed to reduce the number of psychological casualties. Also, troops usually did not go to Vietnam as part of units in which soldiers had spent quite a bit of time together and began to form close bonds. Rather, soldiers went to war and came home alone.

After returning home, soldiers were not given a period of decompression and debriefing. It was common for an infantryman to be on duty in the Vietnam jungle early in a week and back in his hometown visiting with family and friends later in that same week. Such changes were mind-boggling and made the war and its psychic toll seem less than real to these young men. Also, they encountered in the American public an element of vehement opposition to the war—opposition that in the later stages extended to military personnel as well. Paulson (1991), in describing his return home from the war, said,

I felt as if I had ruined my entire life, and I was only 22. I had nowhere to go, no one to explain what had happened to me, and no emotional support. I could only suffer and feel the pain, deep pain. It was not until ten years later, after much psychotherapy, that I could even begin to integrate my war experience positively into my life. (p. 158)

Brende and Parson (1985) report another veteran's homecoming experience that further reveals the confusion and ambivalence that existed between loved ones and the veteran about what the veteran had done in Vietnam:

I got back about 6:00 in the morning. Everybody was asleep. They got up, welcomed me back. I got a few hugs and kisses. The whole scene lasted 15 minutes. . . . They went to bed. Next morning my sisters went to school as usual. . . . Everything seemed the same to them. . . . I felt nervous, tense, jittery. . . . So I walked down to the package store and bought me some liquor to help me out. . . . In spite of all of my efforts to avoid having anyone see me, a long-time friend saw me and really welcomed me home. It was really nice. Then, like out of nowhere, six guys showed up on the scene; I knew most of them. They wanted to know about the good dope in Vietnam. They also wanted to know what it was like having sex with Vietnamese women. One of them yelled out, "How many babies have you burned, man? Yea, you killers, man you heard me." Before I knew it the cops were there. I had beaten up four guys severely. . . . I had done a lot of killing in 'Nam; I just wanted to be left alone. (p. 50)

A final set of factors that figured in the avoidance of dealing with the losses of the Vietnam War were the atrocities that occurred. Well-known instances of American troops slaughtering Vietnamese civilians occurred (e.g., the My Lai massacre). Also, the fact that the enemy often were civilians, including children and elderly, meant that it was common for suspected but innocent civilians to be killed by American troops. The U.S. practice of indexing its military successes in terms of "body counts" also dehumanized the enemy and provided a crass basis for the promotion of officers who were involved in the greatest number of killings. "Waste them" was almost an official policy term applied to the Vietnamese enemy as well as the earth, as Agent Orange and napalm were used extensively. Veterans have expressed grief and guilt about their involvement in America's unclear and at times contradictory war policy. The American forces also used the term "waste them" in reference to their own dead. Body bags were the order of the day after heavy combat, and many a veteran is still terrified at the memory of putting a friend's remains in a "baggie" or of having to identify the remains of friends in body bags. By their language, they transformed the dead bodies of their comrades and enemy into piles of waste—which were in the midst of a much larger wastage. This language made it much easier, then, to deal with the losses. Later, however, the soldiers could not so readily dismiss their losses and pass over their grieving by the magic of language.

It is important to note that many veterans of this war never "came home," in the sense that they never returned to the satisfying, secure lives they may have experienced prior to going away. It has been estimated that as many as 30% of the homeless in this country are Vietnam veterans (Kuenning, 1990). Thousands of veterans have been imprisoned or are on parole. Tens of thousands have had or have serious drug or alcohol addiction problems. Thousands have committed suicide (one Washington, D.C. policeman went to the Wall to take his life in an act symbolic of the Wall's sacredness to veterans).

Why all these consequences? Compared with those who fought in World War II, the Vietnam veteran carried an immense burden of guilt and feelings of unnecessary loss—of friends, health, and time. Dealing with this package was beyond the resources of many men. In their minds, homelessness, crime, and addiction may have appeared to be the only recourse available to them. Many felt as if they were not welcome at home. Many others are still trying valiantly, sometimes unsuccessfully, to deal with the residual horror of this war.

Many veterans encountered lukewarm receptions and rejection upon returning home from people that had previously been close to them. Brende and Parson (1985) report the following fairly typical story told to them by a veteran:

> After a short while, my girlfriend told me she didn't know how to relate to me; or how she really felt about me now. I had expected things to be the way they were; but they weren't. She said she thought I had been killed in the war, because I stopped writing to her. Honestly, I didn't know how to relate to her now either. I dreaded going to bed with her; I just didn't know how I'd do. She said that I wasn't the loving guy she used to know and love, that something horrible must have happened to me over there to change me so completely. . . . She said that the look in my eyes was the look of a deeply terrorized person. . . . She also mentioned that my frightened look . . . my aloofness, you name it . . . made her too uncomfortable to continue our relationship.
>
> She said that besides, she had found somebody else anyway. That really hurt me; it burned me up inside to hear this.
>
> When it came to my family, my mother told me that I wasn't as considerate and sweet as I used to be. My dad felt I wasn't as diligent and committed as he remembered me to be prior to Vietnam. I didn't know what any of these people were saying. I knew I was getting pissed off more and more by hearing all this bullshit, I know that. (p. 46)

Losses and grief deriving from the Vietnam War that only recently have been given national attention are those experienced by the women who served in Vietnam—nurses and Red Cross workers. Many of these women also experienced PTSD symptoms. They too were hurt, angry, and lonely and experienced little emotional support after their service in Vietnam. In 1993, a memorial in the form of a statue showing women assisting wounded soldiers was placed near the Vietnam Wall in Washington, D.C. This step, along with the greater public acknowledgment of their role in taking care of the dead and dying, has contributed much to their own recovery from this war.

Finally, although the losses from Vietnam continue to haunt this nation, Kuenning (1990) quotes Stewart Brown, a Vet Center leader in California, who had this perspective on what the Vietnam War may have given some of the combat veterans who returned: "I think Vietnam combat veterans are much more in touch with important issues of the human experience than the American population in general. This is because veterans experienced life and death in a magnified, graphic form" (p. 334).

Normandy Stories

No one was prepared for this scene from hell.

German machine guns opened up on us when the ramp went down. Several men in front of me were killed. The water was bloody. It was bright red.

The second quote above is a comment made by Harold Baumgarten on his experience as one of the first troops to land in Normandy on June 6, 1944. He was a 19-year-old rifleman with the 116th Infantry Regiment of the U.S. Army 29th Division. In this section, excerpts from stories reported to me in June 1994 by veterans and family members of survivors of D-Day, 1944, the Allied invasion of France, are presented to sketch some of the feelings of horror and loss experienced by soldiers who were among the first to hit the beaches in Normandy. Thousands of people from the United States (30,000 veterans alone), Great Britain, and all over the world assembled along the Normandy beaches in June 1994 to commemorate the 50th anniversary of D-Day.

Many of the veterans and family members were in their 70s and 80s. They were coming to Normandy for one final search for meaning related to the most dramatic event of their lives. They were coming to grieve again and to try to attain a greater completion of their own individual stories surrounding the events of five decades earlier. Many were coming to share their lifelong pain and sorrow with other people who had experienced a similar type of pain and sorrow.

It was reported on *Gettysburg*, a 1994 program on the Discovery Channel, that in the early part of the 20th century, thousands of veterans of the U.S. Civil War made a similar journey to Gettysburg, Pennsylvania, to commemorate the 50th anniversary of that deadly engagement between the Union and Confederate armies. As if to attest to the significance of this reunion and the psychological fulfillment and meaning it signified, many of these men were reported to have died on their return trips home after the Gettysburg reunion.

I went to Normandy to interview veterans and their families about their losses and grief over the 50 years since the Normandy invasion (Harvey, Stein, & Scott, 1995). The stories that were collected from Normandy veterans and relatives of soldiers killed at Normandy contain a range of emotions. Almost all of them point to the necessity of the sacrifice of life to defeat Hitler. Many of them speak with great sadness and sometimes anger about the loss of thousands of young men during the early hours of the assault. Confusion and faulty predictions of the obstacles in landing were common. For example, many troops and tanks were put out of the landing craft too far out at sea to make it to shore. Prior bombing of German installations, particularly above Omaha Beach, had not disengaged machine gun placements that took huge tolls on the early waves of troops landing. Warren Rulien, then a 24-year-old private with the 116th Regiment of the 1st Division said that he was almost enthusiastic about hitting the beach. But as they got nearer to the shore, German bullets began hitting the sides of the landing craft. The ramp was lowered, and he stepped off into water up to his chest. He lost his balance and dropped his rifle. They had been told the Navy Seabees were going ahead of them to get rid of the mines in the water. But the mines were still there, sticking six feet out of the water on steel rails, and there were Navy men floating dead in the water. He took one of the bodies that was floating—and pushed it in front of him toward the shore. He figured that he could not do anything to help the poor guy and his body would stop bullets. Landing crafts were continuing to bring in waves of soldiers and they were bunching up on shore, taking shelter behind a three-foot-high seawall. In short, they were being slaughtered.

All told, however, stories from Normandy reveal more acceptance, healing, and less continuing turbulence in the minds of these World War II combat veterans than do the stories of many Vietnam combat veterans. World War II veterans are approximately 20 to 30 years older than Vietnam War veterans. Compared with the Vietnam veterans, World War II veterans generally had a strong sense of what they were fighting for (i.e., freedom and their way of life) and were given a very positive reception by the American public when they returned home.

This is not to say that World War II veterans escaped a difficult postwar adjustment and even PTSD-type effects. As one Normandy veteran said, "I drank every day for 25 years. If I wanted to sleep, I'd go down to the bar and get drunk." Also, many could not hold jobs, and marriages suffered—although in that generation few divorced. One World War II veteran's son described his father as a brooding, guilt-ridden alcoholic who often woke up screaming and shut himself off emotionally from his children. This son said of his father: "He could never love again. He saw too much. His heart was dead."

Unlike soldiers in the Vietnam War, who were randomly assigned to units, World War II soldiers often fought throughout their time in combat with soldiers from the same home city, state, or region. In fact, one of the hardest hit towns in the United States was Bedford, Virginia, a city of about 4,000 people in 1944. More than 90% of 35 soldiers from Bedford were killed in the initial D-Day landing. This large number of deaths for a relatively small town has been associated with an uncommon degree of mourning in Bedford—mourning that has reverberated over 50 years in the lives of the town's residents.[5] One of the only survivors from the Bedford company of soldiers was Robert Sales. In the June 6, 1994 issue of *The Stars and Stripes,* he commented on the loss of so many of his friends from back home.

Sales said that one could not walk without stepping on a body. It was horribly shocking to see the hundreds of men washing in the surf—men he had grown up with, double-dated with, shared a cigarette with, drank out of the same bottle with—lying there dead. Stark faces with eyes and mouths wide open.

Many men who had been among the first troops to go ashore on June 6, 1944, indicated that they recalled certain events from that day quite vividly. A typical commentary about the early landing experience was provided by William Isenberg:

> There was direct fire coming down at us. We suffered heavy casualties. There were a helluva lot of flashes, a lot of noise, a lot of people on the beach yelling. We were all scared and trying not to show it.
>
> I've tried to wash it all out of my mind. I saw a lot of people murdered that day. But I didn't come back to remember that. I came back to visit my brother's grave [his brother was killed in the invasion]. . . . There were a lot of guys who were heroes at D-Day.[6]

A paratrooper who came down in the small French village Ste. Mere-Eglise at the beginning of the Normandy invasion spoke of the terror of hanging in the night air while being shot at by the Germans. He said that when he landed he saw three of his buddies with their parachutes ensnared, one on a tree and two on poles. Each of them had been killed as they hung there. He said the image reminded him of Christ on the cross. At the church in the center of this city, a model of paratrooper John Steele still hangs from one of the church steeples. His parachute was caught there swaying in the wind. He played dead and was later rescued by American troops. With the vivid image of the paratrooper hanging from the church steeple, Ste. Mere-Eglise now stands as a sacred ground of memory and healing for American and British paratroopers—a place that symbolizes great loss but also great courage. The following quote is from a scroll presented by President Franklin Roosevelt to Mr. and Mrs. Joseph Shimon whose son Joseph Jr. was killed in World War II:

> He stands in the unbroken line of patriots who have dared to die that freedom might live and grow and increase its blessings. Freedom lives, and through it, he lives—in a way that humbles the undertakings of most men.

Conclusion: Finding Peace After
the Ravages of War and Violence

My contribution might have been small, but I walked in the company of very brave men.

This quote is from a veteran reflecting back on being among the first to land on Omaha Beach. Another veteran said the following after visiting the vast U.S. cemetery above Omaha Beach that contains more than 9,000 graves of U.S. soldiers: "I'm all wept out. I can't weep anymore." As we talked with Normandy veterans and family members of those who died on D-Day, it became obvious that this media-hyped, worldwide 50-year recognition was something that they valued greatly. So many spoke of the courage of their buddies who did not return. One veteran commented about the courage it took to continue moving up the beaches and cliffs straight into the teeth of enemy fire:

We were afraid but were able to overcome our fear because we knew we were doing something for a noble cause . . .
    Thinking of another human being more than you think of yourself—that is courage—the capacity to give one's life for another. (Rene Dussaq, now 83, former paratrooper)

These anniversary events have given younger generations much more perspective on "D-Day's dreadful morning." In so doing, the commemorations seemed to give new life, meaning, and hope to thousands of returning veterans, kin, and close friends who have grieved their losses—sometimes in obscurity—for half a century. These events, which included 85-year-old former paratroopers again jumping out of airplanes—to salute their fallen comrades—were cathartic, rejuvenating, and redeeming for many veterans and survivors. Now, new meaning was attached to the fact that thousands of 18-year-old boys lost their lives very soon after they stepped off a landing boat in the choppy sea off Omaha Beach in the wee hours of June 6, 1944. It served as a living statement that might have read,

We remember you gave your life for us. It is time to honor those who gave their lives and those who returned but who also gave much including a prime part of their youth for their country. We are grateful.

Indeed, Normandy veterans and family survivors have their "Wall" now, even more firmly in place than before. It is their image of those beaches, cliffs, bodies, and confusion. It is their image of our collective remembering. For those who returned in actuality and for those who returned in their minds only, this was a rite of passage, a completion of their moment in destiny—not unlike the return of the Gettysburg veterans to that fabled battleground early in the 20th century.

Vietnam veterans also slowly are finding more peace. *USA TODAY*'s Copy Desk Chief Don Ross went back to Vietnam in 1994 where he had served as a young marine in 1969. He said that nothing had prepared him for the feelings he experienced on his return—the sights and sounds whipped his emotions from anger to compassion to pride in having served.[7]

He told of his trip to find the "Valley of Death," the Khe Sanh combat base in central Vietnam (a base that underwent a savage 77-day siege in which 20,000 marines were surrounded by as many as 40,000 North Vietnamese soldiers). Ross said that in 1994 the only reminder of what occurred was the landscape. Although foliage had covered some scars, the terrain was riddled with craters and holes. Many were from bombs and artillery shells. As Ross stood on the former airstrip, a young man diligently working a metal-detector passed. Twenty-six years later the ground still yielded an occasional artifact of war.

Ross went on to say that life had taken many different turns in those years since the war. But he wondered—not with regret—how different his life might have been, how different it would be now, had not events here in some measure, at least, inspired him to enlist. In concluding his deep thoughts on a dreary day, he gave a salute to those marines who had fought there and who had died there and said, "You are not forgotten, by brothers" (1994, p. 1A).

Ross also tells of a train trip in a dimly lighted berth with two North Vietnamese men, one of whom had served in the North Vietnamese army. In a touching encounter, he tells of the ex-soldier taking out four cans of 333 brand beer from his suitcase and sharing them with Ross and a younger Vietnamese man. Ross said that this man, whom he once would have tried to kill on a field of battle, raised his beer in a toast: "To friends." As the train pulled into Danang, Mr. Thong (the former soldier) pointedly asked him why he had made this trip by train. Thong's implication was clear: Ross could have afforded the quicker and more comfortable plane. Ross said, "So I could meet people like you, my friend." Ross concluded that he was very glad he took the train.

Unfortunately, many Vietnam veterans have not and will not find the peace that Don Ross seems to be finding. One who tried valiantly but who couldn't make it was Lewis Puller, Jr. Puller was the only son of legendary Marine General Lewis "Chesty" Puller, Sr. Lewis Puller, Jr. was a Marine lieutenant in Vietnam who lost his legs and parts of both hands after stepping on a booby-trap howitzer round in 1968. He inspired fellow vets with his 1991 Pulitzer Prize-winning autobiography *Fortunate Son* (Puller, 1991), a chronicle of his recovery from depression and alcoholism stemming from his experience in Vietnam. But his depression recurred, as the physical and psychological pain of his losses kept coming back. Senator Bob Kerrey of Nebraska, who lost his right leg in Vietnam and who was close to Puller, said that in the end he could not fight his way out of the deep, dark hole of personal terror (which also included estrangement from his wife of 26 years). In May 1994, Puller shot and killed himself while at home alone. In commenting on his death, *People* magazine reported,

> Puller's sad end seemed to support the belief of many veterans' groups—though no hard statistics are available to back up the claim—that Vietnam vets are committing suicide in alarming numbers. "There are 58,000 names on the Wall in Washington," says Jan Scruggs, a founder of the Vietnam Veteran Memorial. "Probably more than twice as many veterans have committed suicide as were killed in the war."[8]

A March 24, 2000, report by Knight Ridder Newspapers regarding the long-needed restoration of a 217-foot-tall tower in Kansas City that honors World War I veterans posed the following question: Will we forget what the veterans did for us? This report pointed out that only 1,000 of America's 4.5 million World War I veterans are still living. It was accompanied by a news article on World War II veterans, who are dying on the order of approximately 3,000 per month. Many of these vets die alone. According to this report, a Veterans of Foreign War spokesperson stated, "People just forget about them."

Notes

1. From an obituary on the life of Thomas Ferebee, bombardier on the plane Tibbets flew, in *The Economist*, March 12, 2000.
2. From "People," in *APA Monitor*, June 1998, p. 59.
3. From an article by Kenneth Johnson and Larry Copeland in *USA TODAY*, April 22, 1999, p. 1.
4. From *Rocky Mountain News*, May 26, 1994, p. 36A.
5. "For Tiny Town, Innocence Lost," Andrea Stone, *USA TODAY*, April 28, 1994, p. 5A.
6. Quotations from World War II veterans are from interviews with the author.
7. From *USA TODAY*, May 26, 1994, p. 1A.
8. From *People Magazine*, May 30, 1994, p. 68.

9 The Holocaust and Genocide

We have only one task, to stand and pitilessly to lead this race-battle. . . .
The reputation for horror and terror which preceded us we want never to
allow to diminish. The world may call us what it will.

—Heinrich Himmler, 1943
(quoted in Overy, 1997, p. 99)

This quotation reflects the raison d'être of the perpetrators of the Holocaust. The Holocaust was a form of genocide. Genocide may be defined as an attempt to systematically eliminate a whole group of people or a nation. In killing approximately 6 million Jews in Europe (of a total of approximately 11 million), the Nazis set a standard of atrocity the likes of which the world had never previously experienced. In the past decade, stories of genocide from Rwanda in Africa or Kosovo in Serbia still cannot match the systematic character of the persecution of the Jews by the Nazis. It should be noted also that the Nazis systematically killed approximately .5 million to 1 million Gypsies, starting in 1939, even earlier than their program to exterminate the Jews of Europe.

This coverage reflects a broad-scale type of multiple-loss event that was noted as part of the loss and trauma spectrum in Chapter 1. The purpose of this chapter is to sketch some of these loss and trauma aspects. Many survivors (and families of survivors) of the Holocaust suffered incredible losses related to self-identify. Many Holocaust survivors also incurred PTSD-like experiences throughout their lives as a result of their trauma. At the same time, others (e.g., Frankl, 1959) found positive qualities within themselves in their horrific experiences. Some experienced a deeper recognition of the durability of the human spirit, which they could then share with others who might be influenced by their affirmations and courage. The story of the Holocaust is one that has layers of divergent realities and perceptions and so any one account is necessarily incomplete. The purpose of this chapter is to touch on some of these diverse realities.

The Holocaust may be defined as the systematic killing of approximately 6 million Jews by the Nazis in death camps and in other settings from late 1939 well into 1945. The incredibly zealous hate that caused the death of so many people during the Holocaust is illustrated by the fact that well after the liberation of Europe by the Allies in 1944, the Nazis were still shipping Jews and others to concentration camps for slaughter. Anne Frank died in August 1944, well after D-Day on June 6, 1944 and well after the Allies had liberated Paris and stood ready to invade Germany. German soldiers had to know that their cause had been defeated; yet up to a million people were still deported to death camps during this period from late 1944 until the war ended in the spring of 1945. How could any group of human beings be so programmed that even after the certainty of the defeat of their cause they would still go to great lengths to brutalize and kill innocent people? This reality is beyond the pale of understanding well over a half-century after the Holocaust.

Described by Hitler as the "final solution of the Jewish question," the Holocaust also involved the systematic killing of Gypsies, German intellectuals and political socialists and dissidents, homosexuals, and prisoners of various national origins. The Holocaust murders were mainly carried out by gassing prisoners, whose bodies were then burned in crematoriums. Early in the Holocaust, however, the Nazis killed people mainly by shooting them. The gas cha...bers were developed after Nazi commanders and Adolf Eichmann, the head of the SS division responsible for final solution activities, discovered that even elite SS soldiers carrying out the summary executions were showing what we would refer to as PTSD-like symptoms associated with their work (Wiedza, 1993). And "their work" involved killing very young children, the very old, and the disabled. Were these well-indoctrinated SS troops subject to pangs of guilt and a trace of conscience in consideration of their unconscionable acts? It is entirely possible!

Auschwitz: Symbol of Evil

Subsequent discussion of the Holocaust may be assisted by taking a look at Auschwitz, one of the deadliest of the Nazi death camps. As described by Wiedza (1993), Auschwitz was not the first of the hundreds of Nazi concentration camps scattered throughout Central and Eastern Europe, but it was without doubt the most infamous. Auschwitz opened in June 1940, 7 years after the development of the concentration camp system, which occurred shortly after the Nazis took power in Germany in 1933.

Why was Auschwitz so infamous? Because more people were murdered there than in any other camp—approximately 1 million. And because it represented the efficiency of murder perfected by the Nazis. Brought in the cattle cars of trains from all parts of occupied Europe, from as far away as Norway and Greece, the majority of the prisoners were murdered immediately upon arrival. Of those killed, 90% were Jewish. The "selections" were mostly designed to skim off a relative few prisoners who were deemed healthy enough to work for the war cause; all others were not deemed worthy of life. If one was not immediately killed, the average life span in the camp was 6 months. The prisoners who were not killed immediately died of starvation, disease, the rigors of hard labor, beatings, torture, and summary execution—by shooting, hanging, or gassing. As many as a thousand people a day from 1940 to 1945 were killed. When the camp was liberated by the Soviet Army in 1945, only 7,000 totally emaciated people were found alive. These features are what make the stories of any survivor of Auschwitz so valuable.

As Wiedza (1993) describes, Auschwitz (and its later extension to include another camp 2 miles away, Birkenau) became the most efficient death camp because of its massive gas chambers and crematoriums. This technique of industrialized mass murder allowed the Nazis to kill up to 2,000 in a 10- to 20-minute period. The efficiency theme was continued in the crematoriums in that victims' hair was cut off and their fillings and false teeth made of precious metals were removed for use by the Nazi war machine. After the liberation, 7 tons of hair were found in the camp's warehouses.

Lane, Goldman, and Hunt (1954) contend that Auschwitz was set up as the greatest killing field in the system of Nazi death camps because it was in the countryside of Poland (about 100 miles from Warsaw). Thus, it was far removed from the lives of German citizens, who presumably had only a faint knowledge of the depth and breadth of the Nazi regime's atrocities. Furthermore, it is possible that the non-Jewish Polish citizens of that region were, in effect, helpers of the Nazis by being knowledgeable but inactive bystanders (see later discussion of Goldhagen's, 1996, related thesis) or even by assisting the Nazis in identifying Jews and helping carry out the functions of the camp.

What was life like in Auschwitz for prisoners? Prisoners slept in double bunk beds or on the floor, and as many as 800 prisoners were crowded into a space that had been designed for 52 horses; prisoners usually could not move after bedding down for the night. Lavatories were extremely primitive and few in number. Washing facilities were likewise grossly insufficient. Changes of clothing were available only every few months; clothes were always infested with lice. Periodic delousings offered little relief and constituted a further form of torture.

Prisoners awoke at 4:30 a.m. Each day was an unmitigated series of sufferings. This suffering was so extreme that Frankl (1959) wrote that prisoners sought psychological relief mainly at night in their dreams. After a breakfast that consisted of half a liter of a lukewarm liquid that the SS called coffee, the prisoners were driven to work. "Work" meant slave labor in factories, mines, farming operations, and construction— almost all done without equipment. Prisoners, although clearly near death, were forced to carry bricks or push wheelbarrows on the run. The return from work was a terrible sight because the exhausted prisoners had to carry back to the camps the bodies of those who had died during work that day. Even dead bodies had to be present at roll call, which began immediately after the return of the prisoners. The SS deliberately prolonged the roll call to more than an hour as another torment. One roll call on July 6, 1940 lasted 19 hours—and it was not an isolated event! Furthermore, prisoners were often executed at roll call. After the roll call, prisoners got a meal of a small piece of bread, some lard, and sometimes a small piece of salted pork.

Wiedza (1993) states that it is almost impossible to present what happened at Auschwitz in ordinary language. It was not an everyday place. The events and sheer quantity of the atrocities committed defy imagination.

Holocaust Testimonies

> The Holocaust defies literature. . . . We think we are describing an event, we transmit only its reflection. No one has the right to speak for the dead. . . . Still the story had to be told. In spite of all risks, all possible misunderstandings. It needed to be told for the sake of our children. (Weisel, 1960, p. 51)

> The response to *Schindler's List* is proof that the most offensive word in any language is *forget*.[1]

The first quotation is by Elie Weisel, Holocaust survivor and author of important works about the Holocaust. Another quotation that hints at the meaning of the Holocaust in terms of the memory of it is from Lawrence Langer while describing his book *Holocaust Testimonies: The Ruins of Memory* (Langer, 1991): "Holocaust memory is an insomniac faculty whose mental eyes have never slept." The purpose of Langer's book is consistent with Weisel's argument that the Holocaust story must be told. Langer explored how survivors of the Nazi death camps remember the horror of their experience. He asked whether silence would be better. Perhaps for the survivor, because it would spare them much pain; but because memory functions with or without speech, it is difficult to see how not telling the survivor's story could ease that person's distress. Langer asserted that memory cannot be silenced; it might as well be heard.

Langer said that he believed a main effect of these testimonies is to begin to undo a negation—the principle of discontinuity that argues that an impassable chasm permanently separates the seriously interested auditor and observer from the experiences of the former Holocaust victim. Although grim, Langer's analysis paints a very real picture of the survivor, one that cannot be wiped out by time and distance.

Langer's (1991) work is based on hundreds of videotaped interviews in the Holocaust Archive at Yale University. He referred to the type of memory under study as that of "deep memory," which tries to recall the self as he or she existed in the camps, as opposed to "common memory," which attempts to link the self with the present. The Yale Archive was supplemented in the late 1990s by another video archive of interviews being done by *Schindler's List* Director Steven Spielberg. Spielberg is using his project to educate young people about the Holocaust by taking the videos to schools across the United States.

The stories Langer extracts show confusion, doubt, and moral uncertainty. There is survivor guilt: "Why did I survive when so many died?" As Charlotte Delbo's testimony about her nightmarish experience in Auschwitz illustrates, there is immense bleakness in many of these memories (Langer, 1991).

Delbo said that the skin covering the memory of Auschwitz is tough. Sometimes, however, she experienced the bursting of the skin and the memories spilling out. She described a recurring dream in which her will was powerless. In these dreams, she sees herself there again: pierced with cold, filthy, gaunt, and feeling unbearable pain. The pain was exactly the pain she suffered there; she felt it again physically. She felt it again through her whole body, which became a block of pain. She felt it as if it were death seizing her; she could almost feel herself die. Fortunately, in her anguish, she cried out. The cry awakened her, and she emerged from the nightmare, exhausted. It takes days for everything to return to normal, for memory to be "refilled," and for the skin of memory to mend itself. She said that she became herself again, the one who can speak to you of Auschwitz without showing any sign distress or emotion.

As the 1994 movie *Schindler's List* vividly illustrated, fate and caprice were everywhere and often determined who went to the gas chambers. Langer reported Lena Berg's testimony about the terror of the selection procedure (Langer, 1991). She said that every roll call was a selection: Women were sent to the gas chamber because they had swollen legs or scratches on their bodies, because they wore eyeglasses or head kerchiefs, or because they stood at roll call without head kerchiefs. SS men prowled among the inmates and took down their numbers, and during the evening roll call the women were ordered to step forward. They never saw them again. Maria Keiler, Berg's childhood friend and schoolmate, died that way. She had a scratch on her leg, and an SS man took her number. When they singled her out at roll call, she simply walked away without even nodding good-bye. She knew quite well where she was going, and Berg knew it too. She was surprised at how little upset she was.

Liberation from the death camps brought little immediate psychological relief for some of the survivors. In his posthumous volume *The Drowned and the Saved*, Primo Levi (1988) explored the darker side of this dilemma when he said that in the majority of cases the hour of liberation was neither joyful nor lighthearted. For most prisoners, liberation occurred against a tragic background of destruction, slaughter, and suffering. Just as they felt they were again becoming men (i.e., responsible), the sorrows of men returned; the sorrow of the dispersed or lost family; the universal suffering all around them; their own exhaustion, which seemed definitive, past cure; the problems of a life to begin all over again amid the rubble, often alone. They felt "misery the mother of misery." Levi said that leaving pain behind was a delight for only a few fortunate beings or only for a few instants or for very simple souls; almost always it coincided with a phase of anguish.

Philip K.'s testimony reported in Langer (1991) provides a view of this experience that embodies the ambivalence that so many survivors have expressed. He told of people who pretended to seem to be marveling at the fact that he seemed to be so normal, so unperturbed, and so capable of functioning. These people seemed to think the Holocaust passed over, that it is done. But he said the residual of the Holocaust is his coat. You cannot take it off. And it is there, and it will be there until he dies. He said that if Jews were not an eternal people before, they are an eternal people after the Holocaust, in both a very positive and a very negative sense. He said that Jews have not only survived but have revived themselves. In a very real way, they have won. They were victorious. But in a very real way, they have lost. They will never recover what was lost. They cannot even assess what was lost. Who knows what

beauty and grandeur 6 million (i.e., the 6 million Jews who were murdered in the Holocaust) Jewish people could have contributed to the
world? Who can measure it? What standard do you use? How do you
count it? The world lost something, whether it knows it or admits it.

Surviving the Holocaust

Stories of how some people survived the Holocaust provide some of
the most powerful evidence of how humans cope with horrible losses
and trauma and how they adapt after the traumatic event. Viktor
Frankl, a young psychiatrist at the time of his imprisonment, spent 3
years in various death camps and later started a movement of psychotherapy based on his experiences and observations. Starting soon after
World War II, Frankl returned to medicine and began a writing career
(producing 32 books that have been translated into 29 languages). He
traveled, climbed mountains, and gave speeches all over the world until
his death in 1997 at age 92. Despite his traumatic experience during the
Holocaust, he lived life with exemplary verve and vigor. Frankl (1997)
said that he did not mind getting old, as long as he had reason to believe
that he was maturing and contributing. Viktor Frankl's (1959) *Man's
Search for Meaning* is the work that describes his Holocaust experience
and offers lessons for all who read the book. It is a testament to finding
positive ways to cope with unspeakable losses—including having your
father die in your arms after he had been starved and tormented by
camp guards. His Holocaust message serves as a beacon of hope to all
those who encounter great suffering and profound loss. Frankl makes
the "unspeakable" speakable and persuasively advocates the value of
telling one's story of loss. The seeds of Frankl's book began as jottings
on toilet paper in the death camps, but were later discovered and destroyed by a guard.

Frankl survived Auschwitz and three other Nazi death camps between 1942 and 1945. But his parents, wife, and other family members
perished. During his imprisonment and after his liberation, Frankl
dedicated his life to helping people find meaning in their lives, no matter how dismal their circumstances. He developed a new form of psy-

chotherapy called logotherapy, which emphasized the human search for meaning and techniques through which people can find meaning. He contended that the meaning question was one that "burned under the finger nails" of every human (1959, p. 15). His position was called the Third Vienna School of Psychotherapy, after that of Sigmund Freud and Alfred Adler. His teachings emphasize a positive view of humankind and forgiveness—a quality he showed toward even many of the cruel Nazi guards he encountered in the death camps. As Frankl (1997) notes in his autobiography, after the war, his defense of some of the Nazi guards whom he believed had helped prisoners survive became quite controversial among people who viewed all Nazis as equally evil and demented. Logotherapy teaches that people can find meaning in three major ways: (a) by creating a work or doing a deed; (b) by experiencing something or encountering someone—work and love; and (c) by enduring suffering and turning a personal tragedy into a triumph (a tactic that we have seen used by individuals repeatedly in this book in the wake of great personal loss—somehow finding ways to use loss to reach out to others and to advance positive causes). Frankl said that the Nazis could strip the prisoners of all that they had except what was in their minds—their attitude toward life.

Frankl wrote that meaning was more important than food to the inmates of the death camps. He said that his experience in the camps bore witness to the unexpected extent to which people are capable of braving even the worst conditions conceivable. He often quoted Goethe that "he who has a why to live can bear almost any how." Frankl (1959) contended that people can find meaning even in suffering. He paraphrased Dostoyevski: "There is only one thing that I dread, not to be worthy of my sufferings" (p. 87). Frankl said that much of a survivor's success in surviving the selections and cruel conditions was a matter of luck. He said, "We who have come back, by the aid of many lucky chances or miracles—whatever one may choose to call them—we know: the best of us did not return" (1959, p. 24).

In *Man's Search for Meaning*, Frankl (1959) tells how hunger, humiliation, fear, and deep anger at injustice are rendered tolerable by closely guarded images of beloved persons, by religion, by a grim sense of humor, by what he called "tragic optimism," and by glimpses of the healing beauties of nature—snow, a tree, a sunset. Frankl's existential philosophy, which emerged from his survival of the death camps, has riveted and inspired millions of readers, including literally thousands of young persons who have read *Man's Search for Meaning* in my college class titled Loss and Trauma. In fact, a whole college curriculum was designed around Frankl's book at Baker University in Kansas (Frankl, 1997).

Frankl's philosophy can be seen in some of his central ideas. Frankl (1959) suggests that although life is transitory, "nothing is irretrievably lost, . . . everything [is] irrevocably stored" (p. 143). He (Frankl, 1959) argues that life has an unconditional value and meaning:

> Just as life remains potentially meaningful under any conditions, even those which are most miserable, so too does the value of each and every person stay with him or her, and it does so because it is based on the values that he or she has realized in the past, and is not contingent on the usefulness that he or she may or may not retain in the present. (p. 176)

Both in Frankl's work in the death camps trying to restore the morale of the prisoners and afterward in his practice of logotherapy, he said that he had to teach despairing individuals that it did not matter what we expected from life, but rather what life expected from us. He said that life ultimately means taking the responsibility for finding the right answer to its problems and to fulfill the tasks which it constantly sets out for each person (such wisdom is reminiscent of John F. Kennedy's line in his 1961 presidential inaugural speech, "Ask not what your country can do for you, but what you can do for your country").

Frankl (1997) states that frequent thoughts and images of loved ones helped him and other survivors of the death camps. He said,

> In Auschwitz I thought very often of mother. Each time I fantasized how it would be when I would see her again. Naturally, I imagined that the only thing for me to do would be to kneel down and, as the expression goes, kiss the hem of her dress. (p. 22)

Although he did not know that the Nazis had already killed his mother and his wife, he wrote poignantly of his mental reflections of his wife:

> The man marching next to me whispered suddenly, "If our wives could see us now."
> . . . That brought thoughts of my own wife to mind. And as we stumbled on for miles, slipping on icy spots, supporting each other time and again, dragging one another

up and onward, nothing said, but we both knew: Each of us was thinking of his wife. ... Then I grasped the meaning of the greatest secret that human poetry and human thought and belief have to impart: The salvation of man is through love and in love. I understood how a man who had nothing left in this world still may know bliss, be it only for a brief moment, in the contemplation of his beloved.... For the first time in my life I was able to understand the meaning of the words, "The angels are lost in perpetual contemplation of an infinite glory." This intensification of inner life helped the prisoner find a refuge from the emptiness, desolation and spiritual poverty of his existence, by letting him escape into the past. (pp. 56-59)

Frankl also said, "A single moment can retrospectively flood an entire life with meaning" (p. 44). His contribution to the human quest to find meaning and go on living under any circumstance is incalculable.

Primo Levi was also a world-renowned Holocaust writer, producing several important works, including novels such as *If Not Now, When* (1986). He suffered from depression, and he committed suicide in 1987 at age 68. Levi (1988) seconded Frankl's message about the roles of luck and circumstance in survival in his memoir of his Holocaust experience:

The railroad convoy that took us to the Lager contained 650 persons; of these 525 were immediately put to death; 29 women were interned at Birkenau; 96 men, myself among them, were sent to Monowitz-Auschwitz.... Of these only about twenty of the men and women returned to their homes.

I survived imprisonment by a fortunate chain of circumstances; by never falling ill; by the help of an Italian Brick-layer [who brought Levi food]; by being able to work two months as a chemist.... I was liberated thanks to the rapid advance of the Red Army in January 1945. (p. 17)

Goldhagen's Thesis

Daniel Goldhagen (1996) created an uproar with his book *Hitler's Willing Executioners.* This book criticized the claims that Germans were ignorant of the mass destruction of Jews, that the killers were mostly elite SS soldiers, and that those who killed Jews did so reluctantly. Goldhagen reconstructs the scenario of anti-Semitism and the radical persecution of Jews, which made Hitler's pursuit of the final solution possible. He uses archival records to trace how German citizens voluntarily hunted Jews like animals, how regular police herded Jews into synagogues and burned them alive there as they recited prayers. He tells how the typical "man on the street" in Hitler's Germany looked on and cheerfully posed with Jewish victims—sometimes corpses freshly made that way—for photographs. In short, Goldhagen shows how Jews were demonized and scapegoated for the ills that had beset post-World War I Germany so that the Nazis could carry out a societywide campaign of identification, roundup, and massacre.

Goldhagen argued that bystander inaction in the face of obvious atrocities toward innocent German citizens was a major part of the willing executioner campaign. Goldhagen documents the anti-Semitic attitudes that characterized many parts of Central and Eastern Europe that contributed to bystander apathy in the face of the killing of neighboring families and erstwhile friends. Among other nationalities that took part in such inaction, he identifies Polish, French, and Ukranian citizens who likewise stood by without taking action against the atrocities that were being committed.

Goldhagen extends his analysis to include the deplorable conditions and treatment of foreign workers in Germany during the war. His reasoning in regard to this issue was used as evidence to support the attainment of a 5.2 billion dollar settlement by 65 German companies in 1999 with between 1 million and 2 million survivors of Nazi slave labor during World War II. Most of these slaves were not Jews, but the treatment they received was consistent with how the Jews were treated prior to being branded as evil, persecuted, and killed. Goldhagen's thesis also extended to the Swiss banks' acceptance of money and possessions taken by the Nazis from Jewish victims. This banking activity also led to a multi-billion-dollar settlement with Jewish survivors in the late 1990s.

Based on the vast archival evidence he collected and his meticulous approach to the evidence, it is difficult to dismiss Goldhagen's points. Even subtle types of cruelty seem to have been common among German citizens and collaborators in other occupied countries. For example, in long death marches of captured Jews across the countryside of Europe, citizens humiliated, beat, and stripped prisoners of clothing and dignity. The inability of the postwar generation in Germany to come to grips with the Holocaust is further indirect evidence that citizens knew they too had much to hide (and perhaps much guilt as well). Goldhagen (1996) concludes,

The notion that Germany during the Nazi period was an "ordinary," "normal" society which had the misfortune to have been governed by evil and ruthless rulers who, using the institutions of modern societies, moved people to commit acts that they abhorred, is in its essence false. . . . That the world ought to be organized or reorganized according to this conception of an immutable hierarchy of races was an accepted norm. The possibility of peaceful coexistence among races was not a central part of the cognitive landscape of the society. Life within the camp system demonstrated how radically ordinary Germans would implement the racist, destructive set of beliefs and values that was the country's formal and informal public ideology. The camp—Germany's distinguishing, distinctive, indeed perhaps, central institution—was the training ground for the masterly conduct of the ordinary new German "superman," and it revealed his nature. (p. 460)

Only in the past two to three decades have German citizens taken a noble leadership role in recognizing the evil and atrocities of the Holocaust. Expressions of contrition have been common over this period. Jews have been welcomed back to honorable citizenship status in the country by the majority of Germans. There has been much public outcry about complicity with the Nazis. This development will be recognized by the Berlin Holocaust Museum that is expected to open in the early 21st century. There is even a law now in Germany that makes denying the Holocaust a crime (a law that has been directed at the controversial author and historian David Irving, who contended in the 1990s, for example, that Hitler did not approve the mass killing of Jews and that Auschwitz was merely a brutal labor camp with an unfortunately high death rate). Goldhagen (1996) commends the reception of *The Willing Executioners* in Germany:

The reception by the German public that this book has received tells us a great deal what is positive in Germany today. For Germans to confront this horrific part of their past is unpleasant in the extreme. That so many are willing to do so is yet another indication of how radically transformed democratic Germany has become in the second half of the 20th century. (p. 466)

Generational Effects

Daniel Bar-On's (1995) research reported in his book *Fear and Hope* investigated generational effects of the Holocaust via an interview-narrative design comparing generations of survivors living in Israel and in Germany. Generational effects refer to continued traumatization of later generations of children (and sometimes their children) of Holocaust survivors. Bar-On found that in first-generation Jewish persons (who usually were young and either survived the camps or had parents perish there) were often in conflict with second- and third-generation individuals regarding the preservation of the memory of the past and "moving on." Second- and third-generation persons were more interested in moving on than were the first-generation survivors. This national dialogue was occurring from early after the founding of Israel into the 1980s, at the same time that there was too little appreciation of the losses of survivors. Many Israelis held the view that that the victims should have fought harder to withstand or overcome the Nazis.

Bar-On found that second and third generations of Israeli families were affected by "untold" stories in families. They experienced a conflict between fear and hope. In the 1980s, there began to be a greater emphasis on and appreciation of families working through their stories. By the 21st century, in Israel the earlier orientation toward victims has changed to one of compassion, and there is a strong national vow to remember and never let such a genocide of Jews occur again.

Bar-On raised serious doubts about the "conspiracy of silence" that many analysts have claimed characterizes the treatment of the Holocaust by Israelis. He showed that the second and third generations were affected by stories they heard about the Holocaust from first-generation survivors. These "filtered stories," along with countless untold stories, communicated feelings and patterns of thought and behavior to younger generations. For the second generation, the disjuncture and conflict between fear and hope seemed intensified. Still, the second generation seems to be trying to navigate a path between the needs of their children and the demands of their parents. When they are unsuccessful, the disjuncture shows up in the narratives and lives of the third generation—they may feel as if they are outsiders in society. Some families increasingly, however, are helping the younger generations work through the past by promoting an open context whereby children are encouraged to explore the constraints and repressed conflicts of the past (see Ellis, 1995).

Peskin, Auerhahn, and Laub (1997) have referred to the continued difficulties experienced by second- and later-generation Holocaust survivors as the "second Holocaust." The children of survivors may view the world from the vantage point of a graveyard, from the knowledge of a catastrophe that has ravaged the family. The child is witness to the presence of an absence in the family and to behavior of the parents that the child experiences but cannot identify or understand. The parent who is so traumatized may fail to help the child achieve a sense of security when the child is young and highly vulnerable to feeling abandoned. The child may join the parent's sense of "death in life," and feel some of the same void experienced by the survivor.

Peskin et al. (1997) contend that the second Holocaust may appear in the character structure, defensive and adaptive styles, and life choices of survivors and their children as the disintegrative effect of their personal Holocaust trauma that cannot be adequately known, understood, or remembered. There is, in effect, a transmission of this continuing loss across the first and possibly later generations of Holocaust survivors. Why do these transmission effects occur? One possibility is that repression of traumatic memory leads to a distancing attachment style (Shaver & Tancredy, 2000). Still other possibilities are that survivors overinvest in the next generation, maybe even smothering them psychologically, and the next generation may carry a burden of responsibility (R. Weiss, personal communication, September 5, 2000).

Peskin et al. (1997) note that early Holocaust literature formulated the transmission of deep psychopathology from one generation to the next. These scholars do not necessarily agree with the idea that deep psychopathology is transmitted, but they also believe that it is imperative that survivors with major psychological difficulties seek counseling and that therapists and scholars need to be aware of the tendency to pathologize survivors. Peskin et al. are reasonably optimistic that therapists can help children of survivors adapt, deal with a family-produced sense of despair about life, and care more about life and understand better the parents' trauma.

The Holocaust in American Experience

Peter Novick's (1999) book *The Holocaust in American Life* represents one of the fullest and most controversial statements on the Holocaust in American experience during the last half of the 20th century. Novick described the tremendous interest in the Holocaust in the United States during recent decades (e.g., the creation of Holocaust museums in Washington, D.C., Los Angeles, and New York City, Spielberg's movie *Schindler's List,* and Spielberg's video project with survivors known as Shoah). These developments played a role in this interest, but the interest also reflected an opening up of a dialogue in the United States that did not exist for the first three decades after the Holocaust.

Novick argues that the U.S. public did not minimize Holocaust suffering, nor was it callous toward Holocaust causes during World War II. He argues that there was a degree of knowledge of the atrocities. But even when people knew, they usually viewed these reports as part of the constant stream of reports of horrors befalling tens of millions of people around the globe. He notes that the 6 million Jewish deaths occurred in context of a war that killed 50 million. He suggests that the news pictures of Holocaust victims occurred in the context of seeing U.S. soldiers being beheaded by Japanese soldiers. Novick mentions a letter to the editor during World War II saying the horror was too great and that the public didn't need to see such pictures to be involved in the war.

In a more controversial argument, Novick (1999) contends that a "victim culture" is elevated in the United States today. He does not think it is valid to think of the Holocaust as unique (all events are unique on logical grounds). Novick doubts the argument that institutions such as the Holocaust museum teach us. He argues that we view artifacts in the museum in light of our a priori biases and experiences, and we are not necessarily educated by the experience. Novick believes that the Holocaust focus will wane in American culture. He thinks this waning will occur because of the imminent death of survivors (similar to others alive who lived through World War II) and the natural development of other priorities and causes in the society.

The Stigma Associated With
Surviving the Holocaust

The Holocaust exemplified loss at its penultimate. There are count-less aspects of stigmatization and degradation of the human condition associated with the Holocaust. It is important for survivors to tell the stories of what it was like to be "liberated." In truth, as Frankl (1959) described, there could be no psychological liberation for many of these survivors. They had seen too much. Their minds could not block out their Holocaust experiences as they tried to get on with the rest of their lives. Thus, the hour of liberation was neither joyful nor lighthearted for many. It occurred against a tragic background of destruction, slaughter, and suffering the likes of which cannot even be adequately described in words. Just as so many of these liberated individuals felt they were returning to their "normal lives," they encountered the sor-row of dispersed or lost families, the universal suffering all around them in Europe at that time, their own exhaustion, which seemed past cure, and the problems associated with beginning a life all over again amidst the rubble, often alone. Leaving pain behind was possible for only a fortunate few or only for a short time; almost always, this experi-ence coincided with a phase of anguish, severe depression, and a sliver of morale to continue living. Such conditions would be insurmount-able for most of us. They were for quite a few of the Holocaust survi-vors, but some persevered. Still, those who did go on faced stigma and disenfranchised grief.

As described in Langer's (1991) *Holocaust Testimonies,* survivors de-scribed their feelings related to their experience of being stigmatized upon being liberated. They said that a person does not feel at home in this world anymore because of this experience—you can live with it, but it is like constant pain: You never forget, you never get rid of it, but you learn to live with it. And that sets you apart from other people. The images are riveting in their power: the sounds they heard, the smells and stench of burning flesh. They feel as if they cannot excise it. It feels as if there is another skin beneath this skin and that skin is called Auschwitz, and you cannot shed it. It is a constant accompaniment. It

was as if Hitler chopped off part of the universe and created annihila-
tion zones and torture and slaughter areas. They expressed feeling as if
the planet was chopped up into a normal [part]—so-called normal:
their lives are not really normal—and this other planet, and they were
herded onto that planet from this one, and herded back again. They had
to relearn to live again. It all seemed to be too much; it is very hard to get
old with such memories. Survivors went on to tell Langer that life was
one big hell even after the war. So they made believe they could go on.
This is not something that you put behind you. And people think that
they can get away from it or not talk about it. The survivor cannot be
normal. In fact, countless survivors (and even their offspring) never
have felt normal since surviving this great atrocity.

General Ideas About Genocide

In a special issue of *Personality and Social Psychology Review*, edited
by Arthur G. Miller (1999), the topic of evil was considered by a set of
scholars. High on the list of phenomena that epitomize evil is genocide,
or the attempt to exterminate a whole group of people. An example of
genocidal wars include the Crusades of the Christians to rid Europe
and Asia of presumed infidels—mainly persons who were perceived
(incorrectly) to believe in a different god. The Crusades occurred first
in 1095 A.D. and seven more occurred by 1270. The 1999 end-of-the century issue of *The Economist* reported that Europe was quite impressed
with the Crusades and offered this description by one of the Crusader
historians of a typical act by the Crusaders, the sacking of Muslim
mosques:

> Our men took many prisoners in the mosque, men and women, some, and taking
> some alive. . . . They rushed through the city, seizing gold and silver, horses and
> mules, goods of all sorts.
>   Then they went rejoicing and weeping for gladness to worship at the sepulchre of
> our Savior. (p. 68)

This discussion of the Crusaders' acts to "save" the Muslims also notes
similar acts by the Muslims to rid the world of Christians. Other geno-

cidal activities include the mass killing of Armenians in the middle of the 20th century; the "killing fields" approach of the Khmer Rouge in Cambodia; the thousands of "disappearances" of individuals in Argentina in the 1950s; the systematic killing of Muslims in Bosnia by Serbs during the mid-1990s Bosnian War and of ethnic Albanians in Kosovo in 1999; and the almost 1 million Tutsi citizens killed by the Hutu majority in Rwanda in the early 1990s. Recent United Nations investigations of the latter genocide in Rwanda suggest that the UN and the United States turned their backs on this genocide, allowing the number slaughtered to grow fivefold until the time when they finally intervened.

Staub (1989, 1998, 1999) has been one of the most prolific psychological analysts of genocide. Staub notes that evil may be represented both by extremely harmful actions directed toward others and by inaction, such as failure to help innocent people in obvious peril. He argues that the conditions leading to a genocide such as the Holocaust are many and varied in nature. They include (a) low self-esteem, along with a projection of worthlessness in others and limited skills—qualities that Staub suggest are particularly lethal in impressionable young people; (b) authoritarian orientations, leading to reliance on leaders who demand violence be directed toward others and unwillingness to stand up against ruthless leaders—such orientations often are seen in countries that do not have a democratic tradition and freedom of dissent; (c) cultural preconditions, such as the humiliation of Germany and its difficult socioeconomic conditions after World War I—seen widely as setting the table for the development of the Third Reich movement; (d) an outgroup orientation toward others who are different or with whom conflict has occurred in a society, with an accompanying devaluing of these others (e.g., symbolized by the Nazis forcing Jews in occupied countries to wear the Star of David to identify themselves); (e) violent leaders, who in recent times, such as in Kosovo and Rwanda, have had paramilitary organizations operating against minorities with the blessings of still higher-ups in military organizations and governments; and (f) bystander inaction (e.g., Western countries, with the United States and France prominent among them, and the UN, have been accused of standing by too long and not intervening in what was known to be a genocide occurring in Rwanda).

Bandura (1999) argues that in wartime, nations almost always cast their enemies in the most dehumanized and demonic and bestial images to make it easier to kill them (recall that even in the United States, such a tendency could be discerned in government-sponsored images of Iraqi leaders and soldiers during the Gulf War of 1990 and of Serb leaders and soldiers during the Kosovo operation of 1999). Levi (1988) reports an incident in which a Nazi camp commander was asked why the Nazis went to such extreme lengths to degrade their victims, whom they were going to kill anyway. The commander blithely noted that it was not a matter of purposeless cruelty. It was, rather, that the victims had to be degraded to the level of subhuman objects so that those who operated the gas chambers would be less burdened by the distress attendant to their acts!

Hitler and Stalin's Roles in Making the 20th Century the "Bloodiest" Century

Adolf Hitler and Joseph Stalin deserve special note regarding their roles in making the 20th century what historians have called the bloodiest century in history. Few previous regimes had such mad ideas about people and how to govern and the means to so intensively indoctrinate their followers. Few other regimes in history have had the technology and readiness to kill on a grand scale, both by the millions, as Hitler's 12-year reign in Germany (1933-1945) and Stalin's 29-year leadership of the Soviet Union (1922-1953). Hitler's notions rested on concepts such as will, authority, racial superiority, and worship of the leader. Hitler successfully spoon-fed a nation vile anti-Jewish fantasies that somehow were taken seriously by people who clearly had the brain power to see their folly (e.g., Weisel, in a 1998 speech discussed later, noted that the Nazi military leadership was filled with men with PhDs, MDs, and advanced graduate education at the best universities in the world).

Stalin's brutality was couched within a socialist system emphasizing the perfectibility of the human. It was idealistic but won the admiration of poor countries and a large percentage of the Soviet people. But Stalin's cruelty was based mainly on his own paranoia, with an accompanying demonology that worked with a mighty intelligence force designed to root out dissidents and opponents and that turned citizen upon citizen. Stalin's paranoia even caused him to kill some of his own relatives whom he feared might turn on him. By the end of Stalin's life in 1953, his home resembled a prison camp it was so defended. Stalin possessed the following personality traits: self-hatred; low self-esteem; the bearing of grudges against all possible opponents of whatever magnitude; a ferocious temper; disdain for those around him, including family and brilliant generals whose ideas contributed greatly to the defeat of the Nazis; bullying sarcasm that led others to entertain their own paranoia about their own survival; and the ability to induce fear in others because of his unpredictability (Overy, 1997).

As *The Economist* opined in an end-of-the-century opinion piece titled "The Heights of Evil" (1999), Hitler and Stalin shared one common approach to governing: ruthless violence and ferocious internal repression. Hitler's regime convicted 95 Germans a day of political crimes from 1933 to 1939, but this record hardly compares with Stalin's for internal oppression. During Stalin's rule, the Soviet Union had traditions of secrecy and violence that are unmatched in the history of any empire. The number of Stalin's victims in *peacetime* in his own country is estimated to be 11 million, which includes the starvation of whole nations and the maintenance of inhuman labor camps populated by millions of people whom his administration deemed opponents. Furthermore, many people died due to forced collectives (taking food from the farmers and peasants) in the Ukraine and elsewhere from 1928 to 1933. At Stalin's death in 1953, the labor camps had never been as full (see related discussion in Chapter 10 of Romania's period of Stalinist rule).

Overall, the responsibility for the 50 million or so who died in the period of World War II lies with Hitler and Stalin. As *The Economist* argued, Hitler's massacre of European Jews was an act of genocide without millennial equal. This op-ed piece suggested that it was a toss-up whether Hitler or Stalin leads the world's list of infamy.

Conclusions: How to
Avoid Another Holocaust

Staub (1999) makes the reasonable argument that avoidance of genocidal movements such as the one that caused the Holocaust must begin in the socialization of children. He emphasizes the responsibility of parents, teachers, counselors, and relatives to teach caring, helping, compassionate orientations to children, and to model such attitudes in daily life and behavior. Given that many parents work and the influence of peers can be hard to manage, schools are important sites for this socialization (as are programs such as Spielberg's Holocaust video narrative project mentioned earlier). School officials and teachers need to be aware of issues such as bullying (which is said to have been a part of the backdrop of the Columbine school murders in Colorado in 1999), out- and ingroup orientations, authoritarian leaders and followers, bystander inaction, and the like. Baumeister and Campbell (1999) have also written about the undue power of bullying perpetrators in society—with victims invariably losing more than perpetrators gain from violence.

How do we avoid another Holocaust? By keeping the memory alive through the telling of individual stories. We must never forget the Holocaust and genocidal acts throughout history. That is the message of Janusz Bardach and Kathleen Gleeson (1998) in *Man Is Wolf To Man*, who present a compelling story of Bardach's survival of a Soviet gulag during World War II while his wife, parents, and sister were being killed by the Nazis. He too experienced a set of lucky circumstances that saved him, when millions died in Stalin's reign of tyranny. After the war, Bardach became a leading plastic surgeon and medical school professor and now, at age 80, he travels the country telling his story, which exposes the simultaneous atrocities of Hitler and Stalin.

Memory is also the key, according to Elie Weisel. Weisel points out that the memoir is the shield against the acts of humans that could lead to another Holocaust (from Weisel's speech at the University of Iowa, October 14, 1998). He notes that knowledge itself is not enough as an antidote to genocide. Weisel says that many of the Nazi forces who shot innocent women and children without provocation and who led families to the death camps without hesitation were highly educated individuals. Not only did many Nazi officers have college degrees, but many had earned graduate degrees of various types. Weisel also argues that indifference was one of the keys to the Holocaust events of the 1930s and 1940s. He points to the U.S. government's refusal to allow a shipload of Jewish refugees land on its shores in 1939. Our government sent it back to Germany where many of the passengers lost their lives at the hands of Hitler's executioners. Weisel contends that indifference, not hate, is the opposite of love and respect. Unlike the indifference of many countries, including the United States, Denmark distinguished itself during World War II by defying the Nazis and hiding and saving the lives of thousands of Jews who were being hunted by the Nazis. Weisel believes that as we enter the 21st century we must remember the 20th century as one of the bloodiest of all time and not be indifferent to the suffering of anyone anywhere. Weisel argues that we must define ourselves in terms of others and recognize our role as our brother's keeper. Weisel concludes that an emphasis on "other" is the key to peace in the world.

The diminishment of anyone's freedom and justice diminishes our own as well—reminding us of the pervading truth of the following passage from John Donne's (1624) "For Whom the Bell Tolls":

> No man is an island entire of itself; every man is a piece of the continent, a part of the main . . . any man's death diminishes me, because I am involved in mankind; and therefore never send to know for whom the bell tolls; it tolls for thee. ("Devotions Upon Emergent Occasions," Meditation 17)

A 74-year-old woman who survived the Holocaust was quoted in Judith Herman's (1992) *Trauma and Recovery* as saying, "Even if it takes one year to mourn each loss, and even if I live to be 107 [and mourn all members of my family], what do I do about the rest of the six million?" (p. 188).

Finally, Senator John Danforth said the following during a speech at a Days of Remembrance commemoration at the U.S. Holocaust Museum on May 24, 1994:

And that is our duty, those of us who must never forget. It is our duty to intervene, always, every time we see a dehumanized human being, no matter what the cause said to justify the cruelty. It is our duty to step up, speak out, stop it, whenever we see it, wherever we find it.

Note

1. From an article by Richard Corliss in *Time,* March 14, 1994.

10 International Perspectives on Loss and Adaptation

The Case of Romania

This chapter details some of my observations of contemporary losses experienced by citizens of Romania. This chapter will suggest how, because of politics, history, and economic factors, loss may be a general issue confronting a whole people. Societies as a whole may be sustaining or maligning. Unfortunately, 11 years after its liberation from an isolationist Communist dictatorship, Romania remains an example of how the maligning forces of a society can diminish the lives of the society's citizens in large and small ways on a daily basis.

These observations were made in 1998 and were supported by a William Fulbright Research Award. Although these observations pertain to Romania, they hint at the wider, deeper realities of loss that exist around the world—as the opening notes about infant mortality, HIV, and AIDS in Africa suggest.

The Need for a Broader
Perspective on Adaptation

A consideration of the depth and breadth of the psychology of loss can contribute to what is being called positive psychology (Seligman, 1998; Snyder & Lopez, in press). It can do so by helping us learn how people sometimes use major loss to energize their behavior and give back to others in significant, humane ways. Our understanding of loss needs to be accompanied by a deeper appreciation of adaptation processes. This undertaking necessarily will be both interdisciplinary and international in scope. My appreciation of relativity in adaptation was greatly enhanced in a study of loss among contemporary Romanian citizens (Carlson, Johnston, Liiceanu, Vintila, & Harvey, 2000; Harvey, 2000).

In studying loss, it is important to develop a cross-cultural, interdisciplinary approach that is concerned with the historical, cultural, and social contexts in which loss occurs. However, Western psychology is less well informed about the experiences and perspectives of loss across various cultures. Many countries in the contemporary world are seeking greater participation in the international community and greater control over their destinies. The related cultural, political, and social developments are highlighting the need for heightened awareness and understanding of ethnic variations in dealing with social change phenomena and the psychology of loss. One such country whose political history continues to threaten its reintegration into the European community is Romania. An exasperating loss issue for Romanian psychology in the late 1990s is that research is becoming nearly extinct because of the financial deprivations in the universities and the pressure on researchers to work other jobs to survive. However, part of the value in studying Romania now is that a growing number of Romanian psychologists are amenable to collaboration.

The ideas and research findings presented in this chapter resulted from a study I did while spending 4 months living in Romania interviewing more than 100 women in midlife and beyond about the major losses that they have experienced. This special population was chosen not only because women tend to be more open in discussing loss events

(Harvey, Weber, & Orbuch, 1990) but also because they are more likely to have experienced a wider variety of naturally occurring losses due to their age. Also unique to this population is the fact that they have experienced losses as a result of the significant historical and political events that occurred under a repressive and violent communist dictatorship between 1945 and 1989. Although the revolution in 1989 was no doubt a victory for the country of Romania, there continues to be a story of unceasing victimization. The unstable economy, low standard of living, and international isolation created by the communist autocracy of the Ceausescu family continue to threaten the country's reintegration into the European economic, political, and cultural space.

The accounts of loss shared by the Romanian women in our study are embedded within a historical, political, and developmental context. The stories told by these women represent losses incurred as a result of historical and political events (i.e., oppression, loss of employment, loss in socioeconomic status) as well as those losses that may occur naturally throughout the course of one's life (i.e., death, illness, divorce). Our hope is to facilitate a greater understanding and appreciation of the losses experienced by middle-aged Romanian women within a unique historical, political, economic, social, and cultural context.

Historical Overview

As its name suggests, Romania traces its cultural and linguistic roots to Imperial Rome. It has been the target of conquests by the Ottoman Empire, Czarist Russia, the Hapsburg Empire, the German Nazis (in the period of 1939-1945), and the Soviet Union (from 1945 to 1989). Located in Central Europe, Romania has a population of nearly 23 million. The country's largest ethnic minorities are Hungarian and German. Romania is the only country with a Romance language that does not have a Roman Catholic background, with 70% of the population being Romanian Orthodox.

Throughout the communist period, Romania was unique in Eastern Europe for its independent foreign policy, which was based on disarmament, détente, and peaceful coexistence with all countries. Starting in 1945 and continuing to varying degrees throughout President Nicolae Ceausescu's reign, approximately 300,000 Romanians were imprisoned or sent to mental institutions for various "crimes" against communism. Unlike other communist bloc countries that had begun degrees of democratic and market reforms prior to 1990, Romania suffered in brutal isolation under Ceausescu's regime. Ceausescu's efforts to chart an independent course for Romania came at great expense to the Romanian people. To pay off Romania's $10 billion foreign debt, Ceausescu exported Romania's food, which created massive food shortages throughout Romania. Ceausescu also wanted the population to increase despite the inadequate resources of most of the population to care for additional children in their families. In 1966, Ceausescu restricted legal abortion to women who were over 45 years of age. In addition, the importation of contraceptives was prohibited, divorce was severely restricted, and illegal abortion became a punishable offense for women and their service providers. These policies contributed to thousands of illegal and sometimes botched abortions. As a result, many deformed children were born, and thousands more were placed in orphanages.

Throughout the 1980s the population continued to suffer from prolonged scarcities of almost everything. Yet despite the dramatic decline in the population's living standard, Ceausescu initiated several grandiose projects in the country's capital of Bucharest, which came at a huge cost in resources to the Romanian people. To mark his achievements, Ceausescu built imposing buildings and grand boulevards in Bucharest, a program that led to the destruction of thousands of old homes, leaving many people homeless. By 1989, there was no money remaining to finish many of Ceausescu's elaborate and functionless projects. Some of these unfinished buildings and half-built streets still lie dormant in central Bucharest today.

By the late 1980s, with the Soviet bloc quickly disintegrating, it seemed only a matter of time before Romania's citizens challenged the communist regime. In December 1989, the Romanian people spoke out and denounced Ceausescu's rule. After a week of revolutionary activities during which more than 1,000 people were killed, Ceausescu and his wife Elena were captured, tried, and executed.

Although the victory of the revolution opened the way for a reestablishment of democracy, the country of Romania faced a long road to social, political, and economic recovery. The afflictions brought about by Ceausescu's regime continue to live on and threaten the country's postcommunist democracy. Romania continues to have one of the most inflated and harshest economies in Eastern Europe. As a result of Ceausescu's decision in the 1980s to ban abortion to increase the population, nearly 100,000 abandoned children under the age of 18 are living in orphanages. Since 1990, Romania's leaders have shown little effectiveness in turning the country's economy around. As we enter the 21st century, Romania continues to struggle to overcome its political, economic, and social difficulties and heal the wounds from a long history of isolation and oppression.

Accounts of Loss

It has been proposed that people often conceive of their losses in terms of the stories or accounts that contextualize the major events of their lives (Harvey et al., 1990), thus we chose to integrate the stories told by middle-aged Romanian women about their loss experiences into our research. Through personal interviews with the third author, there were common reports of the struggle to find meaning in their losses and to redirect their lives toward opportunities for growth. A 56-year-old Romanian scientific researcher explained her own ideas about loss and the lessons learned from loss:

> I have learned that a loss or a win can't only be considered such. It is something relative, with positive elements in loss and negative elements in win. That is why, a loss must be considered in positive terms because it brings something positive through identify modifications that arise as a result of the loss. You learn from losses, therefore you change. I have reconsidered my relationships and I've become more available to people.

Loss and suffering were not topics that were discussed directly or often. It was typical for these Romanian women to engage in downward social comparison (Wills, 1981) in which they would compare themselves with others less fortunate than themselves or living under more difficult conditions. For example, an accomplished Romanian psychologist shared her story of loss and concluded that her suffering was not that bad relative to countless Romanians who were locked away in communist prisons. In the following passage she describes the loss of her career:

> In 1985, 10 years after I received my Ph.D., I was told by the Romanian Communist Party officials that I would be demoted. I gave an interview in Paris in which I discussed transcendental meditation, a topic that I was studying then. They [Romanian Communist Party] said my interview betrayed state secrets. I was taken out of my university teaching job and given first a factory job, and then I was made a janitor in the plant. These jobs lasted about a year and one-half. Then I was allowed to resume my teaching, but I had to start over as if I had just begun.

Although the Revolution of 1989 opened the way for a democratic government, it has not been an easy transition for the Romanian people. The economic, social, and emotional repercussions are still prevalent more than a decade after the Revolution. For some, there is a sense of loss of community, affliction, and lost identities. For others, there is a sense of victory and optimism:

> One of the most positive experiences for the Romanian people was the Revolution from December 1989. We have more freedom now, but the material (financial) restraints are more acute and serve as a major obstacle for people to enjoy life.

In the face of inconceivable loss, one can find incredible accounts of hope and perseverance. A university professor shared this story:

> There was an accident at a public institution where there was material gathered over a period longer than 20 years for a scientific paper by a 14-person team that I led and worked with for 10 years. Everything was burned down and when the entire staff requested to start it all over, we were not granted permission. Although I suffered much, I never gave up. After 65 years, I wrote and published two books.

One woman told of multiple-loss experiences that included the following losses: the death of her 14-year-old daughter in a car accident; a divorce; the gang rape of her 17-year-old daughter; the imprisonment of her father in a communist jail; and the destruction of her home, which left her family homeless. Yet despite all these losses, which could have left her bitter and devoid of compassion, this woman shared the lessons she learned from her losses: "The losses present in my life have made me better understand other people experiencing loss. I reach out and help people whenever I can."

A university researcher told of her family's experience with the communist regime and how the postrevolution economic conditions negatively affected the quality of life and compromised the country's sense of community:

> Before 1989 during the communist regime, my parents, both professors, were periodically harassed for political reasons. Close relatives were imprisoned for political reasons for long periods of time. Some of them died after they were released as a result of the physical and psychological tortures they suffered.... My researcher wage after 1990 has become entirely insufficient. I am submitted to unimaginable humiliation of material matters in a country that doesn't feel the need for culture and willingly destroys it.

A 57-year-old journalist wrote in great detail about her losses relevant to the historical events in Romania and the subsequent social "freedom" that she experienced:

> The actions of the communist powers had ill-fated consequences on my family. My father lost his job at the ministry as a punishment because he belonged to the [Social Democratic Party]. As a direct result, my family has been deprived of many rights.... I experienced total dissatisfaction as a journalist. I lived the dramatic experience of being required to avoid the truth, which for a journalist meant total alienation. After the Revolution of 1989, I have been able to work at a decision-making level, to make my publications represent truth and incorporate my own beliefs.

An amazing story was shared by a 56-year-old German woman from Transylvania with Romanian citizenship and the cross-cultural difficulties she experienced during a long history of political upheaval which encompassed World War II and the Romanian Revolution of 1989. Here is an excerpt from her story in which she tells of the losses her family incurred as a result of their German heritage:

> Being of German ethnicity, my family was dispossessed of our house, land, vineyard. ... When my mother tried to get our estates back, she discovered that in the local official archives, the evidence of our estates and the personal information of my grandparents, their 10 children, and their descendants were completely erased from the current register.

The experiences of loss as a result of oppression, as evidenced in the stories shared by the Romanian women, are primarily political in nature. Yet another untold story of oppression that existed in the Romanian culture is the ethnic prejudice and oppression experienced by the Hungarian and German minorities in Romania. The preceding quotation signifies a loss of identity of nearly three generations, in essence a loss of one's life history.

The stories of loss that were shared with us were inextricably tied to the political events and the subsequent social and moral degradation suffered by the Romanian people. Their stories are marked by lost opportunities, lost possessions, lost homes, exposure to violence and trauma, and separation from loved ones. Yet intertwined within these accounts of loss one can find evidence of hope and resiliency. Despite the experience of a violently repressive communist regime and insurmountable social and economic conditions, there is evidence that many of the Romanian women in our study have reconstructed their experiences and found new meaning and purpose in their lives.

Quantitative Findings

In addition to the qualitative analysis of the interviews and surveys in which the participants shared their personal stories of loss, I also conducted a quantitative analysis. These findings are based on information collected via interviews and surveys from 40 Romanian female volunteers who were 35 years of age and older.

Demographic Information

Table 10.1 provides a demographic profile of the participants. The sample consisted of 40 Romanian women who ranged in age from 35 to 68 with a mean age of 52. Of the target group, 50% reported that they were married, 2.5% were single, 25% were widowed, and 22.5% had been divorced. The sample represented a wide variety of reported occupations, which were broken down into five occupational categories: education (27.5%), clerical or administrative work (17.5%), business and industry (12.5%), custodial work (10%), and health care (2.5%).

TABLE 10.1 Descriptive Profile for Total Sample

Characteristic	Percentage
Age	
35-45	20.0
46-55	62.5
56-65	10.0
66+	5.0
Marital status	
Single	2.5
Married	50.0
Divorced	22.5
Widowed	25.5
Occupation	
Educational field	27.5
Clerical/administrative	17.5
Business and industry	2.5
Custodial work	10.0
Retired	17.5
Unemployed	5.0

Five percent indicated that they were currently unemployed, and 17.5% reported that they were retired.

Loss Experience Information

Table 10.2 provides a profile of the frequency of losses experienced by these Romanian women, which include the following losses: loss through the death of a loved one, loss of health, loss of employment, loss by divorce, loss as a result of violence, and loss by oppression. It was surprising to note that although all these women survived oppressive political and economic conditions throughout a major portion of their lives only 30% of the sample indicated having experienced loss as a result of oppression. Perhaps what Westerners identify as "oppression" is in fact a way of life that is accepted by the Romanian people. It is also significant to note that half of our sample had experienced loss of employment.

TABLE 10.2 Profile of Loss Experiences for Total Sample

Loss Experience	Percentage
Loss through death of close other	
Yes	82.5
No	15.0
Loss of health	
Yes	67.5
No	32.5
Loss of employment	
Yes	50.0
No	50.0
Loss by divorce	
Yes	27.5
No	70.0
Loss by violence	
Yes	27.5
No	72.5
Loss by oppression	
Yes	30.0
No	70.0

In response to the participants' affirmative response to the specific loss experience, participants were then asked to rate how much more difficult the particular event(s) made their life over the years from "not at all more difficult" to "a great deal more difficult." The means, standard deviations, and range of responses are indicated in Table 10.3. Of those respondents who experienced a loss due to the death of a loved one, a health problem, unemployment, or a divorce, an experience of violence, or oppression, the extent to which they reported experiencing great difficulty over the years was prominent.

In considering the account-making model referred to earlier (Harvey et al., 1990), which posits that our losses, which are constructed and reconstructed through storylike accounts, become part of who we are, I was interested in finding out how these Romanian women may have changed as a result of their losses (from their own subjective

TABLE 10.3 Difficulty Associated With Loss

Loss Experience	Mean	SD	Range
Death of close other(s)	6.06	2.38	0-8
Loss of health	6.58	1.74	0-8
Loss of employment	6.33	2.28	0-8
Loss by divorce	5.17	2.98	0-8
Loss by violence	6.10	2.56	0-8
Loss by oppression	7.33	.98	0-8

point of view). Thus, participants were asked to indicate what their history of losses had taught them about life and how these losses had affected their philosophy of living and their relationships with others. Five categories of responses emerged, which included the following: increased sensitivity to or compassion for death, dying, and loss in general (37.5%); increased focus on living (12.5); increased commitment to loved ones and close others (12.5%); increased service to one's community (7.5%); and increased commitment to a cause (5%). One category of responses emerged which was indicative of a negative effect from one's losses. Specifically, this negative effect was reported as difficulty in interpersonal relationships (i.e., difficulties related to trust, compassion, or closeness to others). This negative effect was only indicated as a response to loss by 25% of the sample. Remarkably, 75% of the sample reported positive changes in their philosophy of living and derived meaning from their losses about the value of life and their relationships with others.

Central to the account-making model is the premise that the confiding experience is crucial to the person's assimilation of and adaptation to the loss. This confiding experience includes not only the personal, private work on one's own story but also the social interaction of telling part of his or her story to close others over time. We found our results to be consistent with this premise. When asked how helpful it was to confide in others by telling them about their loss, 65% indicated that it was helpful, whereas only 15% indicated that it was not at all helpful. This result was further clarified in the accounts of the stories shared via the interviews and written responses in the surveys. Family, friends, and spirituality were commonly reported sources of support relied upon by these Romanian women as they coped with the variety of losses throughout their lives. In fact, 92.5% of our sample reported that they relied on religion or spirituality to cope with the loss experiences in their life. This points to the important place that religion and spirituality has in Romanian culture. Finally, when asked to rate how happy they were with their current life, 75% of the sample indicated that they were happy with their current life.

Correlations of Interest

Pearson product-moment correlations were calculated in order to identify relationships between variables of interest. Several significant findings were found. Specifically, the relationship between difficulty associated with loss of employment and reported helpfulness of spirituality was found to be statistically significant ($r = .61; p < .01$), indicating that the more difficulty experienced with the loss of employment, the greater spirituality was found to be helpful. With a reported 70% of the population in Romania being Romanian Orthodox (Stanley, 1991, cited by A. Liiceanu, personal communication, April 27, 1999), the Orthodox perspective on life and loss is prominent. An underlying belief of the Orthodox religion is that tragedy, loss, and hard times are considered to be God's challenges, and thus are to be accepted and faced with heroism (A. Liiceanu, personal communication, April 27, 1999).

A second significant positive correlation emerged between the extent to which participants found confiding their loss experiences to others to be helpful and the extent to which one's losses stimulated a personal growth experience ($r = .70; p < .01$). This indicates that the greater the perceived helpfulness of confiding in others about loss experiences, the greater the impact the losses reportedly had on their lives. This significant relationship can be referenced in the findings of Harvey, Barnes, Carlson, and Haig (1995) in which they investigated the differential emotional and coping responses of individuals at midlife and beyond who had recently experienced the loss of a close loved one. In their findings, Harvey, Barnes et al. (1995) suggested that confiding in others by sharing stories of loss facilitates the meaning re-construction process in which one begins to adapt to the loss, assimi-late the loss experience into one's identity, and recognize the contribu-tions of the deceased and the loss experience itself on one's life. As with the Romanian women in our study, confiding in others about loss was significantly related to the extent to which they reported experiencing a significant impact from their losses. The growth-related confiding ex-perience can be witnessed in the account of a retired architect and uni-versity lecturer:

> I tell my confidant about my problems, worries, fears, and difficulties. After I talk with her, I feel more optimistic and peaceful and thanks to her, I have more confi-dence in my ability to get through difficult times. . . . I have learned that loss is a change and from each loss one gains something, too. One learns something, one changes in his or her relationships, one becomes more careful with people, more tol-erant, and values their worth.

Consistent with the aforementioned finding, a significant relation-ship was also found between the extent to which confiding was found to be helpful and the participants' overall rating of their happiness ($r = .54$; $p < .01$), indicating that those who reported that confiding was helpful to them in coping with loss also reported greater happiness in their current life. The helpful interaction of confiding in others can contribute to the healing process. Research on the account-making process has suggested that account-making and confiding activities are vital to recovery, in terms of both psychological and physical health (Harvey, Barnes, et al., 1995, p. 217). Harvey, Barnes, et al. (1995) sug-gested that the greater the extent to which the account-making and confiding activities have occurred, the healthier the individual should feel in the long run.

A significant positive correlation emerged between participants who reported a growth experience as a result of their loss and their reported level of happiness ($r = .47$; $p < .01$). The account-making model posits that through confiding activities, meaning reconstruction of the loss takes place. Thus, it would seem that this process facilitates an experience of growth through which one comes to recognize the purpose and value of the loss, thus enhancing one's personal outlook on loss and life.

Two significant correlations emerged between the various loss experiences that were evaluated. A positive correlation emerged between participants reporting loss due to divorce and loss due to violence ($r = .47; p < .01$). This finding had relevance for this particular sample in that in many of the qualitative accounts of loss by divorce, participants often cited spousal abuse as a reason for the separation and divorce. In Romania, the divorce rate for the past two decades has been between .7 and 1.7 in 1,000 persons (A. Liiceanu, personal communication, April 27, 1999). Yet despite this small population of divorcees, nearly 23% of our particular sample reported being divorced. Although divorce in Romania is preferable to never being married, it is considered a social failure that affects the entire family.

A second correlation relating two loss experiences was loss experienced as a result of oppression and loss of employment ($r = .44; p < .01$). This result was not found to be surprising given the history of communist oppression that led to job replacement and job loss for many Romanian people. Yet in Romania, as in many other countries that broke away from communist rule, people are left to deal with the aftermath of the destruction of the economy. Today, Romania has one of the most inflated and harshest economies in Eastern Europe.

A negative correlation that was of interest was between whether participants found confiding about their losses to be helpful and how often they attended religious services ($r = -.42, p < .05$). This finding suggests that the less participants found confiding to be helpful, the more often they attended religious services. This points once again to the reliance on religion as a coping mechanism.

Another significant relationship was found between loss due to oppression and the extent to which one's losses stimulated a personal growth experience ($r = .52; p < .05$), indicating that perhaps the experience of oppression serves as a catalyst for personal growth to occur. Many of the accounts that were shared with us were characterized by elements of extraordinary strength, resilience, and hope. Snyder (1996) posits that it is hope that gets us through our lowest moments and enables us to move ahead from our loss-filled present to an imagined brighter future that is better. For many hopeful Romanians, they are determined to address the country's problems and create a better place for future generations. A university researcher shared this account:

> The events from 1989 along with the loss of those closest to me have changed my relations with others. I now have more patience and I understand better people who suffer. I place a great deal of weight on moral values, responsibility for others, involvement in community life, and the solidarity for a high goal regarding the destiny of our country and of our children. (Snyder, 1996, p. 15)

Personal Observations

I supplement the preceding accounts and research findings with some personal observations of loss in Romania. Dogs, children, beggars, and Gypsies bear a considerable burden of the daily loss in this country.

Hundreds of thousands of stray dogs roam the streets of Bucharest because Ceausescu's administration tore down many central city neighborhoods and built huge concrete block apartments so that people would be "more equal." People moving to these apartments abandoned their pets, who now have bred in the streets for two decades and who depend on the mercy of shopkeepers and passersby to survive (Yossif-Vickery, 1998).

In a similar vein, Ceausescu's policies regarding the family led to terrible results. He wanted to increase the country's population. Thus, he dictated that couples would not use birth control and made abortion illegal, even though financially most people in the country could not afford more children (David & Baban, 1996). These policies led to the abandonment of newborn children. Upon birth, couples would leave them at state-run orphanages. Approximately 100,000 children remain in orphanages as of 1998. The challenges related to making a decent living in Romania continue to contribute to the abandonment of children. It also is estimated that there are a few thousand street children. Space does not permit a full discussion of the magnitude of loss issues facing Romania, and this situation continues despite the presence of millions of well-educated, multilingual, proud citizens who make up 21st-century Romania.

The relative nature of loss, coping, and adaptation is illustrated by the plight of beggars in Bucharest. Beggars are a common sight in the large cities of Romania. Many are Gypsies, who for centuries have endured prejudice and hardship in Romania and all of Europe (Fonseca, 1995). But the beggars represent a variety of ethnic groups and ages. The old and disabled as well as the young and apparently destitute can be found at most subway stops in Bucharest at most times every day. Some are quadriplegics. The young include many grimy-faced kids no older than 5 to 7 years old. A colleague reported seeing a father leading his young daughter around in the subway as she held a sign saying she needed help because she had AIDS.

A story that unfolded each weekday in the Bucharest metro system was that of the tenacious solicitations of a young man in his 20s who had no legs and slid around the floor of the subway car with a box into which riders sometimes put money. "The Slider" went about his work when the subway was not as crowded and did not stop his movement until the trip ended; then he would move to a different subway car for another trip. I found him resting early one morning behind a large post at the end of the subway station. It was as if that post gave him sanctuary from the onslaught of his daily grind. It is unclear how he managed the more than 80 steps of stairs leading to the subway platform or how he interacted with food vendors given his short stature and probable difficulties in negotiating crowded, chaotic sidewalk scenes and store areas. But he was a regular and had found ways to survive in these circumstances. We as researchers and scholars of loss and trauma can learn valuable lessons about resiliency, courage, and coping by paying greater attention to the millions of persons in this world who face losses and levels of ongoing stress similar to those encountered by The Slider.

Observations such as these regarding begging in Bucharest suggest the value not only of a psychology of loss, but also of a broad interdisciplinary and international approach to studying loss. This work likely would involve multimethod techniques, including observational, questionnaire, narrative approaches with groups, and case studies. It would involve the integration of ideas and methods from disciplines such as anthropology, sociology, political science, and psychology. Furthermore, essential to such inquiry would be collaboration with scholars representing the cultures being studied.

Limitations

There are several limitations to this research. Although I was fortunate to have had the opportunity to consult with various Romanian sources, I still found myself lacking in sufficient culture-specific knowledge that could have enriched our understanding of the research findings. Second, most of the qualitative interviews and questionnaires were gathered in Bucharest and in a few other large Romanian cities. Thus, the experiences of people living in the outlying villages and rural areas are not represented. However, in its size and complexity, Bucharest probably represents Romania's woes and its promise better than any other place in the country. Third, although I had the questionnaires translated into Romanian, it is uncertain whether our "Western" concepts and terminology delivered the same inquiry that was intended (i.e., the question posed may have gotten lost in the unclear translation) thus making it difficult to extract the precise meaning from the response. Furthermore, the argument that our understanding of loss and coping may be enhanced by taking careful note of the Romanian situation may be naive. Thus, with regard to the generalizability of the results, the ideas and conclusions of our analysis must be viewed with caution. However, what we can learn from studying loss in Romania are the contextual and cultural influences that contribute to the unique social and psychological dynamics intertwined in the loss experience and process.

Although there are certainly instances of greater suffering and more daunting losses and coping circumstances throughout the world that might be studied, scientific research in Romania is becoming nearly extinct because of financial deprivation in the universities. Thus, there is a need to pay attention to Romania and other similar countries in hopes that through scientific research, we will gain the knowledge necessary to address prevalent societal issues and psychological phenomena to further benefit humanity.

An Update on
Conditions in Romania

The 2 years since the preceding observations were recorded have not brought positive news to Romania. The economy has continued to stagger. Effective steps toward becoming a member of the European Union are estimated as requiring maybe more than two decades to complete. The lei has gone from 10,000 per U.S. dollar in 1998 to almost 25,000. The environment continues to be polluted, with a cyanide spill in early 2000 threatening neighboring countries because it got into the river system of Romania. The country is still struggling with the issue of what to do with its approximately 100,000 orphans. It is almost impossible for Romanians to get mortgages or credit from a banking system plagued by bad loans and political interference. Six banks have folded in the past 18 months.

There continues to be tremendous uncertainty about the political leadership of the country. As a *New York Times* editorial on November 30, 2000, explained, the presidential elections of 2000 presented the possibility that the country would revert further into a pariah state. In the elections, voters chose between Ion Iliescu, a former president, who once was the protégé of Nicolae Ceausescu, and Corneliu Vadim Tudor, an ardent nationalist who has blamed the country's problems on Jews, Gypsies, and Hungarians. Tudor had 30% of the electorate behind him in the primary election.

In late fall of 2000, the Romanian–American Chamber of Commerce took the unusual step of supporting Iliescu in this election as the lesser of two evils when it argued in a press release that "Vadim Tudor feeds upon the fears and frustrations of a beleaguered people with promises that he can never fulfill and demagogical diatribes against national minorities."[1]

Fortunately, as of this writing, it appears that Romanians elected Iliescu by a landslide, with more than 70% of the vote. Iliescu promised to try to move the country toward entry into the European Union and NATO at the earliest possible time.

Conclusions

In studying the loss experiences of Romanian women in their midlife and beyond, we are reminded of the universal existence of loss in human life. Yet the experience of loss cannot be separated from our individual uniqueness and the cultures that surround us. Concepts such as "death" and "grief" have culture-specific meanings. Thus, it is misleading to assume that our Western understanding of these concepts and experiences apply generally from culture to culture and from person to person. People from other cultures understand and classify their experiences and perceptions differently and place them in the context of their own beliefs about the origins of events, the nature of the person, the proper way to behave, and the meaning of losses (Irish, Lundquist, & Nelsen, 1993, p. 15). Thus, in studying loss from a multicultural perspective, we are able to gain insight into the unique historical and social influences that contribute to the conceptualization and experience of loss from both an individual and a cultural perspective.

Harvey (1996) argues that the key to transforming losses into something positive lies in our efforts to give our losses meaning, to learn and gain insights from them, and to impart something positive to others based on the loss experience. Thus, in coping with loss, the process of finding meaning in one's losses is crucial. Although reconstruction of meaning can be accomplished through a variety of social, psychological, or spiritual processes, perhaps the most omnipresent approach to dealing with and finding meaning in loss is through storytelling, or what Harvey et al. (1990) refer to as account making. As people share their stories with others, they give meaning to their unique life experiences. Yet sharing one's story of loss has the power to not only have profound effects on the teller but on the listener as well. In listening to and reading the narratives of the Romanian women in our study, I find validation of the important role of telling one's stories, confiding in others, and finding meaning. These efforts were also associated with loss-related growth, identity transformation, and giving back to others and to one's community. The lessons learned from losses that were shared should serve as a reminder of the resiliency of the human spirit. Despite the oppressive history that Romania has endured, the poor economic and social conditions that continue to persist, and the personal losses of these Romanian women, I found common themes of strength, courage, hope, and graciousness:

> My brother's disease determined me to contribute my time to a humanitarian foundation aimed at people with disabilities.

> I hope from the bottom of my heart that my suffering and losses have made me more understanding, tolerant, and generous. I believe that a person who has suffered has gained greater wisdom.

> I regard my losses as integral parts of life. My philosophy of life is that everything must be balanced. Evil is followed by good, and good by evil. We shouldn't despair when things get hard, nor should we ever take things for granted when things get better. I have compassion for others in sorrow, and I get involved in their problems by encouraging them.

> I could never understand why a toddler or infant dies, why a very young friend of mine was exiled a few months ago, why the parents are the ones who have to deal with all of these things. But each loss has made me think about the greatness of some of our actions. Life is our greatest present that must be lived all the way, meaning that each of us has to give him- or herself completely to one or more activities, and to improve the relationship among people. Each "little" thing one does in life in good faith means a lot and with will power, we can all move on in life.

> I have learned with great difficulty to become more independent, to accept loneliness, to have more self-esteem, to better understand differences and to accept them. I have become more receptive to other people's problems and to support them. I have revised some rigid and categorical opinions of mine, and I have come to accept my losses and overcome my desperation by getting involved in different activities of political and social order.

In the face of major loss, we can observe the immense capability of the human spirit to renew and be generative. In a fragile country continually challenged by adversity, Romania represents a place where we can learn invaluable lessons about the interdependent relationship between loss and life. I hope that these observations, findings, and the stories of loss shared in this chapter will provide insight into the rich psychological phenomena that are present in the unique loss experiences of these Romanian women.

Note

1. From *Bucharest Business Week,* December 5, 2000.

11 Adaptation and Therapeutic Approaches

When we are no longer able to change a situation . . . we are challenged to change ourselves.

—Viktor Frankl (1959, p. 135)

Can Some People Recover Without Grieving?

Can people heal from great pain and suffering without grief, stories, and actions designed to reconstruct their lives? Perhaps. Some people, such as emergency room medical personnel and police working in violent neighborhoods, become inured to the sights and sounds of death and grieving. They have to put aside their feelings to keep going. The same is true of soldiers in combat. Becoming hardened to death, however, is not the same as healing. What has been argued throughout this book and in much of the literature reviewed in this book is that grieving major loss and putting one's life back together requires considerable work and the good fortune of good friends and confidants. The question remains, do some people move on readily without much grief?

Researchers Camille Wortman, Roxane Silver, and their colleagues have reported on the experience of parents who have lost children to sudden infant death syndrome (e.g., Wortman & Silver, 1992). They interviewed parents soon after their infant's death and reinterviewed them 18 months later. Wortman and Silver reported that parents showed some initial anxiety on the measures of bereavement, but they also showed positive emotions and little major distress. Were these parents in denial? No, according to the researchers. Eighteen months later, the parents continued to show strong signs of adaptation without major grief. Wortman and Silver have found that religious devotion and participation of the parents were positively related to their ability to cope with their loss. The mediating factor apparently was their feeling that they would see their children again healed someday in heaven.

However, it could be argued that even 18 months may be too soon to see the effects of denial. It is possible that the parents who grieved little in this first 18 months will need to come to grips with the grief they put aside. Otherwise, they may suffer in various physical and psychological ways in the long run.

In another study in their program, Wortman and Silver (1992) reported evidence showing that in a sample of older persons who had lost spouses, only a moderate degree of distress was felt by the survivors. Wortman and Silver speculate that such persons may have grieved prior to their spouses' deaths and that the deaths in many cases may have been seen as positive events because of the extended period of suffering prior to death.

Wortman and Silver (2001) revisit the idea that some people may cope well without grieving major losses. In this chapter, they reassert their earlier argument about the myths of coping with loss (e.g., that everyone grieves losses intensely, including those of children, or becomes depressed). They discuss recent evidence from a study of persons who had lost spouses. Yet these same individuals continued having some negative feelings about the loss for years. These data are for elderly spouses; Wortman and Silver admit that "working through" likely will be more difficult than for other losses, such as the loss of a child. They conclude with the point that "working through" is not well understood and deserves further theoretical and empirical attention.

Wortman and Silver's work suggests the intricacies of the grieving experience and that we still know too little about its convolutions. Certainly, many of us who have lived long lives begin to regularly experience the deaths of our kin and friends. It is the nature of things that we have learned to expect and accept.

Selected Approaches to Therapy for Traumatic Losses

Logotherapy (Meaning Therapy)

Fabry, Bulka, and Sahakian (1995) edited a collection of authors writing about the use of logotherapy, or meaning therapy, which developed from Frankl's (1959) analysis of the importance of meaning to humans. Below I incorporate ideas derived from Fabry et al. (1995) with points made by Frankl in his 1959 statement of logotherapy.

Frankl survived Auschwitz, where 3 million people died, and three other concentration camps between 1942 and 1945. His teachings that led to logotherapy have been described as the Third Vienna School of Psychotherapy, after that of Sigmund Freud and Alfred Adler. Frankl learned from his experience in Nazi death camps and his mentor Alfred Adler, the originator of individual psychology, that distress was often not physical or psychological. Instead, distress many times evolves from a lack of purpose. Thus, he began to develop a therapy based on redirecting clients toward meaningful pursuits. As Frankl (1959) suggested in *Man's Search for Meaning,* these quests for meaning may involve simple steps such as creating a work, or doing a deed, or experiencing something or someone. Frankl wrote that his task was to help clients find meaning in their lives, no matter how dismal their circumstances. Most important, Frankl believed that meaning was found in one's attitude. He said that he had learned in the death camps the invaluable quality of adopting an attitude to transcend personal suffering. Regardless of what the Nazis did to him or took from him, he controlled his mind and his attitude to find meaning (sometimes referred to as "tragic optimism").

Logotherapy is therapy through meaning (*logos*). The logotherapist does not "prescribe" meanings. The therapist cannot tell the client what the meanings of her or his life are. But the client can be shown that meaning does in fact exist. We all have millions of moments of meaning, whether heroic (e.g., saving another person's life) or prosaic (taking a refreshing walk in the country). Logotherapy helps the individual

recognize the uniqueness of these meanings. Such recognition provides a more meaningful life in general. Logotherapy does not dwell on
people's limitations, although they need to be acknowledged. Socrates
demanded of the person, "Know thyself;" Freud put the emphasis on
"Know your unconscious;" and Frankl argues, "Know your potentials."
The greatest waste, therefore, of the human is in terms of that human's
potential to accomplish.

A person's greatest motivation, in this system, is the will to find
meaning. Frankl (1959) believed that no activity is satisfying unless it
satisfies a spiritual hunger for meaning. This spiritual hunger was not
conceived within a religious meaning but, rather, a basic humanistic
meaning. Frankl diagnosed the existential vacuum as the common
problem of people in contemporary society. The logotherapist, then,
may treat a variety of persons, including an alcoholic, a drug addict, a
juvenile delinquent, a person who has attempted suicide or thought of
doing so, or an aimless searcher looking for meaning.

As it relates to existential concerns in people's lives, logotherapy is
quite similar to Yalom's (1980) existential psychotherapy. Yalom describes existential psychodynamics as involving the frequent conflicts
flowing from the individual's confrontation with the givens of existence such as the inevitability of death and the essential isolation of human life. Yalom's approach is aimed at helping the client realize his or
her personal freedom to construct a personal life design and make
choices that affect one's personal fate—which is similar to the attitudinal framing that Frankl (1959) advocates.

Specifically, logotherapy makes a contribution to dealing with neu-
rotic problems caused by (a) the difficulties of day-to-day living, which
may be sharpened by the threat of war, even nuclear war, pollution, and
all manner of public disasters and activities that degrade the human
spirit; (b) fatalism, an attitude that may cause one to consider a search
for meaning hopeless because the human's fate is determined by psychological drives, early environment, and other influences (all of which
Frankl challenges); (c) conformism, an attitude that tempts a person
who no longer trusts traditional guidelines to meaning and has not yet
developed personal values to do what most other people find meaning-

ful (e.g., go on binge drinking because one's buddies seem to find meaning by doing that); regarding conformity, Frankl (1959) remarked that humane humans are and probably will remain a minority, but it is precisely for this reason that each of us is challenged to join the minority; and (d) fanaticism, an attitude that accepts uncritically the meaning dictates of a leader or movement, such as the Third Reich movement.

One of the most cogent lines of reasoning in Frankl's (1959) statement of logotherapy concerns his view of love. Frankl, who died in 1997 at age 92, has written that he had wonderful relationships with his two wives (his first wife died in a Nazi death camp) and his family of origin. In a close relationship, Frankl believes that love triggers an upward spiral that causes both partners to attain heights otherwise unreachable. The loved one wants to be worthy of the lover, to grow more and more in the image the lover holds. Each one, in a manner of speaking, outbids the other to be worthier and thus elevates the other. In a good relationship, the partners bring out the best in each other, just as in a bad relationship they bring out the worst. Frankl emphasizes that although love can give meaning to life, a life without love is not meaningless. Meaning is unconditional, and love is an effective means to meaning, but other avenues can also lead to meaning fulfillment. Meaning is realized not merely through what is given or denied but, rather, through the attitude or approach taken. An unhappy love can start a process of self-investigation leading to true fulfillment. Meaning is never anticipation. It is recognized retroactively through the quality ones sees in each situation.

Telling and Writing Our Stories of Loss as Therapy

Loss is a general concept that may bring together under the same conceptual umbrella a host of diverse human experiences that may be understood better by viewing them as part of a life's constellation of losses. Focusing on stories of loss in different spheres can help synthesize a sense of the meaning of loss across different experiences and aspects of loss for different people. Available evidence suggests that such writing, teaching, and research on this topic will help people grow in their capacity to be empathic with others who suffer and also give them greater strength in dealing with their own inevitable losses.

The storytelling approach to dealing with major loss highlights the idea that *loss becomes gain* as we heal and particularly as we use our losses and what we learn from them to contribute to others who also suffer. In fact, that is the central idea of this whole book. What is important is how we deal with loss. What is important is how we see our lives and our losses as inextricably related to those of others in the past, present, and future and how we choose to make use of what transpires in our lives for the benefit of humanity as a whole. As Erikson (1963) defined it, such use of our lives is "generative" in its contribution to future generations. That is the message that the stories in this chapter will reveal.

Why do some losses heal and become generative? My answer, which has been illustrated with stories throughout this book, is that there is a crucial set of steps that needs to occur. The general social psychological model that I refer to as the story-action model involves the following set of events: A major loss leads to the development of a story about or understanding of the loss, which leads to storytelling or confiding about the loss, which leads to identifying possibilities for change, which leads to some sort of action that addresses the loss in some constructive way.

The idea of action aimed at redressing loss or gaining from it has been pervasive in stories presented throughout this book. In this context, "action" is defined as behavior that reflects a person's beliefs and values as reflected in that person's story of loss and grief. Identity change refers to the idea that who we think we are in the most fundamental sense changes drastically at the time of major loss. When we lose a spouse, we may choose to stop thinking of ourselves as a member of a "couple." Or we may continue to maintain a sense of our pre-loss identity for a long time (e.g., by continuing to wear a wedding ring to symbolize that identity). Similarly, when we lose our job, we have to reorient our self-image as someone employed by a certain employer with certain perquisites associated with that employment.

It has been argued that, on occasion, major loss does not necessarily require a person to take action in order to heal (Berscheid, 1994). Rather, time alone is sufficient to healing. In fact, we often tell survivors that "you just need time." Logically, however, there is every reason to believe that it is *what people do* during the time after major loss that matters most. Time itself is not a healer. Furthermore, simply not thinking about, or even avoiding thinking about, one's loss does not appear to be a viable way of dealing with the loss—however long a person actively avoids it.

The story-action model involves elements that are conducive to adaptive responding and generative behavior. Sometimes, these elements may be arranged in a different order. For example, after a loss, confiding and story development sometimes occur simultaneously. Also, as Neeld (1990) and other analysts of their own grieving have suggested, story development, confiding, and identity change probably go on simultaneously, as well as recursively, cycling in one direction and then the next.

Each element also is composed of several subelements. Story development and storytelling, for example, involve the release of emotions that build up after a loss and that must be partially released for the survivor to recover. In their stories of loss, grief, and healing, many people have provided powerful examples of transforming even the most crushing forms of loss into rays of hope and meaning for themselves and others. Later, I review other models of adaptation that involve storytelling as a significant component.

Is the storytelling approach effective in contributing to adaptation for everyone dealing with major loss? We do not have enough evidence to suggest that this approach applies to everyone. And in fact, there are some people (e.g., Holocaust survivors) who may have discovered that they cannot bear to tell of the horrors they have experienced. They may have found that they feel they can heal better in private without confronting these "unspeakable" losses. Most of us, though, very likely will benefit from this approach. Also, there are countless stories in the scholarly and popular literatures suggesting that the failure to tell one's story of major loss may ultimately cause one to suffer more as a result of the avoidance of the loss.

Emotional Expression

James Pennebaker's (1990) influential emotional expression argument about the value of opening up and expressing emotions about serious losses has been noted in Chapter 1 and elsewhere in this book.
This approach emphasizes the importance of narrative work, whether
in writing or talking. Pennebaker and colleagues have argued that writing reduces the physical and mental stress involved in inhibiting
thoughts (i.e., thoughts designed to avoid or distract oneself from
thinking about personal traumas). Furthermore, they contend that
writing is a powerful tool that can be used to organize thoughts and
feelings about overwhelming events and make them manageable. Writing takes these chaotic thoughts and feelings and helps the person gain
a sense of control in dealing with them.

More recently, however, Pennebaker, Zech, and Rime (2001) have
provided a somewhat more qualified view of the value of emotional expression in dealing with major loss. Pennebaker et al. admit that emotional expression usually stimulates victims to report that they feel
better, but they suggest that it may do little to help develop adaptive behavior (or it may even reduce such behavior). They cite studies that
have failed to find positive behavioral outcomes for emotional expression of loss. They predict that people suffering trauma likely will benefit more from disclosure than will people suffering a predicted loss (no
evidence yet); further, they predict that people who are not naturally
able to talk about loss may benefit most from disclosure. They believe
more research is necessary, comparing talking and writing for different
types of loss.

Related to Pennebaker et al.'s (2001) qualified logic about whether
narrative is always helpful is the work of Nolen-Hoeksema (2001). She
shows that ruminative coping (a personality style), which usually
involves incessant talking about loss, is not beneficial and contributes
to continued depression, anxiety, and anger. Why? Nolen-Hoeksema
provides the following answers: (a) Ruminative coping makes negative
thoughts more salient and accessible by stimulating negative moods;
(b) ruminative coping interferes with problem solving; (c) ruminative
coping impairs instrumental behavior by reducing motivation to do

everyday chores that can increase a sense of control and enhance mood; and (d) ruminating reduces social support from others.

Nolen-Hoeksema asks, "What is a ruminator to do?" Her answer seems to be to try to distract oneself. Suppression is hardly ever effective in the long run.

Stress and Coping

Donald Meichenbaum, a cognitive behavioral theorist and therapist, has developed what he calls stress inoculation training (SIT) to help people cope with imposing stresses in their lives. At the heart of this approach is the individual telling of his or her narrative about the stressful event.

As described by Meichenbaum (1985) and Meichenbaum and Fitzpatrick (1992), SIT involves (a) a (re)conceptualization phase, (b) a coping skills acquisition and rehearsal phase, and (c) an application and follow-through phase. Initially, it is critical for the therapist or trainer to establish a nurturant, compassionate, nonjudgmental set of conditions in which distressed individuals can tell their stories at their own pace. The therapist may use reflective listening, Socratic dialogue, sensitive probes, imagery reconstruction of stressful experiences, and other techniques to help the individual relate what happened and why it happened from his or her perspective. The exchanges between the therapist and client help the client make sense of difficult experiences and give meaning to those experiences. The therapist may ask, "Has anything positive come out of this experience for you?" Because meaning can determine the extent to which a given circumstance is a stressor and because meaning varies among people and with time, those in the same circumstances may be coping with qualitatively different stressors. It is important to understand this meaning so that it can be confronted and its implications can be considered.

In the second phase, a type of narrative repair is begun by the therapist. The therapist tries to help the client normalize his or her reactions to the stressor. The therapist helps the client appreciate that his or her reaction to the stressor is not abnormal. Rather, these reactions reflect one of a set of normal ways of perceiving and reacting to a difficult situation. The therapist may help the client reframe the stressful symptoms being experienced as a normal spontaneous reconstructive process and not a sign of weakness. Thus, emotional numbing and denial are characterized as ways individuals who have experienced trauma dose or pace themselves because they can deal with only a limited amount of stress at a given time.

A later aspect of SIT involves a reconceptualization of the distress process. The therapist helps the distressed client develop a more differentiated and integrated view of the stress by helping the client break down complex distressing reactions into manageable component parts that go through different phases and that vary across situations and time. The therapist may also help clients rescript what they say to themselves. The idea is to break down global stress descriptions into specific concrete, behaviorally prescriptive stressful situations. Clients, in other words, are taught the difference between changeable and unchangeable aspects of stressful situations. Clients are also taught to practice these coping skills so that they can collect "data" and review the results of their efforts. Consistent with my own view of the power of storytelling and reframing, what matters most about this type of narrative reconstruction is not its historical truthfulness but, rather, its narrative truthfulness—that is, the coherence of the story for the individual's life, goals, and new plans for action.

Pathologic Grief and Complicated Mourning

It has been argued that most therapy is mourning (Winer, 1994). Mourning makes it possible, using Loewald's (1960) phrase, "to turn ghosts into ancestors." Although all people will suffer losses and grieve, pathologic grief has a particular meaning among therapists working in this area. Jacobs (1993), in a book titled *Pathologic Grief,* defines this type of grief as a state that occurs when a bereaved individual experiences chronic, intense depression or separation distress or both. Separation distress involves yearning or pining for the lost loved one. Jacobs indicates that this type of grief occurs in 20% of acutely bereaved individuals, which is a huge number considering the fact that most humans will be "acutely bereaved" on multiple occasions in their lives. Jacobs also notes that this type of grief is most often associated with "haunting memories," and intrusive thoughts, images, and flashbacks. When chronic grief occurs after a major traumatic, fear-producing event, such as a war or a natural disaster, Jacobs indicates that the survivor may engage in dissociative behavior (showing "multiple personalities" or separation from one's normal personality). When chronic grief occurs in the context of personal loss, such as the death of a loved one, Jacobs indicates that the survivor is more likely to show disbelief and numbness. Unexpected death is the type of personal loss most often associated with pathologic grief. For almost 30% of the individuals who experience the sudden, unexpected loss of a loved one, PTSD-type symptoms such as depression have been reported.

Jacobs discusses a clinical case of pathologic grief that has some similarity to the stories reported in this book. Mr. D is a 45-year-old businessman whose daughter was assaulted and murdered by a stranger who was high on drugs. Mr. D then experienced severe bereavement for more than a year before seeking counseling. His grief was compounded by his anger at the failure of the judicial system to bring the alleged murderer to justice in a prompt manner. He was tortured with images of his daughter's actual death act, which left him feeling helpless, violated, and revengeful. He also experienced severe depression, thoughts of suicide, and thoughts of taking violent action against the alleged murderer. Mr. D was the key player in his family's work to bring the alleged murderer to trial and was very frustrated by defense actions that led to delays in the trial.

Fortunately, Mr. D did seek and receive therapy. That step, plus his constructive action to prod the judicial system to act more efficiently, led to a reduction in his intense grief. He could see a "light at the end of the tunnel" in gaining some justice for his daughter. Jacobs notes that therapists often have effectively treated pathologic grief such as Mr. D's with antidepressant drugs and psychotherapy. From the perspective of the story-action model, Mr. D's case supports the roles of the development of a story, confiding in a therapist, and taking action—in this case, action directed at the judicial system—as key factors in improvement.

Elizabeth Neeld (1990) developed valuable ideas about grief after her husband's sudden death. Neeld provides a convincing argument that people in deep mourning face a series of choices that can facilitate their successful recovery. She outlines the following seven choices in this process:

1. The choice of whether or not to experience the effect of the event and express grief fully
2. The choice of whether or not to suffer and to endure
3. The choice of whether or not to look honestly at oneself and one's life
4. The turning-point choice of whether or not to make an assertion with one's life
5. The reconstruction choice of whether or not to take action
6. The working-through choice of whether or not to engage in the inevitable conflicts that come after major loss
7. The integrative choice to continue to make choices—that is the nature of life—and to feel freedom from the domination of grief

Neeld's "map of the grieving process" is quite idealized. Do people engaged in powerful mourning have to go through this whole process? Will failures to choose at some interim point preclude the ultimate freedom from the domination of grief? Neeld's analysis has value in understanding the consequences of loss because she outlines how each of these choices was involved in her own recovery. People do not make these choices in a vacuum. Neeld suggests that survivors can best deal with their choices when they have strong support from family and friends, when they already have dealt with past major losses, and when their social, economic, and personal circumstances afford them the time and opportunity to grieve fully. This latter factor is too often neglected in scholarly analyses of grieving: Do people have so little energy left from trying to scrounge out a living that giving time to grieving becomes an impossible luxury? Neeld persuasively notes that the behavior of family and friends is critical in the grieving process. For example, she argues that if these close others are uncomfortable with mourning, if they act as if the grieving person should already be done with grieving, then grieving may be extended indefinitely.

Neeld's approach to healing bears considerable similarity to the position Therese Rando (1993) takes in *Treatment of Complicated Mourning*. Rando provides a thorough analysis of different aspects of mourning and recovery. She devotes considerable attention to the concept of "complicated mourning." This concept is quite similar to Jacobs's (1993) notion of pathologic grief. It is mourning that exceeds what is considered to be the norm and that defies modest attempts at intervention. In a way, this concept flies in the face of some of the logic of this book, which argues that all mourning is complicated. However, it is true that some people reach a point of peace and move on with their lives more readily than others. As important, it is true that some people desire to move on but cannot readily do so. For them the mourning process is most definitively complex in nature. Rando (1993) lists a set of risk factors that predispose any individual to complicated mourning: (a) sudden, unexpected death (especially involving trauma, randomness, or violence); (b) death from an overly lengthy illness; (c) the loss of a child; (d) the mourner's perception of the death as preventable; (e) a predeath relationship with the deceased that involved high degrees of anger, dependence, or ambivalence; (f) other losses that the mourner still is grieving; and (g) the mourner's perceived lack of social support.

Rando believes that the mourner experiences six major mourning processes.

1. Recognition and acknowledgement that the loss has occurred

2. Reaction to the separation by being willing to experience the pain—to feel, identify, and accept

3. Recollection and reexperiencing the deceased and the relationship, which involves an attempt to plan times to review and remember realistically

4. Relinquishment of the old attachments to the deceased and the old assumptive world, which means giving up the ways of viewing the world that were idiosyncratic to the lost relationship

5. Readjustment to move adaptively into the new world without forgetting the old

6. Reinvestment in new relationships and acts of meaning

These six correspond closely to the steps in the story-action model that I mentioned earlier. Rando (1993) makes the following specific recommendations to the caregiver about working with a mourner in her or his act of confiding:

> Help the mourner understand that it is precisely those emotions that go unexpressed that prompt loss of control and that there is great value in expressing a little emotion at a time in order to avoid an accumulation that will explode later on....
>
> Encourage expression of feelings with those people and in those places that are comfortable and without threat. If none exist, work to establish them (e.g., enlist the aid of an appropriate family member or provide referral to a support group). Given that social support is critical in the mourning process, it is inadvisable for the mourner to remain isolated. (pp. 402-403)

Support Group Movement

> A loving relationship is the therapy for all disorders of the human spirit. (Patterson, 1985, p. 91)

Stories and storytelling are vital activities carried out in grief support groups and in hospices. In support groups, one hears countless stories and experiences a plethora of vicarious emotions as tellers share their struggles with the group. After an early period of grieving, when being alone may be quite essential to the survivor, it may help to join a support group. In most cities, there are many different kinds of support groups. Survivors need to do research before they join one. It probably will help to inquire of both leaders and regular members about the goals and activities of the relevant groups.

In *I'm Grieving as Fast as I Can,* Linda Feinberg (1994) describes the value of a grief support group for young widowed persons after she lost her husband. She suggests that widowed people need to laugh and are good at it when given the chance. Sitting with a group for 10 minutes as people tell their stories can be an emotional roller-coaster. People quickly learn that they just thought they were the only ones sitting at home feeling miserable. Feinberg says that widowed young parents with children at home may feel a special sense of isolation. If left to their own devices, they will probably never even meet another young widowed person. That is where well-run relevant grief groups are valuable. Survivors meet people like themselves. The group members can struggle together in dealing with the common feelings related to being cheated out of a long and happy marriage.

Actress Gilda Radner endeavored to develop and publicize cancer-related support groups before she died, and there now are many excellent cancer wellness programs around the country. Central to these programs are support groups made up of survivors of cancer. They may be dying of their cancer, but they are also trying to live as hopefully and fully as they can. And they are helping other survivors in the process. Survivors find that they can tell their stories without restraint in these groups. Survivors often note that friends and family soon began to find stories of the cancer disease progression and treatment scary. Humor bubbles up regularly during these meetings. The humor may be black, but it is appreciated.

Many of us would like to die at home. But we may need medical assistance in the form of nursing help or some form of medical technology. Hospices exist to provide a feeling of being at home coupled with appropriate medical assistance. In a hospice, which is often a regular home in a community, the emphasis is on the quality of life. The medical care is aimed primarily at controlling pain and restoring normal functioning. Hospice services are requested only after the person or physician believes that no treatment or cure is possible. Clients and their families are viewed as a unit. An attempt is made to keep clients free of pain. The role of the staff is focused on being with the client, rather than doing something for the client as may be true in a hospital. An emphasis is placed on emotional and social support (Saunders, 1977).

Psychological Trauma
and Its Complications

Trauma may occur in a variety of circumstances. The sudden loss of a loved one may be traumatic to the survivor, very much in the same way that the experience of combat war veterans may be traumatic when they lose friends and have their own close calls with death. As an initial question, are there certain types of people who are more capable of withstanding and healing after trauma than others? That is, are certain types of personalities more resistant to the consequences of trauma?

One interesting study of Holocaust survivors and the lives they made in America after liberation was conducted by William Helmreich and reported in his 1992 book *Against All Odds.* Helmreich reviewed available data on the 140,000 Jewish Holocaust survivors who came to the United States and conducted more than 6 years of interviews with survivors. His study points to the incredible resilience of the survivors under the worst possible conditions. He argues that 10 general traits or qualities characterized the survivors who were able to lead positive, useful lives in the United States. These qualities were the following: flexibility, assertiveness, tenacity, optimism, intelligence, distancing ability, group consciousness, the ability to assimilate the knowledge that they survived, the ability to find meaning in their lives, and courage. Helmreich notes that not all these qualities were present in each individual, nor did all people who succeeded possess most of these attributes. However, at least some of these qualities were present in the majority of those survivors who did well in their postwar work and personal lives. Furthermore, the greater the number of these traits present within an individual, the greater the likelihood of successful adjustment.

A related story was published in Eva Fogelman's (1994) book *Conscience and Courage,* which tells the stories of rescuers of Jews during World War II. One of the people she highlighted was a businessman in Warsaw, Poland at the time of the Nazi takeover of Poland. When the Nazis created an imprisoned Jewish ghetto, from which Jews soon were shipped to concentration camps, this man said that he was curious about what was happening in the ghetto and found a way to visit it. *He said that one powerfully transforming moment in that visit motivated him to spend the next 4 years risking his life and the lives of his family to help Jews hide from the Nazis. This moment was the sight of dead and dying young children with flies swarming over their bodies.*

A well-written analysis of psychological trauma appears in Judith Herman's (1992) *Trauma and Recovery.* In this book, Herman suggests that a number of types of survivors, including combat veterans, concentration camp survivors, crime victims, battered and abused children and spouses, and prisoners of war, frequently are traumatized by their experiences, and sometimes to an extreme degree (thus the term "complicated trauma").

Complicated trauma involves such behaviors as denial, withdrawal, and aggression, as well as feelings of shame, hopelessness, and helplessness. Herman argues that the first principle of all recovery is the empowerment of the survivor. She believes that there are three major phases involved in helping people deal with such trauma. The first is helping the survivor feel safe. This step is a prelude to effective healing. It involves creating an environment in which the survivor feels safe to confide details of an event that may have greatly violated and degraded the self. It also involves helping the survivor reestablish a sense of personal control such that he or she can begin to work on the meanings of the trauma.

The second phase involves facilitating a survivor's remembrance of the traumatic event and helping the survivor mourn the loss involved. Obviously, this is the most difficult and potentially lengthy phase in the healing process. It involves telling the story of the traumatic event. In this phase, the survivor actually reconstructs the event so that it eventually can be integrated into her or his overall life story. Part of the difficulty in the survivor's work in the story phase is that his or her trauma may lead to emotionless, stereotyped reporting of what happened. Thus, it is important that the survivor be helped to achieve a comfort level wherein she or he can express emotions, mental images, and bodily sensations as part of the interpretive, communicative act.

This act of confiding, or telling about one's loss and pain, may be fraught with anxiety on the part of the survivor (as well as the person to whom the story is told). A person who had experienced incest made the following comment to Herman (1992) about what it felt like to confide in her family:

> Initially I felt a sense of completion. . . . Then, I began to feel very sad, deep grief. It was painful and I had no words for what I was feeling. . . . This was just raw feeling. Loss, grief, mourning . . . I knew there was nothing unspoken on my part. . . . I had said everything I wanted to say in the way I wanted to say it. I felt very complete about it and was very grateful for the lengthy planning, rehearsals. . . . Since then I have felt free. . . . I feel HOPE! (p. 201)

It should be noted that Herman (1992) argues, and I strongly agree, that we never achieve total completion in our grieving and interpretive reconstruction. New reflections about loss will recur at various points in our lives, particularly at new turning points. Our regrets and horrors, as well as our joys, never completely leave our minds, and sometimes return in our thoughts and emotions when we least expect them. Whereas total completion may be impossible, we nonetheless may achieve a high degree of completion and in so doing free ourselves to take on new challenges.

The third and final phase in Herman's (1992) model of recovery from trauma involves helping the survivor reconnect with the world and create a new future. It may involve reeducation regarding what is typical, what to expect, and what is possible. The survivor needs to reestablish personal control over how he or she continues to work on the trauma. For example, Herman presents the following quote from an incest survivor who was arriving at this point in her recovery:

> I decided, "Okay, I've had enough of walking around like I'd like to brutalize everyone who looks at me wrong. I don't have to feel like that any more . . ."
>   I thought, "How would I like to feel?" I wanted to feel safe in the world. I wanted to feel powerful. And so I focused on what was working in my life, on the ways I was taking power in real-life situations. (p. 197)

Herman suggests that reconnection involves a conscious decision to be willing to face danger in the future. It also involves an emerging tenacity, a learning how to fight in the face of vulnerabilities. It may involve some concrete act such as learning self-defense. I personally believe that another approach to dealing with past loss and continued feelings of vulnerability involves focusing on helping others in need.

Herman (1992) argues that the simple statement "I know I have myself" could stand as the emblem of a survivor's recovery and reconnection with the world. Reconciling with oneself probably will require creativity and energy, just as does reconciling with loved ones in one's environment. There is a new focus on identity and intimacy in these resolutions. Survivors often form close bonds with other survivors and plan futures together. A person introduced to an incest survivor's group commented on the affirmative nature of the group acceptance:

> I will look to this group experience as a turning point in my life, and remember the shock of recognition when I realized that the strength I so readily saw in the other women who have survived this . . . violation was also within me. (p. 216)

As suggested in the story-action model described earlier in this chapter, Herman (1992) also believes that an important aspect of reconnection is "finding a survivor mission." This step involves using one's experience and renewed capacity for action to work with others facing personal difficulties. Common to various types of social action is a dedication to raising public awareness about issues and problems facing various types of survivors. A Vietnam veteran told Herman about the value of his work with homeless veterans:

> This is about being an American, this is about what you learn in a fourth-grade civics class, this is about taking care of our own, this is about my brother. This feels personal to me. That feeling of isolation, it's gone. I'm so connected into it, it's therapeutic to me. (p. 209)

Coping With Disenfranchised Grief

Disenfranchised grief can be defined as the grief that persons experience when they incur a loss that is not or cannot be openly acknowledged, publicly mourned, or given much social support (Doka, 1989). As an illustration of disenfranchised grief, a widow wrote to "Dear Abby" in 1994 about her friends who seemed to be ignoring her loss of her 23-year-old husband 9 months earlier. She said that some of her friends avoided her to the point of ducking in the supermarket aisles and then acting as if nothing had happened when they did encounter her. This woman did not appreciate the tendency of many people to be threatened by the early death of one of their friends. She said that all she wanted was to have her loss acknowledged—just a simple "I'm so sorry." She also pointed out that only other widowed people knew how she felt and took her feelings seriously. She concluded that the best thing anybody (who did not know her husband personally) said to her was "I was so sorry to read about your husband's death. Would you like to talk about it?"

This woman has learned a lot about human reactions to death the hard way. Humans frequently are fickle in their friendships when they feel threatened, and nothing is more threatening than death. Support groups serve an invaluable role in our world in providing a forum with others who have experienced similar losses and know what it is like to have friends avoid you in your time of need.

As Doka (1989) suggests, the concept of disenfranchised grief recognizes that societies have sets of norms, or grieving rules. These norms specify who, when, where, how, how long, and for whom people should grieve. Doka perceptively notes that even in organizations personnel policies may reify these norms, as when a worker is permitted a week off for the loss of a spouse or child but only 3 days off for the loss of a parent or sibling.

Doka argues that a survivor's grief is most often unrecognized in three types of situations. The first situation is when a relationship is unrecognized. For example, people often grieve the loss of a non-marital close relationship profoundly (Orbuch, 1988). Yet we have no support systems for nonmarital partners. The same is true for persons who are homosexuals. It has been shown that homosexual men who lose a partner to AIDS may experience bereavement for as long as 1 year before the death of their partner and for years afterward and that this bereavement affects their patterns of future close relationships (Mayne, Acree, Chesney, & Folkman, 1998).

The second in which a survivor's grief may go unrecognized is when the loss itself is not recognized. There are many examples of this situation of disenfranchised grief. Parents whose child develops a serious mental illness or a serious chronic illness may experience the same grief as those who experience the death of a child. As one grief counselor noted, the grief of parents facing these types of loss are not recognized or validated by society.[1] As a result, healthy expression of parental grief is impaired. A type of loss that falls into the "nonloss" category in the behavior of people is the loss of a parent. Miriam Moss, a senior research scientist at Philadelphia Geriatric Center, quoted in *Chicago Tribune,* contended, "People tend to see an old mother or father, and the reaction to their death is, 'What do you expect?' The ethos is it's just not a big deal."[2]

Parents who have missing children also may experience disenfranchised grief because others do not know how to respond to their long-term (and likely unending if the child is not found) grief. One example of this type of situation is the experience of the family of Jacob Wetterling in Minnesota. Jacob was 11 years old when he was abducted in October 1989. Dirk Johnson of the *New York Times* interviewed Jacob's parents in December 1998 to find out how the family was coping with this loss. Johnson described the effect of Jacob's disappearance on their lives:

> For the Wetterling family, the uncertainty has meant nearly a decade of life lived in the half-step, not quite there, reluctant to lose themselves completely to the moment, moving ahead with daily routines, because there is no choice, learning to sing again, even to laugh, but never as freely, or lightly, as before.
>
> Theirs is the burden of doubt known to people who live with mysterious holes in the family fabric, voids that go unexplained, losses that are never properly mourned.[3]

Ms. Wetterling still clings to the belief that her son is alive. Her burden has resulted in great bouts of depression. As she said, "One morning I lay in bed and couldn't go on anymore. . . . It was too hard. I pulled the covers up over my head and decided I was never going to get out of that bed again." But she has tried to cope by writing a letter to the captor beseeching him to listen and to have compassion and has started a foundation for missing children called Jacob's Hope. As she said, "For my own survival, I have had to let go a lot of anger or I would be swallowed up in it" (p. 13).

Johnson points out that Jacob's family has changed in many ways since his abduction. His siblings are just about done with college, his high school class has moved on to college and careers, his dog has died, and his grandfather has died. In addition to the prolonged grief of his parents and close friends and relatives, one must wonder if Jacob and other lost or abducted persons are out there somewhere experiencing their own insuperable grief at the loss of hopes and dreams and a fate so cruel that we as outsiders may never begin to understand how they feel.

In a third type of situation involving disenfranchised grief, the grieving person is not recognized as capable of grief. Doka (1989) argues that there are situations in which a person is viewed as incapable of grief. The very old, the very young, and the mentally disabled frequently are viewed in this light. Somehow, we may consider people in these categories as unable to cognize their major losses, and hence unable to feel the depth of pain that most people feel about such losses. Yet each person is capable of grief, and it is naive to believe that some of us have deeper feelings of loss or a less profound sense of grief.

Doka (1989) points out that disenfranchised grief poses major problems for those who experience it. It can exacerbate grieving and lead to complicated reactions such as guilt and anger. Disenfranchised grief is often associated with a strong sense of ambivalence. For example, ambivalence often accompanies abortion or the breakup of a relationship and is intensified in the absence of recognition and support from close others.

C. S. Lewis (1961), whose writings about the loss of his wife were discussed in Chapter 4, described the embarrassment he experienced in public after the death of his wife. He articulated his discomfort with others because he was "now alone because of death": "To some, I'm worse than an embarrassment. I am a death's head. Whenever I meet a happily married pair I can feel them thinking, 'One or the other of us must some day be as he is now'" (p. 11).

The avoidance of associates who have a fatal or disabling illness both stigmatizes them and prevents them from grieving their loss, or possible loss, openly. Similar to the survivors of persons who die, they sometimes become "pariahs." In an article in the *Washington Post,* Victor Cohn discussed what pariahs sometimes experience and how they feel in our society:

> Those of us who lose a loved one begin to feel as though we have some loathsome, contagious disease. After the Emily Post proprieties—and the flowers, cakes and fruit baskets of the official mourning period—the friends disappear. . . . Whether we've lost a mother on whose guidance we depended or a life-long spouse . . . or [have experienced] a child's suicide, the ultimate, rejection, we feel lonely or abandoned.[4]

Cohn went on to suggest that avoidance by our friends is hardly what we need when we experience such losses. Cohn further suggests that we may simply need the reassurance of continuity with the nongrieving world. (Although, as I argued at the outset of this book, I think experience will teach us that there is no nongrieving world!)

Cohn also describes the experience of David Rabin, Professor of Medicine at Vanderbilt University, who in 1980 was dying of Lou Gehrig's disease, but who desired to attend one more European meeting in his field before he died. His physical condition was quite serious, but he was able to make the trip. This professor spoke of people walking past him with eyes averted or saying hurried "hellos." He said that the nonverbal message clearly indicated what others now thought of him: that what Susan Sontag has called "the passport of the healthy" had been revoked. Rabin later wrote in a medical journal about his experience of being shunned at the meeting. He received hundreds of letters from physicians and other people who had had similar experiences. He said that this flood of support helped him feel that he was not somehow to blame for inflicting the sight of his condition on his colleagues. Cohn concluded his piece with the admonition that all of us should learn how to take responsibility for looking at, talking to, and showing simple acts of support to our colleagues who are suffering the from loss of their loved ones or their own grave conditions. Saying "I didn't know what to say" is easy, but it is a cop out on friendship and responsibility—and on the decency we hope others will afford us when we are in a similar situation.

Coping With "Silent Losses"

Closely related to disenfranchised grief is the sorrow felt by persons whose close pet companions die. This type of loss sometimes is not seen as a "big deal" in society. Morales (1997) perceptively wrote about the great loss many people experience when their pets die or become permanently lost. She states that there are more than 50 million dogs and even more cats serving as animal companions in the United States.

Morales argues cogently that such losses typically are "silent" and too little recognized by many people in society. People reacting to pet losses often say, "Well why don't you go buy a replacement dog or cat, etc.?" These reactions are not helpful. As Morales notes, animal companions provide a shoulder to cry on, become trusted confidantes, and help us in untold ways during times of crises. She also points to work showing that petting a dog or stroking a cat can reduce blood pressure.

Animal companions often are connected to key passages in our lives and their loss may be linked in our master account to our other losses. We may grieve intensely and connect the loss of humans to losses of animal companions during the same period. How we grieve and adapt in general may apply just as much to our mourning when we lose valued animal companions. Morales (1997) quotes Dora in Charles Dickens's *David Copperfield* as reflecting well what our animal companions may mean to us:

> I couldn't be friends with any other dog but Jip; because he wouldn't have known me before I was married, and wouldn't have barked at Doady when he first came to our house. He has known me in all that has happened to me. (Morales, 1997, p. 248)

Conclusions

Dealing with major loss cannot be easy or simple—despite the modicum of evidence that some people do not show the standard signs of significant grieving reactions. On a practical level, loss takes away resources. On an emotional level, loss may even take away our will to live and likely is involved in our most daunting psychological disorders and difficulties.

Nonetheless, as discussed in this chapter, there are useful approaches to dealing with major loss. I will treat this topic of coping in a more personal way in the final chapter on adjustment in general.

> The greatest use of a life is to spend it on something that will outlast it. (William James)

Notes

1. From an article by Peggy MacGregor, LSW and child and family advocate, in *Alliance for the Mental Ill Newsletter of Iowa,* Winter 1995.
2. From WOMANEWS, *Chicago Tribune,* December 6, 1998, sec. 13, p. 8.
3. From *New York Times,* December 31, 1998, pp. 1, 13.
4. From *Washington Post,* May 24, 1990, p. 6B.

12 Perspectives on Personal Adjustment to Loss

An Integrative Commentary

I am the sum of my commitments, or in other words, I am what I choose to stand up and be counted for, and those choices define me.

—Martin Buber

The credit belongs to the man who is actually in the arena; who strives valiantly; who errs and comes short again and again; who knows great enthusiasms, the great devotions, and who spends himself in a worthy cause.

—Theodore Roosevelt

In this chapter, I present different perspectives aimed at common real world loss and trauma dilemmas and then some integrative comments focusing on principles of loss revealed across the different topics covered in this text. Much of this material derives from teaching the loss and trauma course that was described in Chapter 1. The first part of this chapter is based on my own personal experience and not on the literature. It reflects my living experience and should be taken as potentially biased because it emphasizes a particular point of view, even to a greater degree than have other chapters.

Framing

One of the most important things we all have to learn about loss is how to frame the experience. As argued in Chapter 1, all loss is relative. When stresses of living occur, we have to learn how to frame them within the context of other events, and how these stresses compare to other events in our own lives and the lives of others. Framing can help us cope, work through problems more effectively, and give us greater acceptance and peace about our losses. As the Frankl quote beginning Chapter 11 suggested, when in times of crisis we cannot change the outside world, we have to look into ourselves and make changes there. That is what cognitive framing helps a person do.

Another perspective on framing loss is provided by Dr. Virginia Geary-Shen (personal communication, October 15, 2000). She argues that loss is a transition. The love felt for the lost other is reinvested; thus, from this standpoint, loss does indeed become gain. Geary-Shen is suggesting that we use our lessons of loss to imbue ourselves with greater love and compassion for others.

Geary-Shen's message is reinforced by a book titled *Missing Still* (1993), which was put together by the family and friends of Stephanie Schmidt, a young woman who was abducted and killed by a coworker while she was attending college at Pittsburgh State University in Kansas (see Wilson & Allison, 1993). This book contains many testimonials to Schmidt's contributions in her 20 years of living. It also describes her family's efforts to effect state legislation to have greater public attention given to persons who have previously been convicted for sexual crimes. Schmidt's killer had been released after serving 10 years of a 20-year sentence for sexual molestation. The book is a wonderful statement of remarkable graciousness exhibited by family and friends whose grief was enormous but who refused to withdraw from tackling their grief in a highly constructive way. *Missing Still* concludes with this poem on loss:

> Measure thy life by loss and not by gain,
> Not by the wine drunk, but by the wine poured forth,
> For love's strength standeth in love's sacrifice,
> And he who suffers most has most to give. (p. 38)[1]

As described at the beginning of Chapter 2, the experience of missing a loved one (as in instances of missing persons) is particularly devastating to families. In that discussion, I told of an Indiana University coed who disappeared in late spring 2000 (and had not been found as of this writing), who law enforcement authorities believe was abducted. As the family of this coed expressed, grief in these situations is daily, debilitating, and open-ended. The losses for the family may far transcend the loss of the individual and their interaction with her. They may include what the young person would have achieved in the future, possible relationship difficulties in their own family, as parents and other relatives attempt to cope both individually and collectively over an indefinite period, and health-related difficulties caused by the stress and grief.

This type of loss speaks to the principles of loss outlined in Chapter 1, especially the ideas that people often experience a loss of control and that losses often have cumulative impacts over time. The framing task of someone who has suffered a big loss like this is so colossal they may not know when to start full-blown grieving or how long to hold out hope that their loved one will be found alive.

Some of the long-term influences of the loss of a loved one and the profound adaptation task involved were described in *Chicago Tribune Magazine* in a piece titled "Seasons of Grief." This piece by Julia Keller described how the people of Huntington, West Virginia, coped with the loss of the 75 members of the Marshall University football team, coaches, and others who died when their plane crashed as it was approaching Huntington on November 14, 1970. The scars of that great loss—all who were on the plane—remain etched in the city, the university, and the families of the victims 30 years later. One father who lost his son in the crash said,

> The pain still is fresh each morning ... almost as if it renews itself overnight, culling from the new day power to hurt ... you don't forget it. You don't. It's something that happened and you can't do anything about it. I have to accept it. I have my bad moments. I do. I get in the car and ride out to the cemetery and visit his grave. I have a cry. Sometimes I can't talk about it. (p. 10)[2]

Like the family with the missing loved one, another mother of one of the Marshall University victims said, "It makes you never quite believe it. You think he'll come walking along" (p. 14). As ways of coping and remembering, Marshall University has created a memorial at the football stadium that lists the names of the victims. And in 1999, a documentary was being made about the crash—a documentary that members of the community say could not have been made sooner because of the depth of the collective bereavement process.

Framing the Loss of a Close Relationship

To better illustrate cognitive framing, let us use an example of framing by a grieving partner in a close relationship that has lasted a substantial period of time, but that now is coming to an end. In our example, let's say Bob tells Ann that he no longer loves her and does not want to be with her anymore. This news comes out of the blue for Ann. After all, Bob had spent years courting Ann and telling her how much he loved her. They had planned their lives—'til death—together and had taken various steps toward that eventuality. Yet now Bob had changed his mind, and he was adamant in his feeling that he no longer loved Ann. Indeed, her world of assumptions was shattered (Janoff-Bulman, 1992).

Many of us have been in Ann's shoes, and many of us will be there in the future, however much we believe that we have a stable world that cannot take cruel turns such as this one. What can Ann do? Nothing? She can take some adaptive steps, slowly. First, though, there are very normal passages of grief that will unfold. Very much like the account-making confiding model described in Chapter 1 suggests, she is likely to be quite numb, shocked, and in a state of wildly vacillating emotions—from panic, despair, and depression to a period of ecstasy arising from the thought that maybe there will be a wonderful new life out there for her. The more common experience is that of deep grief accompanied by thoughts about loving times with Bob in the past. In addition, she may ask the question over and over, why did this happen? Other recurring questions may include the following: Did I do something to make him fall out of love with me? Did he find someone else?

How could this happen after all we went through to achieve a feeling of mutual love?

Ann probably will then begin her process of confiding in close others about this loss. Hopefully, she has caring others who will be there for her, listen to her, and even have a few gems of wisdom to offer on occasion. Hopefully, these close friends will know that it is good for Ann to stay busy, fight off bitterness and hostility toward Bob, and think about positive steps she can take with her life. Psychoanalyst Carl Jung emphasized the value of working in the garden or on arts and crafts projects and being with one's pets in times of great loss. Maybe Ann will have some of those inclinations. She should not be deluded that Bob will come back to her. He may try to. But the high probability is that once this dissolution process starts, it will go all the way. Even if Bob ultimately wants Ann back, Ann may be so hurt and feel so betrayed that there may be no way the relationship can be renewed. Renewal works best when it is begun while the relationship still involves a mutual commitment to make it work and involves tinkering rather than miracles cures.

Despite the work reviewed in Chapter 11 about some people who did not need to grieve much when they lost a loved one to death, most of us will experience high degrees of grief in these situations and many others in our lives, including the one faced by Ann. Ann somehow has to first find a way to continue on, to survive! Then, she has to take the baby steps to restore her sense of selfhood, who she is, what she expects and hopes for in life, and what she has learned from her relationship with Bob. She has to fight the negative, revenge-oriented inclinations that are so common when people are hurt by others. Why? Because these inclinations will hurt her more in time than anything else. She will be restored more by grace in the heat of loss and will find redemption much sooner with gracious acceptance of her partner's decisions. She has to look inward, as Frankl said and so marvelously did in surviving the Nazi death camps. Easily said but not easily done, I know.

One of the most difficult areas of activity in a breakup is what to do about practical areas of interdependence with one's ex-partner. You may have a home together, a mutual bank account, many common possessions, and yes, all those photos of the good times. I do not have a recommendation other than these tasks all will have to be addressed and dealt with. You may wish to put the photo albums away (gently filed rather than burned or destroyed). Why? See the discussion below about "embracing" past memories. Someday you may want to see those photos again and treasure them. Give that possibility a chance, I would suggest, though I know some people find it cathartic to destroy them. But you cannot destroy memories and especially intrusive memories. These thoughts, feelings, and memories will come back at us, just as dreams will too.

Ann has to give herself a break. She may make many mistakes in her adaptation. She has to be focused, though, on positive steps forward. Sure, she will experience many bouts of nostalgia and regret. But she cannot repress these thoughts, memories, and feelings. They will happen. Daniel Wegner and colleagues (Wegner, 1989, 1999; Wegner & Schneider, 1989), experts on thought control, have recommended wallowing in these remembrances and pangs of regret—don't run from them. Let them happen. By doing that enough, presumably you can gain a sense of control over the memories rather than having the memories control you. As one of my book titles suggests, you learn to "embrace their memory" (Harvey, 1996) rather than being "imprisoned or haunted by their memory." It is a matter of practiced thought, acceptance of the grueling nature of pain from loss, and actually taking small steps to begin a new life. It is a matter of cognitive framing and action consistent with the frames developed.

Physical Fitness and Tenacity

The importance of physical fitness in relieving stress and prolonging quality of life is increasingly recognized. In the discussion of life span processes in Chapter 7, Bland's (1997) thesis on "live long, die fast" was described. Bland emphasizes the value of lifelong physical fitness in contributing to a long life, and a life that has a better chance of death by natural processes rather than those associated with smoking, overeating, and self-destructive behavior in general. I personally have benefited greatly from a lifelong commitment to rigorous physical fitness and have heard many stories of the value of exercise from my students taking my loss and trauma course. As we who exercise regularly know well, physical fitness activities help us confront our mental demons, just as much as they help us achieve better physical health.

In December 2000, the *Washington Post* reported on a soon-to-be published study done at Duke University Medical Center that showed the value of exercise in fighting depression. In this study, 156 people with depression were divided into one of three groups, an exercise group, a medication group, and a group that exercised and received medication. The participants were 50 years of age or older, and the medication was Zoloft. The people in the exercise group spent 30 minutes, 3 times a week, on a treadmill or stationary bicycle at 70% to 85% of their maximum heart rate. After 4 months, about two-thirds of the people in all three groups had overcome their depression. The researchers checked the mental status of those people again after 10 months. People in the exercise group had less than half as many relapses as the people in the other two groups. The researchers suggested that the higher relapse rate among the exercise-plus-medication group may have been due to the belief of the group members that the medication helped them—not the exercise. Importantly, after the study, more than half of the exercise group participants continued to exercise (believing that it was continuing to help them). Only a quarter of the participants taking only Zoloft continued taking Zoloft after the study (believing that it was not helping them that much).

Related to the value of physical fitness is one's tenacity regarding living life constructively. This message was delivered cogently by Frankl (1959) in his report of surviving the Nazi death camps. In Albert Ellis's (1975) *A Guide to Rational Living,* he makes good points about the imperative of having the correct attitude that can guide actions aimed at overcoming adversity. Ellis puts it in his typically colorful way, saying, "You have to push your ass" (lecture at Governor's State University, Illinois, Oct. 14, 1994). He says that when loss or adversity strikes us, we have the choice of whether to fall into depression and despair—and, essentially, not move out of those states—or to choose grief, sadness, regret, and similar "movement-oriented" emotions. According to Ellis, they are movement oriented because most of us learn the pathway through them to adaptation and recovery, whereas depression and despair lead nowhere.

Guidance From Darkness

Shelton (2000) used her own experience with divorce and the losses she experienced with her congregation as a minister in California to develop some thoughtful advice about dealing with adversity. She noted the common experience of loss as that of feeling limitation and a sense of "being broken" introduced into one's life. She argued that only through a transformation (similar to what Ann must do in the above example) will the feelings of limitation and being broken begin to subside. But, unfortunately, not everyone gets that far. Some may pretend that change is occurring. But it is not. We have to be realistic in evaluating our lives, lest we take the same rutted paths over and over again. Some people have all the right information, read all the right books, but the steps are not taken, the changes are not made. Camus said that there can be no happiness if the things we believe are not consistent with the things we do. To make these critical transformations in the context of loss, we must be diligent in pursuing behavioral compliance with such a philosophy of living.

Similar to the example given for Ann, Shelton (2000) describes the sense of being broken when a loss, such as divorce, occurs:

> Times of brokenness are shocking and difficult. In the midst of them we are likely to experience an emotional roller coaster. From hope to despair; from bargaining to blaming; from rage to guilt; from terror to peace—loss rockets us from one emotion to the next with little rest or comfort. Just when we think we have regained our balance, the rug seems to be pulled out from under and the cycle of emotions begins again. (p. 87)

Shelton's quote is so true. Throughout life, people experience these recurrent moments of deep angst about loss—even loss that is years in the past. As described in Chapter 8, Harvey, Stein, and Scott (1995) documented the lifelong despair and grief among Normandy invasion veterans who still felt so much grief about the loss of their buddies 50 years earlier. The story about the Civil War veterans of the bloody Gettysburg battle of 1863 also informs us about the powerful and lasting nature of loss and grief. Fifty years after the famous battle, they traveled to Gettysburg for a reunion, and many of them died on their way home after the reunion. They stayed alive to remember with other veterans the trauma of that defining experience in their lives!

I have also encountered so many senior citizens, including my parents, who must remember and talk about their many losses (as well as triumphs) as they move inexorably toward the end of their lives. That is just the way it is with the human condition and another reason I believe we must honor all our memories. Our memories have the potential to humanize us. We will experience greater peace in the long run if we treasure these memories, even the sad and crushing ones, as the stimuli that make us who we are.

Shelton (2000) discusses death and her experience with many people getting ready to die. She stresses that we know too little about this preparation and near-death experience in general. She is right. People near death often report seeing and hearing things from "the other side," or seeing people who have gone on before them—as if these close departed others are beckoning them forward, as if they can serenely make their transitions. Shelton describes how the "veil" between the worlds becomes thin for these people. We tend to spend time in both this world and the one we think we are going to next.

Shelton (2000) notes that all of us want the dream life: We want to be wealthy without responsibilities. We want to be healthy without regular exercise, a good diet, and practices for dealing with stress. We want the perfect mate. Yet how realistic are these desires? A devotion to realism comes in handy over and over again in life. And realism usually means that we will have to work hard to succeed in any area, including adaptation to loss. Shelton argues that the event of loss opens the way to changing us at a deep level. It is inconvenient, but amazingly transformational.

Shelton also makes the excellent point that many of us do not show our feelings related to loss easily to others. We hide it or avoid the topic. Thus, those closest to us may think that all is fine with us. It is not. This fact can leave us feeling even more lonely and ashamed, and we may feel as if we are a failure. We buy into the term "loser" that gets thrown around indiscriminately in our culture. We buy into the term "failed marriage" as if there were a scoreboard in the sky and a godlike score-keeper who could readily help us all know who succeeded and who failed and what the score was. Forget that nonsense. It is all relative. Take a microscope to any marriage, any life, and one will discover pain, probably different types and degrees, but pain nonetheless.

One of Shelton's (2000) most vivid examples of the pain of loss is when she started her own divorce and how crushing the immediate sensations were. She described this event as follows:

> The day my husband and I decided to divorce after ten years of marriage, I remember sitting in the living room of our house in the rocking chair where I had spent so many hours nursing and rocking our son as an infant. It was a gorgeous, sunny September day in Seattle. The weather seemed to be mocking me. I couldn't understand how life could go on as if nothing had happened, when the universe was shattering within and around me.
>
> Although I never identified the end of my marriage as a failure, the feelings of loss were so profound I truly felt like a bruised and beaten loser. I had lost my vision for the future. The bible wisely says, "Where there is no vision, the people perish." (pp. 99-100)

How many of us have had similar sensations? Many, I bet. Harvey (1996) describes the paradox of feeling an internal sense of despair and pain on a great sunny day when so much of nature is so lovely. And what is inside takes precedence over what is outside any day.

Shelton (2000) contends that the quality of our lives in the end reduces to the choices we make. That is the point of the Buber quote that introduces this chapter. Our choices define us. If we have had a close relationship end and feel very hurt by our ex-partner, the responsibility finger should be pointed first at ourselves because we chose to be involved with that partner. Certainly, a realistic view of relationships and life in general is that responsibility is shared by multiple sources in complex events. Nonetheless, remember Frankl's advice that we may only be able to change that which is within us. Similarly, we will use our experience best by holding ourselves responsible for our own decisions and behavior in many of the dilemmas we encounter.

This advice supplements Neeld's (1990) "seven choices" logic in how she regrouped after the sudden death of her husband. She clearly was not responsible for that event. Bad luck occurs. Yet she was responsible for her reactions to the loss and how she tried to cope and develop a new identity. She did make choices in coping with that loss; she left teaching and moved into the business world, and she formed new close relationships and hopes for her life. She made these decisions and moves while keeping clearly in mind the great blessing of having had her long-term relationship with her departed husband.

A final important story repeated by Shelton (2000) about transformation concerns how the song "Amazing Grace" was written. A slave ship captain was called to address a problem in the hold of his vessel. His vessel contained hundreds of African men, women, and children being transported to be sold into slavery. In seeing the filthy conditions in which these people were traveling, this captain for the first time saw the cruel plight of these fellow human beings. He decided to turn the ship around to take them home and set them free. He also went to his cabin to pray for forgiveness and in so doing wrote the lyrics of "Amazing Grace": "Amazing grace, how sweet the sound, that saved a wretch like me./I once was lost, but now I'm found; was blind but now I see."

Grappling With Bereavement

Over the years, I have found certain recommendations quite helpful in dealing with loss and bereavement. These are simple ideas that also can be readily communicated to others when they grapple with loss. Professionals in this area emphasize a set of activities to use in grappling with bereavement. In my loss and trauma class, I summarize these ideas into the following three Rs: *Recognize, Respond, Remember.*

Let me elaborate. At some point after major loss, we need to recognize the nature, magnitude, and implications of the loss in our lives. In so doing, we may need to take time to allow nature's healing and pamper ourselves with rest and routine activities. We may need to recognize that forgiveness (of ourselves and others) is a vital part of the healing process. As has been argued in this book, we need to realize that any new major loss or crisis will bring up feelings about past losses. Our losses accumulate and cohere together in our minds and in our unconscious.

This process of recognition and response often occurs in an awkward, stuttering way. We have to recognize further that there will be many times that we are overwhelmed by our losses. They may keep us awake at night and in feelings of deep regret and yearning. As this book has emphasized, key steps to dealing with major loss are to be vulnerable, to share pain with close others, and to be humble enough to accept support. Experts suggest that surrounding oneself with life, such as plants, animals, and friends, may be a valuable step.

Ultimately, the step of remembering, what we have called memorialization in this book, is essential. This may involve regular memorial work—for example, the use of photo albums, letters, and visits to graves. A further helpful step may be to keep a diary and record successes, memories, and struggles during this time. As important may be engaging in positive activities to recognize and honor the causes in which a loved one most believed and worked. We have seen this latter type of generative, memorial work in many of the examples of adaptation to loss discussed in this book. In the arena of the loss of close relationships, it very likely will be helpful to avoid rebound relationships, as well as making big decisions quickly, or doing anything that is negatively addictive. As is realistic, we need to embrace the blessings of our lives. All of us have things in our lives that we are grateful for, possibly including health, family, friends, a job, or whatever we value and appreciate. Write them down so you can refer to them whenever you feel there is nothing positive in your life.

Another set of recommendations pertains to significant moments in time, as in anniversaries and special holidays. We need to know that holidays and anniversaries can bring up painful feelings, even if you thought you had successfully worked through these feelings. Grief counselors suggest that we should be realistic during these times. Don't have the expectation that the holidays will produce a magical feeling or be a solution to your problems. We need to recognize our feelings as what they are and feel them without suppression. Cry as much as you need to. Understand that the holidays may intensify your sense of loss. During these times of intense bereavement, we may want to lower our expectations of what we think we should or should not do. Consider whether you need to accept every invitation. Don't try to make things happen or force happiness. It only creates the opposite effect. If it is physically possible, people will benefit from rigorous exercise as a stress release and a health benefit for body, mind, and soul; that is true year-round, particularly so at special times. Also, during this time, choose to be with the people who support you the most. Make special plans for special days in advance. Let your family know your plans in advance. Tell them what you need and what you expect of them. Maintain and even cultivate your sense of humor. Try not to take the holidays too seriously. If you find life too serious or intense, have a good laugh. Do something ridiculous and funny. Laughing is a good way to relieve tension and stress. Many people will rely on their own source of spiritual strength.

The holidays are special times for all families, and that is true for families who have lost children too. How should we approach such families? Should we avoid mentioning the lost loved one? No. *Tribune Media Services* columnist Jacquelyn Mitchard echoed this point in a December 8, 2000, column.[3] She suggested that friends may not recognize that parents who have lost children would like their friends to discreetly inquire about their loss, especially during special seasons and at birthdays. Parents likely will want to talk about the life and accomplishments of their child. They may especially want to remember qualities such as their child's grace, humor, intelligence, and the like—dear qualities that are now invisible but live on in memory.

Mitchard said that one parent whose son committed suicide in 1994 noted how much it helped that her best friend never forgets to acknowledge their son in her yearly Christmas card. This woman contended that it helps when people don't pretend it never happened. Finally, Mitchard mentioned that the leader of a Compassionate Friends group said that when bereaved parents come to the group they do not believe that there will come a time when they will feel better. Parents who lose children do not forget.

Searching for Forgiveness

Much of what families do who have suffered violent losses, such as murder, is search for forgiveness. Forgiveness is a topic that is drawing widespread contemporary attention in psychology both in practice and research (e.g., Enright & North, 1998; Fincham, 2000). A main premise behind this movement is that harboring hatred and grudges, or the desperate desire for revenge, can be damaging. Elie Weisel, although embracing the ideas of forgiveness, has said that some things cannot be forgotten or forgiven—the Holocaust is a prime example.

Parade Magazine did a feature piece on people who are trying to forgive. As a police officer in New York, who had been made a quadriplegic by the bullets of an attacker, said about his attacker: "Every day I have to forgive again."[4] Thus, trying to forgive for major acts of harm is similar to grief work. It is ongoing and relentless. Scholars of forgiveness (e.g., Fincham, 2000) tell us that it is an important step we all must learn for our own benefit and that of society. It removes the barrier for relating, helps us understand better the dynamics of human behavior, and helps us be more empathic to other people's pain.

Tears That Last

When we grieve major losses, we often grieve about our history of loss, and possibly the losses of others as well. We grieve by thinking about and telling ourselves our stories of loss and putting them together in some sort of meaningful account (Harvey, Weber, & Orbuch, 1990). We also may tell and grieve the stories of loss experienced by others. As we age, it is helpful to have confidants with whom to share these stories of loss (Harvey & Hansen, 2000).

On the ABC news program "Nightline," host Ted Koppel interviewed Morrie Schwartz a couple of times in 1995. I show a video of this interview to my class on loss and trauma. It is immensely touching and instructive. Schwartz (who also was the person interviewed in the best-selling 1997 book *Tuesdays with Morrie* by Mitch Albom) was in his mid-80s and in the final stages of dying from ALS, Lou Gehrig's disease.

In one interview segment, Koppel asked Schwartz what he was grieving the most as his life neared its end. Schwartz said that without question he grieved the loss of his mother when he was an 8-year-old boy the most. That was the insuperable pain that he felt most even as his own body was quickly becoming dysfunctional. He had felt very much alone then, and in thinking about that loss he always felt lonely. He also said that when he grieved, he felt some of the pain of the whole world and of people through the ages who suffered great losses. Schwartz's grace as he finishes his valuable life was inestimable. He modeled a way to die with dignity, hope, and a broad, loving approach to humankind and human history.

Finding Peace

I have argued that we all grieve at some level during a good portion of our lives (Harvey, 1996). The grief may be acute about a recent major loss, or as with Morrie's story, it may be ongoing at a low level, periodically rising higher in our thoughts and feelings over many years. Some of us grieve more than others. Some of us are more demonstrative in our grief than others. But make no mistake about it, when you encounter a thoughtful, sensitive adult person, you will find someone who grapples with grief and that grief is never far from the surface.

Does this pervasive grief also suggest that we must be hopeless and helpless in our ability to react positively to our grief? No, we all have the capacity to use our grief as a motivator to devote the precious moments of our lives to constructive action. I conclude this chapter with a perceptive story told by Earl Yarborough (1988) that deals with what all of us want—peace. The message, I think, is that even if we must experience loss and grief, we still can find peace through our contributions to others:

> Once there was a man lost in the woods. For days and nights he wandered around in the deep woods and found that there were no roads leading out. One long and lonely night as he walked through the dark, he came upon a monastery. He knocked at the door. A monk came, and before opening the door he called out and asked the man what he wanted. The lonely, lost man didn't answer the monk. Again the monk asked him, "What do you want?" Finally the man said, "All I want is peace."

Peace is what we all are searching for most of the time. Even the monk, who in this story was the helper, was looking for peace. The monk could never have found peace had he refused to open the door to this lonely, lost man. We are all, at some point in our lives, standing and knocking at the door of the monastery, crying out for peace. ... Until all of us learn the true meaning of giving, we ourselves are helpless people, not helpers.... The lost, hurting stranger is still knocking at the door of our monasteries. All he wants is peace.... Will you open the door for him? (pp. 179-181)

Some Integrative
Comments on Central Ideas

Returning to the basic ideas presented in Chapter 1 that span much of the loss material in this text, let's now take stock of how well those ideas and others we have reviewed have captured some of the essence of what loss is. These basic principles were discussed in Chapter 1 and then woven into various discussions throughout the text:

1. Our major losses are relative.
2. Our major losses have cumulative impacts.
3. When major losses occur, they contribute to new aspects of our identity.
4. Major losses involve adaptations related to a loss of a sense of control.
5. Valuable coping strategies for dealing with major losses include working on the meanings of the losses and learning how to give back to others based on our lessons of loss.

We have seen how these ideas have currency across diverse topics including death, divorce, accidents and disease, life span losses and aging, war and violence, genocide, international trauma, and, in a more subtle way, in prejudice, stigmatization, and suicide.

Life and grieving are processes that do not stop. We have seen in the course of developing the various topics of loss that people are often taken aback by the ongoing nature of grief and pain. For losses such as the death of a child, we learn that for the parents of that child each day is a new day of negotiation and a battle with that new reality. The same is true for persons living their lives in wheelchairs or as invalids or with brain injuries or with the memories of being a victim of war crimes. The lessons of loss also apply to the experience of losing a valued intimate relationship. We somehow hope that time will heal. We heal in ways; we renew in ways; we change in ways. But usually it takes work to engage in the process of healing, which can be a lifelong process in many instances.

A related idea is that the experience of grief is integrated into the basic psychological functioning of a person, even from the earliest age. Therefore, there exists both the potential for personal growth and personal deterioration throughout life in response to the experience of loss.

More generally, loss is such a fundamental part of our lives that it beckons us to begin negotiating it early in life. Grief and bereavement are normal human processes that likely start early and are with us every day, to varying degrees. We have argued that ideas such as those mentioned above lead to a wealth of similarities across different loss experiences. Also, as was argued in Chapter 1, it has been contended that each loss experience has its own character, just as each person experiences universal and unique qualities in her or his own history of losses.

Finally, I think that across the many stories of loss reported in this text, we discover the great privilege of listening to the diverse voices of loss and renewal. It is a privilege that is timeless and cross-cultural. This book has emphasized the power of stories and storytelling in dealing with major loss. As Robert Coles (1989) argued, each of us has the bedrock capacity to develop and tell our personal narrative of pain and hope. Similarly, Raphael and Dobson (2000) argued that narratives of mourning, in a way, serve a resurrective function for the griever. They engender hope and establish a bond with other grievers of similar types of loss. These narratives also provide a "life" for the deceased and a sense of a bond with lost loved ones who continue to live on in the stories of the living.

I conclude with a story. Elizabeth Kim (2000) described her journey of sorrow in her book *Ten Thousand Sorrows*. She says in the opening paragraph, "I bring a smorgasbord of pain to the table: Witnessing the murder of my mother in postwar Korea; physical and emotional torture because of my mixed heritage; internment in a hellish orphanage; and years of atrocities that seemed, to me, just a normal part of life" (p. 1). Kim, now a journalist in California, shows how the power of the pen can help alleviate such a vast reservoir of pain—just as Viktor Frankl showed. With this book she feels that she has done a lot of the job of exorcising her many demons. We all have that capacity. When we bemoan our losses, it may help to remember the courage of Frankl, Kim, and so many others who do not dig a hole in the sand and cover their heads. Rather, they tell their stories and in so doing touch the hearts of so many others who are in pain and looking for an outlet.

We must accept infinite disappointment, but never lose infinite hope. (Martin Luther King)

Live your life as if you were to die tomorrow, and learn as if you were going to live forever. (Mahatma Gandhi)

In the midst of winter, I finally learned that there was an invincible summer. (Albert Camus)

Notes

1. Poem by Ugo Bassi, Italian patriot.
2. From "Seasons of Grief," by Julia Keller, *Chicago Tribune Magazine*, September 5, 1999, pp. 9-17.
3. Reprinted in *Cedar Rapids Gazette*, p. 2A.
4. From *Parade Magazine*, April 23, 2000, p. 6.

References

Abbey, A. (1982). Sex differences in attributions for friendly Behavior. *Journal of Personality and Social Psychology, 42*, 830-838.

Ackner, L. F. (1993). *How to survive the loss of a parent*. New York: Morrow.

Ahrons, C. (1994). *The good divorce*. New York: HarperCollins.

Aiken, L. R. (1995). *Aging: An introduction to gerontology*. Thousand Oaks, CA: Sage.

Albom, M. (1997). *Tuesdays with Morrie*. New York: Doubleday.

American Psychiatric Association. (1994). *Diagnostic and statistical manual of mental disorders* (4th ed.). Washington DC: Author.

Auden, W. H. (1994). *Tell me about truth and love*. New York: Random House.

Bailey, B. L. (1988). *From front porch to back seat*. Baltimore: Johns Hopkins University Press.

Balk, D. E. (1996). Models for understanding adolescent coping with bereavement. *Death Studies, 20*, 367-387.

Bandura, A. (1973). *Aggression: A social learning analysis*. Englewood Cliffs, NJ: Prentice Hall.

Bandura, A. (1999). Moral disengagement in the perception of inhumanities. *Personality and Social Psychology Review, 3*, 193-209.

Bardach, J., & Gleeson, K. (1998). *Man is wolf to man*. Berkeley: University of California Press.

Barnes, M. K., Harvey, J. H., Carlson, H., & Haig, J. (1996). The relativity of grief: Differential adaptation reactions of younger and older persons. *Journal of Personal & Interpersonal Loss, 1*, 375-392.

Barnett, O. W., Miller-Perrin, C. L., & Perrin, R. D. (1987). *Family violence across the lifespan*. Newbury Park, CA: Sage.

Bar-On, D. (1995). *Fear and hope*. Cambridge, MA: Harvard University Press.

Baron, R. A. (1971). Reducing the influence of an aggressive model: The restraining effects of discrepant modeling cues. *Journal of Personality and Social Psychology, 20*, 245-250.

Bass, E., & Davis, L. (1988). *The courage to heal*. New York: Harper & Row.

Baum, A. S., & Burnes, D. W. (1993). *A nation in denial*. Boulder, CO: Westview.

Baumeister, R. F. (1991). *Meanings of life*. New York: Guilford.

Baumeister, R. F. (1997). *Evil: Inside human cruelty and violence*. New York: Freeman.

Baumeister, R. F., Bushman, B. J., & Campbell, W. K. (2000). Self-esteem, narcissism, and aggression: Does violence result from low self-esteem or from threatened egotism? *Current Directions in Psychological Science, 9,* 26-29.

Baumeister, R. F., & Campbell W. K. (1999). Intrinsic appeal of evil. *Personality and Social Psychology Review, 3,* 210-221.

Baumeister, R. F., & Staub, E. (1999, January). Point-counterpoint column. *APA Monitor,* pp. 8-9.

Baxter, E., & Hopper, K. (1981). *Private lives/public spaces: Homeless adults on the streets of New York City.* New York: Community Service Society.

Baxter, L. A., & Montgomery, B. M. (1996). *Relating: Dialogues and dialectics.* New York: Guilford.

Beck, A. T., Steer, R. A., Kovacs, M., & Garrison, G. (1985). Hopelessness and eventual suicide: A 10-year prospective study of patients hospitalized with suicidal ideation. *American Journal of Psychiatry, 142,* 559-563.

Belsky, J. (1994). Aging in later life. In J. L. Ronch, W. V. Ornum, & N. C. Stillwell (Eds.), *Counseling approaches throughout the lifespan* (pp. 484-485). New York: Crossroads.

Berscheid, E. (1994). Interpersonal relationships. *Annual Review of Psychology, 45,* 79-129.

Berscheid, E. (1999). [Review of the book *Cupid's Arrow*]. *Contemporary Psychology, 44,* 425-426.

Bland, J. H. (1997). *Live long, die fast.* Minneapolis, MN: Fairview.

Blumstein, P., & Schwartz, P. (1983). *American couples.* New York: Pocket Books.

Bonanno, G. A. (2000). Evolving (finally) toward new insights on grief and bereavement [Review of the book *The nature of grief*]. *Contemporary Psychology: APA Review of Books, 45,* 490-493.

Bowlby, J. (1960). Separation anxiety. *International Journal of Psychoanalysis, 41,* 89-113.

Bowlby, J. (1979). *The making and breaking of affectional bonds.* London: Tavistock.

Bowlby, J. (1980). *Attachment and loss: Vol. 3. Loss: Sadness and depression.* London: Hogarth.

Bregman, L., & Thiermann, S. (1995). *First person mortal: Personal narratives of illness, dying and grief.* New York: Paragon.

Brende, J. O., & Parson, E. R. (1985). *Vietnam veterans: The road to recovery.* New York: Plenum.

Brewer, B. W. (1993). Self-identity and specific vulnerability to depressed mood. *Journal of Personality, 61,* 343-364.

Brickman, P., Ryan, K., & Wortman, C. B. (1975). Causal chains: Attribution of responsibility as a function of immediate and prior causes. *Journal of Personality and Social Psychology, 32,* 1061-1067.

Brink, T. L., Yesavage, J. A., Lum, O., Heersema, P. H., Adey, M., & Rose, T. L. (1982). Screening tests for geriatric depression. *Clinical Gerontologist, 1,* 37-43.

Bruner, J. (1990). *Acts of meaning.* Cambridge, MA: Harvard University Press.

Buchwald, A. (1994). *Leaving home.* New York: Putnam.

Bushman, B., & Baumeister, R. F. (1998). Threatened egotism, narcissism, self-esteem, and direct and displaced aggression. *Journal of Personality and Social Psychology, 75,* 219-229.

Carlson, H. R., Johnston, A., Liiceanu, A., Vintila, C., & Harvey, J. H. (2000). Lessons in the psychology of loss: Accounts of middle-aged Romanian women. In J. H. Harvey & B. G. Pauwels (Eds.), *Posttraumatic stress theory, research, and application* (pp. 83-100). Philadelphia: Brunner/Mazel.

Chang, I. (1997). *The rape of Nanking.* New York: Basic Books.

Charcot, J. (1889). *Clinical lectures of the disease of the nervous system.* London: New Syndenham Society.

Chwalisz, K. (1998). Brain injury: A tapestry of loss. In J. H. Harvey (Ed.), *Perspectives on loss: A sourcebook* (pp. 189-200). Philadelphia: Brunner/Mazel.

Clelland, M. (1982). *Strong at the broken places.* New York: Chosen Books.

Cochran, L., & Claspell, E. (1987). *The meaning of grief.* New York: Greenwood.

Coles, R. (1989). *The call of stories.* Boston: Houghton Mifflin.

Coontz, S. (2000). *The way we are.* New York: HarperCollins.

Corr, C. A., Nabe, C. M., & Corr, D. M. (1994). *Death and dying: Life and living.* Pacific Grove, CA: Brooks/Cole.

Cosmides, L., & Tooby, J. (1999). Toward an evolutionary taxonomy of treatable conditions. *Journal of Abnormal Psychology, 108,* 453-464.

Cousins, N. (1989). *Head first.* New York: Penguin.

Crompton, V. (1993). *Teen dating violence.* Unpublished manuscript, University of Iowa.

Dabbs, J. M., Frady, R. L., Carr, T. S., & Buesch, N. F. (1987). Saliva testosterone levels and criminal violence in young adult prison inmates. *Psychomatic Medicine, 49,* 174-182.

David, H. P., & Baban, A. (1996). Women's health and reproductive rights: Romanian experience. *Patient Education and Counseling, 28,* 235-245.

DeSpelder, L. A., & Strickland, A. L. (1992). *The last dance* (3rd ed.). Mountain View, CA: Mayfield.

Doka, K. J. (1989). Disenfranchised grief. In K. J. Doka (Ed.), *Disenfranchised grief: Recognizing hidden sorrow* (pp. 1-11). Lexington, MA: Lexington Books.

Dollard, J., Doob, L. W., Miller, N. E., Mowrer, O. H., & Sears, R. R. (1939). *Frustration and aggression.* New Haven, CT: Yale University Press.

Drake, R. E., Osher, F. C., & Wallach, M. A. (1991). Homelessness and dual diagnosis. *American Psychologist, 46,* 1149-1158.

Durkheim, E. (1951). *Suicide: A study in sociology* (J. A. Spaulding & G. Simpson, Trans.). Glencoe, IL: Free Press.

Eddy, D. M. (1994). A conversation with my mother. *JAMA, 272*(3), 179-181.

Ehlers, A., Mayou, R. A., & Bryant, B. (1998). Psychological predictors of chronic posttraumatic stress disorder after motor vehicle accidents. *Journal of Abnormal Psychology, 107,* 508-519.

Ehrenreich, B., Hess, E., & Jacobs, G. (1986). *Re-making love.* New York: Anchor/Doubleday.

Ellenberger, H. F. (1970). *The discovery of the unconscious: The evolution of dynamic psychiatry.* New York: Basic Books.

Ellis, A. (1975). *A guide to rational living.* Englewood Cliffs, NJ: Prentice Hall.

Ellis, C. (1995). *Final negotiations.* Philadelphia: Temple University Press.

Enright, R. D., & North, J. (Eds.). (1998). *Exploring forgiveness.* Madison: University of Wisconsin Press.

Erichsen, J. E. (1882). *On concussion of the spine: Nervous shock and other obscure injuries of the nervous system in their clinical and medico-legal aspects.* London: Longman, Green.

Erikson, E. (1963). *Childhood and society* (2nd ed.). New York: Norton.

Evans, G., & Farberow, N. L. (1988). *The encyclopedia of suicide.* New York: Facts on File.

Fabry, J. B., Bulka, R. P., & Sahakian, W. S. (Eds.). (1995). *Finding meaning in life: Logotherapy.* Northvale, NJ: Jason Aronson.

Farnsworth, J., Lund, D. A., & Pett, M. A. (1989). Management and outcomes of loss in later life: A comparison of bereavement and divorce. In D. A. Lund (Ed.), *Older bereaved spouses* (pp. 155-166). Washington, DC: Hemisphere.

Fawcett, J., Scheftner, W. A., Fogg, L., Clark, D. C., Young, M. A., Hedeker, D., & Gibbons, R. (1990). Time-related predictors of suicide in major affective disorders. *American Journal of Psychiatry, 147,* 1189-1194.

Fassler, D. G. (1999). *Help me! I'm sad.* New York: Penguin.

Feinberg, L. (1994). *I'm grieving as fast as I can.* Far Hills, NJ: New Horizon Press.

Feshbach, S. (1956). The catharsis hypothesis and some consequences of interaction with aggressive and neutral play objects. *Journal of Personality, 24,* 449-462.

Figley, C. R. (1978). Introduction. In C. R. Figley (Ed.), *Disorders among Vietnam veterans: Theory, research, and treatment* (pp. 3-10). New York: Brunner/Mazel.

Figley, C. R. (1993). Foreword. In J. Wilson & B. Raphael (Eds.), *International handbook of trauma stress syndromes* (pp. xvii-xx). New York: Plenum.

Fincham, F. D. (2000). The kiss of the porcupines: From attributing responsibility to forgiving. *Personal Relationships 23,* 1-23.

Fincham, F. D., & Bradbury, T. N. (1987). The impact of attributions in marriage. *Journal of Personality and Social Psychology, 53,* 510-517.

Fiske, A. P. (2000). Complementarity theory: Why human social capacities evolved to require cultural complements. *Personality and Social Psychology Bulletin, 4,* 76-94.

Fogelman, E. (1994). *Conscience and courage: Rescuers of Jews during the Holocaust.* New York: Anchor.

Fonseca, I. (1995). *Bury me standing: The gypsies and their journey.* New York: Vintage.

Frankl, V. (1959). *Man's search for meaning.* New York: Washington Square Press.

Frankl, V. (1997). *Viktor Frankl recollections: An autobiography.* New York: Insight Books.

Freud, S. (1961). Mourning and melancholia. In J. Strachey (Ed. & Trans.), *The standard edition of the complete psychological works of Sigmund Freud* (Vol. 14, pp. 239-260). London: Hogarth. (Original work published 1923)

Fromm, E. (1941). *Escape from freedom.* New York: Holt, Rinehart & Winston.

Fulton, R. (1979). Anticipatory grief, stress, and the surrogate griever. In J. Tache, H. Selye, & S. Day (Eds.), *Cancer, stress, and death* (pp. 234-254). New York: Plenum.

Furstenberg, F. F., & Cherlin, A. (1991). *Divided families.* Newbury Park, CA: Sage.

Furstenberg, F. F., & Spanier, G. B. (1987). Remarriage and reconstituted families. In M. B. Sussman & S. K. Steinmetz (Eds.), *Handbook of marriage and the family* (pp. 419-434). New York: Plenum.

Gately, D., & Schwebel, A. I. (1992). Favorable outcomes in children after parental divorce. In C. A. Everett (Ed.), *Divorce and the next generation* (pp. 57-78). New York: Haworth.

Gillis, E. (1986). A single parent confronting the loss of an only child. In T. A. Rando (Ed.), *Parental loss of a child* (pp. 315-319). Champaign, IL: Research Press.

Glick, I. O., Weiss, R. S., & Parkes, C. M. (1974). *The first year of bereavement.* New York: John Wiley.

Goffman, E. (1959). *The presentation of self in everyday life.* Garden City, NY: Doubleday-Anchor.

Goldhagen, D. (1996). *Hitler's willing executioners.* New York: HarperCollins.

Gottfredson, M. R., & Hirschi, T. (1990). *A general theory of crime.* Palo Alto, CA: Stanford University Press.

Gottman, J. (1994). *What predicts divorce? The relationship between marital processes and marital outcomes.* Hillsdale, NJ: Lawrence Erlbaum.

Gottman, J. (1995). *Why marriages succeed or fail.* New York: Fireside Books.

Green, B. L., Grace, M. C., Lindy, J. D., Gleser, G. C., Leonard, A. C., & Kramer, T. L. (1990). Buffalo Creek survivors in the second decade. *Journal of Applied Social Psychology, 20,* 1033-1050.

Greenberger, D. (1993). *Duplex planet.* Boston: Farber & Farber.

Gubrium, J. F. (1993). *Speaking of life: Horizons of meaning for nursing home residents.* New York: Aldine De Gruyter.

Hansson, R. O., Fairchild, S., Vanzetti, N., & Harris, G. (1992, June). *The nature of family bereavement.* Paper presented at the Sixth International Conference on Personal Relationships, Orono, ME.

Harvey, J. H. (1987). Attributions in close relationships: Research and theoretical developments. *Journal of Social and Clinical Psychology, 4,* 420-434.

Harvey, J. H. (1995). *Odyssey of the heart.* New York: Freeman.

Harvey, J. H. (1996). *Embracing their memory: Loss and the social psychology of storytelling.* Needham Heights, MA: Allyn & Bacon.

Harvey, J. H. (2000). *Give sorrow words: Perspectives on loss and trauma.* Philadelphia: Brunner/Mazel.

Harvey, J. H., Barnes, M., Carlson, H., & Haig, J. (1995). Held captive by their memories: Managing grief in relationships. In S. Duck & J. Wood (Eds.), *Relationship challenges* (pp. 211-230). Thousand Oaks, CA: Sage.

Harvey, J. H., Flanary, R., & Morgan, M. (1986). Vivid memories of vivid loves gone by. *Journal of Social and Personal Relationships, 3,* 359-373.

Harvey, J. H., & Hansen, A. (2000). Loss and bereavement in close romantic relationships. In C. Hendrick & S. Hendrick (Eds.), *Sourcebook on close relationship* (pp. 359-370). Thousand Oaks, CA: Sage.

Harvey, J. H., Orbuch, T. L., Chwalisz, K., & Garwood, G. (1991). Coping with sexual assault: The roles of account-making and confiding. *Journal of Traumatic Stress, 4,* 515-531.

Harvey, J. H., Stein, S. K., & Scott, P. K. (1995). Fifty years of grief: Accounts and reported psychological reactions of Normandy invasion veterans. *Journal of Narrative and Life History, 5,* 315-332.

Harvey, J. H., Weber, A. L., & Orbuch, T. L. (1990). *Interpersonal accounts: A social psychological perspective.* Oxford: Blackwell.

Harvey, J. H., Wells, G. H., & Alvarez, M. D. (1978). Attribution in the context of con-
flict and separation in close relationships. In J. H. Harvey, W. Ickes, & R. F. Kidd
(Eds.), *New directions in attribution research* (Vol. 2, pp. 235-259). Hillsdale, NJ:
Lawrence Erlbaum.

Hazan, C., & Shaver, P. (1987). Romantic love conceptualized as an attachment process.
Journal of Personality and Social Psychology, 52, 511-524.

Heaton, T. B., & Albrecht, S. L. (1991). Stable unhappy marriages. *Journal of Marriage
and the Family, 53,* 747-758.

Heide, K. (1995). *Why kids kill parents: Child abuse and adolescent homicide.* Thousand
Oaks, CA: Sage.

Heide, K. (1999). *Young killers: The challenge of juvenile homicide.* Thousand Oaks, CA:
Sage.

Heider, F. (1958). *The psychology of interpersonal relations.* New York: John Wiley.

Helmreich, W. (1992). *Against all odds.* New York: Simon & Schuster.

Herek, G. M. (2000). The psychology of sexual prejudice. *Current Directions in Psychological Science, 9*(1), 19-22.

Herman, J. (1992). *Trauma and recovery.* New York: Basic Books.

Hetherington, E. M., Cox, M., & Cox, R. (1982). Effects of divorce on parents and children. In M. Lamb (Ed.), *Nontraditional families* (pp. 233-288). Hillsdale, NJ: Lawrence Erlbaum.

Hollander, E. M. (in press). Cyber community in the valley of the shadow of death.
Journal of Personal and Interpersonal Loss.

Holtzworth-Munroe, A., & Jacobson, N. J. (1985). Causal attributions of married couples. *Journal of Personality and Social Psychology, 48,* 1399-1412.

Horowitz, M. J. (1976). *Stress response syndromes* (2nd ed.). Northvale, NJ: Jason
Aronson.

Hunt, M. (1966). *The world of the formerly married.* New York: McGraw-Hill.

Irish, D. P., Lundquist, K. F., & Nelsen, V. L. (Eds.). (1993). *Ethnic variations in dying,
death, and grief.* Washington, DC: Taylor & Francis.

Jacobs, S. (1993). *Pathologic grief: Maladaption to loss.* Washington, DC: American Psychiatric Press.

Jamison, K. R. (1999). *Night falls fast: Understanding suicide.* New York: Knopf.

Janis, I. L. (1982). *Victims of groupthink* (2nd ed.). Boston: Houghton-Mifflin.

Janoff-Bulman, R. (1992). *Shattered assumptions.* New York: Free Press.

Jones, W. H., & Burdette, M. P. (1994). Betrayal in relationships. In A. L. Weber & J. H.
Harvey (Eds.), *Perspectives on close relationships* (pp. 243-262). Needham Heights,
MA: Allyn & Bacon.

Jones, E. E., Farina, A., Hastorf, A. H., Markus, H., Miller, D. T., & Scott, R. A. (1984). *Social stigma.* New York: Freeman.

Kastenbaum, R. (1981). *Death, society, and human experience* (2nd ed.). St Louis, MO:
Mosby.

Kayser, K. (1994). *When love dies.* New York: Guilford.

Kelley, P. (1998). Loss experienced in chronic pain and illness. In J. H. Harvey (Ed.), *Perspectives on loss: A sourcebook* (pp. 201-220). Philadelphia: Brunner/Mazel.

Kelly, G. (1955). *The psychology of personal constructs.* New York: Norton.

Kim, E. (2000). *Ten thousand sorrows: The extraordinary journey of a Korean war orphan.* New York: Doubleday.

Kirmayer, L. J., & Young, A. (1999). Culture and context in the evolutionary concept of mental disorder. *Journal of Abnormal Psychology, 108,* 446-452.

Klass, D., Silverman, P. R., & Nickman, S. (Eds.). (1996). *Continuing bonds.* Washington, DC: Taylor & Francis.

Kleber, R. J., & Brom, D. (1992). *Coping with trauma: Theory, prevention, and treatment.* Amsterdam: Swets & Zeitlinger.

Krahe', B. (2000). Childhood sexual abuse and revictimization in adolescence and childhood. In J. H. Harvey & B. G. Pauwels (Eds.), *Posttraumatic stress theory, research, and applications* (pp. 49-65). Philadelphia: Brunner/Mazel.

Kramer, H., & Kramer, K. (1993). *Conversations at midnight.* New York: Morrow.

Koss, M. P., & Leonard, K. E. (1984). Sexually aggressive men: Empirical findings and theoretical implications. In N. M. Malamuth & E. Donnerstein (Eds.), *Pornography and sexual aggression* (pp. 213-232). New York: Academic Press.

Kubler-Ross, E. (1969). *On death and dying.* New York: Collier.

Kuch, K., Cox, B. J., & Evans, R. J. (1996). Posttraumatic stress disorder and motor vehicle accidents. *Canadian Journal of Psychiatry, 41,* 429-434.

Kuenning, D. E. (1990). *Life after Vietnam: How veterans and their loved ones can heal the psychological wounds of war.* New York: Paragon.

Lane, F. C., Goldman, E. F., & Hunt, E. M. (1954). *The world history* (Rev. ed.). New York: Harcourt Brace.

Langer, L. L. (1991). *Holocaust testimonies: The ruins of memory.* New Haven, CT: Yale University Press.

Larson, D. (1993). *The helper's journey.* Champaign, IL: Research Press.

Lawson, A. (1988). *Adultery.* New York: Basic Books.

Lazarus, R., & Folkman, S. (1984). *Stress, appraisal, and coping.* New York: Springer.

Leash, R. M. (1994). *Death notification.* Hinesburg, VT: Upper Access.

Lerner, M. J. (1980). *The belief in a just world.* New York: Plenum.

Levi, P. (1986). *If not now, when?* (W. Weaver, Trans.). New York: Penguin.

Levi, P. (1988). *The drowned and the saved* (R. Rosenthal, Trans.). New York: Summit.

Levinson, D. S. (1997). Young widowhood: A life change journey. *Journal of Personal & Interpersonal Loss, 2,* 277-291.

Levinger, G. (1992). Close relationship loss as a set of inkblots. In T. L. Orbuch (Ed.), *Close relationship loss* (pp. 213-221). New York: Springer-Verlag.

Lewis, C. S. (1961). *A grief observed.* New York: Bantam.

Lindemann, E. (1944). Symptomatology and management of acute grief. *American Journal of Psychiatry, 101,* 141-148.

Loewald, H. W. (1960). On the therapeutic action of psycho-analysis. *International Journal of Psycho-Analysis, 41,* 16-33.

Lokhandwala, T. M., & Westefeld, J. S. (1998). Rational suicide and the crisis of terminal illness. *Journal of Personal & Interpersonal Loss, 3,* 143-159.

Lopata, H. Z. (1996). *Current widowhood: Myths & realities*. Thousand Oaks: Sage.

Lund, D. A., Caserta, M. S., & Dimond, M. F. (1989). Impact of spousal bereavement on the subjective well-being of older adults. In D. A. Lund (Ed.), *Older bereaved spouses* (pp. 3-15). Washington, DC: Hemisphere.

Lyons, R. F., & Sullivan, M. J. L. (1998). Curbing loss in illness and disability: A relationship perspective. In J. H. Harvey (Ed.), *Perspectives on loss: A sourcebook* (137-152). Philadelphia: Brunner/Mazel.

Macdonald, B. (1983). *Look me in the eye: Old women, aging, and ageism*. San Francisco: Spinsters Ink.

Malamuth, N. M. (1989). Predictors of naturalistic sexual aggression. In M. A. Pikrog-Good & J. E. Stets (Eds.), *Violence in dating relationships* (pp. 219-240). New York: Praeger.

Maltsberger, J. T. (1988). Suicide danger: Clinical estimation and decision. *Suicide and Life-Threatening Behavior, 18,* 47-54.

Maltsberger, J. T. (1998). An explication of rational suicide: Its definitions, implications, and complications. *Journal of Personal & Interpersonal Loss, 3,* 177-192.

Maltsberger, J. T., & Goldblatt, M. J. (1996). Introduction. In J. T. Maltsberger & M. J. Goldblatt (Eds.), *Essential papers on suicide* (pp. 1-8). New York: New York University Press.

Mayne, T. J., Acree, M., Chesney, M. A., & Folkman, S. (1998). HIV sexual risk behavior following bereavement in gay men. *Health Psychology, 17,* 403-411.

Mayo, D. J. (1998). Rational suicide? *Journal of Personal & Interpersonal Loss, 3,* 193-203.

McCrae, R. R., & Costa, P. T. (1988). Psychological resilience among widowed men and women: A 10-year follow-up of a national sample. *Journal of Social Issues, 44(3),* 129-144.

McGue, M., & Lykken, D. T. (1992). Genetic influence on risk of divorce. *Psychological Science, 3,* 368-373.

Mead, G. H. (1934). *Mind, self, and society*. Chicago: University of Chicago Press.

Meichenbaum, D. (1985). *Stress inoculation training*. New York: Pergamon.

Meichenbaum, D., & Fitzpatrick, D. (1992). A constructivist narrative perspective on stress and coping. In L. Goldberger & S. Breznitz (Eds.), *Handbook of stress* (pp. 28-43). New York: Free Press.

Messman, T. L., & Long, P. J. (1996). Child sexual abuse and its relationship to revictimization in adult women: A review. *Clinical Psychology Review, 16,* 397-420.

Milgram, S. (1963). Behavioral study of obedience. *Journal of Abnormal and Social Psychology, 67,* 371-378.

Miller, A. G. (Ed.). (1999). [Special issue on stereotyping]. *Personality and Social Psychology Review, 3.*(2).

Morales, P. C. (1997). Grieving in silence: The loss of companion in modern society. *Journal of Personal & Interpersonal Loss, 2,* 243-254.

Morrell, D. (1988). *Fireflies*. New York: Dutton.

Morse, G. A. (1998). Homelessness and loss: Conceptual and research directions. In J. H. Harvey (Ed.), *Perspectives on loss: A sourcebook* (pp. 269-280). Philadelphia: Brunner/Mazel.

Morse, G. A. (2000). On being homeless and mentally ill: A multitude of losses and the possibility of recovery. In J. H. Harvey & E. D. Miller (Eds.), *Loss and trauma: General and close relationship perspectives* (pp. 249-264). Philadelphia: Brunner-Routledge.

Moss, M. S., & Moss, S. Z. (1995). Death and bereavement. In R. Blieszner & V. H. Bedford (Eds.), *Handbook of aging and the family* (pp. 422-439). Westport, CT: Greenwood.

Mueller, L. (1986). Face lift. In *Second Language, 21,* Baton Rouge: Louisiana State University Press.

Murphy, S. (2000). Deaths: Final data for 1998. *National vital statistics report* (Vol. 48, No. 11). Hyattsville, MD: National Center for Health Statistics. (Available online at www.cdc.gov/nchs/data/nvsr/nvsr48/nvs48_11.pdf)

Myers, D. G. (1992). *The pursuit of happiness.* New York: Morrow.

Neeld, E. (1990). *Seven choices: Taking the steps to a new life after losing someone you love.* New York: Delta.

Nolen-Hoeksema, S. (2001). Ruminative coping and adjustment to bereavement. In M. S. Stroebe, R. O. Hansson, W. Stroebe, & H. Schut (Eds.), *Handbook of bereavement research: Consequences, coping, & care* (pp. 545-562). Washington, DC: American Psychological Association.

Novick, P. (1999). *The holocaust in American life.* Chicago: University of Chicago Press.

O'Bryant, S. L., & Hansson, R. O. (1995). Widowhood. In R. Blieszner & V. H. Bedford (Eds.), *Handbook of aging and the family* (pp. 440-458). Westport, CT: Greenwood.

O'Connor, P. (1994). Salient themes in the life review of a sample of frail elderly respondents in London. *The Gerontologist, 34,* 224-230.

Orbuch, T. L. (1988). *Responses to and coping with nonmarital relationships terminations.* Unpublished doctoral dissertation, University of Wisconsin, Madison.

Orbuch, T. L. (1997). People's accounts count: The sociology of accounts. *Annual Review of Sociology, 23,* 455-478.

Orbuch, T. L., Harvey, J. H., Davis, S. H., & Merbach, N. (1994). Account-making and confiding as acts of meaning in response to sexual assault. *Journal of Family Violence, 9,* 249-264.

Overy, R. (1997). *Russia's war: Blood upon the snow.* New York: TV Books.

Page, H. (1885). *Injuries of the spine and spinal cord without apparent medical lesion.* London: J. & A. Churchill.

Palmer, L. (1987). *Shrapnel in the heart.* New York: Random House.

Parkes, C. M. (1972). *Bereavement: Studies of grief in adult life.* London: Tavistock.

Parkes, C. M. (1988). Bereavement as a psychosocial transition: Processes of adaptation to change. *Journal of Social Issues, 44,* 53-65.

Parkes, C. M., & Weiss, R. S. (1983). *Recovery from bereavement.* New York: Basic Books.

Parry, A., & Doan, R. E. (1994). *Story re-visions: Narrative therapy in the post-modern world.* New York: Guilford.

Patterson, C. H. (1985). *The therapeutic relationship.* Pacific Grove, CA: Brooks/Cole.

Paulson, D. S. (1991). Myth, male initiation and the Vietnam veteran. In E. Tick (Ed.), *Healing a generation* (pp. 156-165). New York: Guilford.

Pennebaker, J. (1990). *Opening up.* New York: Morrow.

Pennebaker, J., Zech, E., & Rime, B. (2001). Disclosing and sharing emotion: Psychological, social and health consequences. In M. S. Stroebe, R. O. Hansson, W. Stroebe, & H. Schut (Eds.), *Handbook of bereavement research: Consequences, coping, & care* (pp. 517-544). Washington, DC: American Psychological Association.

Peskin, H., Auerhahn, N. C., & Laub, D. (1997). The second holocaust: Therapeutic rescue when life threatens. *Journal of Personal and Interpersonal Loss, 2,* 1-26.

Petry, S., & Avent, H. (1992). Stepping stone: A haven for displaced youths. In M. J. Robertson & M. Greenblatt (Eds.), *Homelessness: A national perspective* (pp. 299-305). New York: Plenum.

Phillips, D. H. (1982). *Living with Huntington's disease.* Madison: University of Wisconsin Press.

Phillips, J. (1998, Autumn). My stroke. *Phi Beta Kappa Key Reporter,* pp. 5-9.

Pipher, M. (1999). *Another country: Navigating the emotional terrain of our elders.* New York: Riverhead.

Popenoe, D. (1993). American family decline, 1960-1990: A review and appraisal. *Journal of Marriage and the Family, 55,* 527-555.

Powell, J. (1994). *Things I should have said to my father.* New York: Avon.

Price, R. H., Friedland, D. S., & Vinokur, A. D. (1998). Job loss: Hard times and eroded identity. In J. H. Harvey (Ed.), *Perspectives on loss: A sourcebook* (pp. 303-318). New York: Brunner/Mazel.

Puller, L. B. (1991). *Fortunate son: The autobiography of Lewis B. Puller, Jr.* New York: Grove Weidenfeld.

Radner, G. (1989). *It's always something.* New York: Simon & Schuster.

Rando, T. A. (1993). *Treatment of complicated mourning.* Champaign, IL: Research Press.

Raphael, B. (1980). A psychiatric model for bereavement counseling. In B. Schoenberg (Ed.), *Bereavement counseling: A multidisciplinary handbook* (pp. 121-154). Westport, CT: Greenwood.

Raphael, B. (1983). *The anatomy of bereavement.* New York: Basic Books.

Raphael, B., & Dobson, M. (2000). Bereavement. In J. H. Harvey & E. D. Miller (Eds.), *Loss and trauma: General and close relationship perspectives* (pp. 45-61). Philadelphia: Brunner-Routledge.

Reese, P. (1993). *Ten million steps.* Waco TX: WRS Publishing.

Robertson, M. J., & Greenblatt, M. D. (Eds.). (1992). *Homelessness: A national perspective.* New York: Plenum.

Rosenblatt, P. (1983). *Bitter, bitter tears.* Minneapolis: University of Minnesota Press.

Ross, E. B. (1997). *Life after suicide: A ray of hope for those left behind.* New York: Insight.

Ross, M., & Holmberg, D. (1992). Are wives' memories for events in relationships more vivid than their husbands' memories? *Journal of Social and Personal Relationships, 9,* 585-604.

Rothman, B. (1991). *Loving & leaving.* Lexington, MA: Lexington Books.

Rusbult, C. E. (1980). Commitment and satisfaction in romantic associations: A test of the investment model. *Journal of Experimental Social Psychology, 16,* 172-186.

Ryan, D. R. (1992). Raymond: Underestimated grief. In K. J. Doka (Ed.), *Disenfranchised grief: Recognizing hidden sorrow* (pp. 127-133). Lexington, MA: Lexington Books.

Sacks, O. (1970). *The man who mistook his wife for a hat.* New York: HarperPerenniel.

Saunders, C. (1977). Dying they live: St. Christopher's Hospice. In H. Fiefel (Ed.), *New meanings of death* (pp. 45-55). New York: McGraw-Hill.

Sanders, C. M. (1980). A comparison of adult bereavement in the death of a spouse, child and parent. *Omega, 10,* 303-322.

Sanders, C. M. (1982). Effects of sudden vs. chronic illness death on bereavement outcome. *Omega, 13,* 227-241.

Savage, J. A. (1989). *Mourning unlived lives: A psychological study of childbearing loss.* Wilmette, IL: Chiron.

Schachter, S. (1959). *The psychology of affiliation.* Stanford, CA: Stanford University Press.

Schaie, K. W. (1983). The Seattle longitudinal study: A twenty-one year exploration of psychometric intelligence in adulthood. In K. W. Schaie (Ed.), *Longitudinal studies of adult psychological development* (pp. 64-135). New York: Guilford.

Schleifer, S. J., Keller, S. E., & Stein, M. (1979, May). *The influence of stress and other psychosocial factors on human immunity.* Paper presented at the annual meeting of the American Psychosomatic Society.

Schoenberg, B., Carr, A., Peretz, D., & Kutscher, A. (1970). *Loss and grief.* New York: Columbia University Press.

Schulz, R., & Heckhausen, J. (1996). A life span model of successful aging. *American Psychologist, 51,* 702-712.

Schulz, R., O'Brien, A. T., Bookwala, J., & Fleissner, K. (1995). Psychiatric and physical morbidity effects of Alzheimer's disease caregiving: Prevalence, correlates, and causes. *The Gerontologist, 35,* 771-791.

Seligman, M. E. P. (1975). *Helplessness: On depression, development, and death.* San Francisco: Freeman.

Seligman, M. E. P. (1998, August). Call for a new discipline: Positive psychology. *APA Monitor,* pp. 1, 15.

Selye, H. (1956). *The stress of life.* New York: McGraw-Hill.

Shaver, P. R., & Tancredy, C. M. (2000). Emotion, attachment, and bereavement: A conceptual commentary. In M. Stroebe, W. Stroebe, R. Hansson, & H. Schut (Eds.), *Handbook of bereavement research: Consequences, coping, and care* (pp. 63-88). Washington, DC: American Psychological Association.

Shaw, C. (1982). *Come out, come out, wherever you are.* New York: American R. R. Publishing Co.

Shelton, M. M. (2000). *Guidance from the darkness.* New York: Tarcher/Putnam.

Shneidman, E. (1996). *The suicidal mind.* New York: Oxford University Press.

Shuchter, S. R. (1986). *Dimensions of grief.* San Francisco: Jossey-Bass.

Sittser, G. L. (1996). *A grace disguised.* New York: HarperCollins.

Snyder, C. R. (1994). *The psychology of hope.* New York: Free Press.

Snyder, C. R. (1996). To hope, to lose, and hope again. *Journal of Personal & Interpersonal Loss, 1,* 3-16.

Snyder, C. R., & Lopez, S. J. (Eds.). (in press). *Handbook of positive psychology.* New York: Oxford University Press.

Spanier, G. B., & Thompson, L. (1987). *Parting: The aftermath of separation and divorce.* Newbury Park, CA: Sage.

Sprecher, S. (1994). Two sides to the breakup of dating relationships. *Personal Relationships, 1,* 199-222.

Staub, E. (1989). *The roots of evil: The origins of genocide and other group violence.* New York: Cambridge University Press.

Staub, E. (1998). Breaking the cycle of genocidal violence. In J. H. Harvey (Ed.), *Perspectives on loss: A sourcebook* (pp. 231-240). New York: Brunner/Mazel.

Staub, E. (1999). The roots of evil: Social conditions, culture, personality, and basic human needs. *Personality and Social Psychology Review, 3,* 179-192.

Stroebe, M. S., Stroebe, W., & Hansson, R. O. (1993). Bereavement research and theory: An introduction to the *Handbook.* In M. S. Stroebe, W. Stroebe, & R. O. Hansson (Eds.), *Handbook of bereavement* (pp. 3-19). New York: Cambridge University Press.

Stroebe, W., & Stroebe, M. S. (1986). Beyond marriage: The impact of partner loss on health. In R. Gilmour & S. Duck (Eds.), *The emerging field of personal relationships* (pp. 203-210). Hillsdale, NJ: Lawrence Erlbaum.

Stroebe, W., & Stroebe, M. (1987). *Bereavement and health: The psychological and physical consequences of partner loss.* New York: Cambridge University Press.

Styron, W. (1990). *Darkness visible: A memoir of madness.* New York: Random House.

Sutker, P. B., Uddo, M., Brailey, K., Vasterling, K., & Errera, P. (1994). Psychopathology in war-zone deployed Operation Desert Storm troops: Assigned graves registration duties. *Journal of Abnormal Psychology, 103,* 383-390.

Thompson, S. C. (1998). Blockades to finding meaning and control. In J. H. Harvey (Ed.), *Perspectives on loss: A sourcebook* (pp. 21-34). New York: Brunner/Mazel.

Thompson, S. C., & Janigian, A. (1988). Life schemes: A framework for understanding the search for meaning. *Journal of Social and Clinical Psychology, 7,* 260-280.

Thornton, A. (1989). Changing attitudes toward family issues in the United States. *Journal of Marriage and the Family, 51,* 873-893.

Tick, E. (Ed.). (1991). *Voices: Healing a generation.* New York: Guilford.

Uchino, B. N., Kiecolt-Glaser, J. K., & Cacioppo, J. T. (1994). Construals of preillness relationship quality predict cardiovascular response in family caregivers of Alzheimer's disease victims. *Psychology and Aging, 9,* 113-120.

Valliant, G., & Blumenthal, S. (1990). Introduction: Suicide over the life-cycle. In S. Blumenthal & D. Kupfer (Eds.), *Suicide over the life-cycle* (pp. 1-16). Washington, DC: American Psychiatric Press.

Vaughan, D. (1986). *Uncoupling.* New York: Oxford University Press.

Veiel, H. O. F., Brill, G., Hafner, H., & Welz, R. (1988). The social supports of suicide attempters: The different roles of family and friends. *American Journal of Community Psychology, 16,* 839-861.

Veith, I. (1965). *Hysteria: The history of the disease.* Chicago: University of Chicago Press.

Viorst, J. (1986). *Necessary losses.* New York: Fawcett.

Volkan, V. D., & Zintl, E. (1993). *Life after loss.* New York: Scribner.

Wakefield, J. C. (1999). Evolutionary versus prototype analyses of the concept of disorder. *Journal of Abnormal Psychology, 108,* 374-399.

Walker, L. E. (1999). Psychology and domestic violence around the world. *American Psychologist, 54*(1), 21-20.

Wallerstein, J., & Lewis, J. (1998). The long-term impact of divorce on children: A first report from a 25-year study. *Family & Conciliation Courts Review, 36,* 368-383.

Wallerstein, J. S., & Kelly, J. B. (1980). *Surviving the breakup.* New York: Harper Torch.

Wallerstein, J. S., Lewis, J. M., & Blakeslee, S. (2000). *The unexpected legacy of divorce.* New York: Hyperion.

Weenolsen, P. (1988). *Transcendence of loss over the life span.* New York: Hemisphere.

Wegner, D. M. (1989). *White bears & other unwanted thoughts: Suppression, obsession, and the psychology of mental control.* New York: Penguin.

Wegner, D. M. (1999, January/February). The seed of our undoing. *Psychological Science Agenda,* pp. 10-12.

Wegner, D. M., & Schneider, D. J. (1989). Mental control: The war of the ghosts in the machine. In J. S. Uleman & J. A. Bargh (Eds.), *Unintended thought* (pp. 287-305). New York: Guilford.

Weisel, E. (1960). *Night.* New York: Bantam.

Weiss, R. S. (1975). *Marital separation.* New York: Basic Books.

Weiss, R. S. (1988). Loss and recovery. *Journal of Social Issues, 44,* 37-52.

Weiss, R. S. (1993). Loss and recovery. In M. S. Stroebe, W. Stroebe, & R. O. Hansson (Eds.), *Handbook of bereavement: Theory, research, and intervention* (pp. 271-284). Cambridge, UK: Cambridge University Press.

Weiss, R. S. (1998). Issues in the study of loss and grief. In J. H. Harvey (Ed.), *Perspectives on loss: A sourcebook* (pp. 343-352). New York: Brunner/Mazel.

Weiss, R. S. (2000). Grief, bonds, and relationships. In M. S. Stroebe, R. O. Hansson, W. Stroebe, & H. Schut (Eds.). *Handbook of bereavement research: Consequences, coping, & care* (pp. 47-62). Washington, DC: American Psychological Association.

Welwood, J. (1990). *Journey of the heart.* New York: Collins.

Wiedza, K. (1993). *Auschwitz: A history in photographs.* Bloomington: Indiana University Press.

Williamson, G. W., & Shaffer, D. R. (1998). Implications of communal relationships theory for understanding loss among family caregivers. In J. H. Harvey (Ed.), *Perspectives on loss: A sourcebook* (pp. 173-187). New York: Brunner/Mazel.

Wills, T. A. (1981). Downward comparison principles in social psychology. *Psychological Bulletin, 90,* 245-271.

Wilson, A., & Allison, J. (Eds.). (1993). *Missing still.* (Available from Speak Out for Stephanie Foundation. P.O. Box 7829, Overland Park, KS 66207)

Winer, R. (1994). *Close encounters.* New York: Aronson.

Woodson, M. (1994). *The toughest days of grief.* Grand Rapids, MI: Zondervan.

Worden, J. W. (1996). *Children and grief.* New York: Guilford.

Worden, J. W. (1982). *Grief counseling and grief therapy: A handbook for the mental health practitioner.* New York: Springer.

Wortman, C. B., & Silver, R. C. (1989). The myths of coping with loss. *Journal of Consulting and Clinical Psychology, 57,* 349-357.

Wortman, C. B., & Silver, R. C. (1992). Reconsidering assumptions about coping with loss: An overview of current research. In L. Montada, S. Filipp, & M. J. Lerner (Eds.), *Life crises and experiences of loss in adulthood* (pp. 341-365). Hillsdale, NJ: Lawrence Erlbaum.

Wortman, C. B., & Silver, R. C. (2001). The myths of coping with loss revisited. In M. S. Stroebe, R. O. Hannson, W. Stroebe, & H. Schut (Eds.), *Handbook of bereavement research: Consequences, coping, and care.* Washington, DC: American Psychological Association.

Yalom, I. D. (1980). *Existential psychotherapy.* New York: Basic Books.

Yarborough, T. E. (1988). Finding peace in crisis. In O. S. Margolis, A. Kutscher, E. Marcus, H. Raether, & V. Pine (Eds.), *Grief and the loss of an adult child* (pp. 26-45). New York: Praeger.

Yossif-Vickery, A. Y. (1998). *From an old world value into post-communist refuse: Romania's vagabond dogs as key metaphor in the transition to a new world order.* Unpublished manuscript, Tulane University.

Index

About the Author

John H. Harvey is Professor of Psychology at the University of Iowa. Formerly, he taught at Vanderbilt, Ohio State, and Texas Tech Universities and was Educational Affairs Officer at the American Psychological Association from 1981 to 1982. He is a social psychologist specializing in the study of close relationships, attribution and account making, and loss and trauma phenomena. He is a Fellow of Division 8 of the American Psychological Association and was a Fulbright Research Fellow studying loss in Romania in the spring of 1998. He has authored and/or edited over 20 books and has published over 130 articles and chapters. He was editor of *Contemporary Psychology* from 1992 to 1998 and was founding editor of the *Journal of Social and Clinical Psychology* and the *Journal of Personal and Interpersonal Loss*. His books include *New Directions in Attribution Research* (with Ickes and Kidd); *Perspectives on Attributional Processes* (with Weary); *Close Relationships* (with Kelley et al.); *Interpersonal Accounts* (with Weber and Orbuch); *Odyssey of the Heart: The Search for Intimacy, Closeness, and Love; Embracing Their Memory: Loss and The Social Psychology of Storytelling; Minding the Close Relationship: A Theory of Relationship Enhancement* (with Omarzu); and *Perspectives on Loss: A Sourcebook*.